Separado

***

Paul Cox

ISBN: 1494228416
ISBN 13: 9781494228415

Paul Cox

Separado

T he heavy stench of rotting garbage soured in the midday heat, but Conway Fargo was nearing the end of the back alley. Just ahead was Randolph Street and fresh air. He would wait there until Ned Turpine appeared. Turpine was worse than a thief. He was a cheat. West of the Mississippi, his kind would have been shot. But this was no backwater frontier town scratching out an existence on the edge of civilization. This was Chicago.

Thirty feet from Randolph Street, Fargo stepped around a pile of moldy vegetable crates, then stopped suddenly. Someone stood in the shadows to his left. Reaching inside his coat, Fargo rested his palm on a Colt pistol hidden in a shoulder holster.

"You there, step out nice and easy so I can see you."

A gray-haired man stumbled over a rotting head of cabbage and then took a few steps. A ragged frock coat and threadbare pants hung loosely over a scrawny frame. Grime covered his face and beard. He wiped his lips with the back of his sleeve.

"Friend, could you grubstake a fellow citizen down on his luck?"

Frowning, Fargo took his hand from his coat. Even with the distance between them, he could smell whiskey.

"I've never sent a man away hungry, mister, luck or no luck. But it looks to me like you'd sooner satisfy your thirst than your appetite."

The old man clutched his coat together as if a cold wind were blowing through it. "Even one such as I must eat from time to time."

Fargo studied the man for a moment. He took out his pocket watch, checked the time, and then glanced into the street ahead. "You talk like you're an educated man," said Fargo, replacing the watch. "A man like you shouldn't be living in an alley."

"I deserve nothing better."

Fargo scoffed. "Why's that?"

"I lost everything. I was a wealthy man once. I had a wife and child. But I failed my wife and left my son with nothing. He has no inheritance save the watchword that I preached so often to him: 'God suffers fools to reap what they have sown.' Little did I know that I would become living proof of my own incessant lecturing."

Fargo pulled a silver dollar from his pocket. Tossing it, Fargo said, "We're all fools from time to time."

The old man leaned forward, catching the coin with both hands. Standing erect, he looked at the coin. His eyes widened. "You are a fine Christian gentleman, sir! God will reward such charity."

"God helps those who help themselves," said Fargo as he started for Randolph Street. "You can eat with that money or drink with it. It's up to you. A man has to live with the choices he makes."

Fargo stepped out of the shadows of the alley onto the crowded boardwalk. Its wooden planks rumbled from the rapid-fire pounding of leather heels. Everyone seemed to be in a hurry. He took a deep breath and glanced around.

It was almost noon in the business district. Horse-drawn trolleys rattled over steel rails. Clanging bells and the rhythmic clatter of hooves on pavement competed with the babble of countless conversations. Truck wagons were making deliveries while the men unloading them called out one to another. Here and there a child's voice could be heard above the melee.

Both sides of the street were walled with seven- to eight-story stone or brick buildings. Above them, a narrow strip of sky could be seen through dozens of drooping, black telegraph wires and a haze of factory smoke.

Looking up, Fargo tried to find the sun, but in the narrow strip of sky, there was no room for it. He shook his head. He hadn't carried a watch in twenty years, but in Chicago, he needed one. People in the city lived by the clock. More than that, they were slaves to it.

A few steps from the alley, Fargo tipped his bowler hat to two women dressed in the latest French fashion and then flattened himself against a building to avoid the stampede of pedestrians. Turpine was to come out of the hotel across the street shortly after noon. Fargo's assignment was to follow and investigate, nothing more.

Fargo reached into his vest pocket and took out a card. It was a trade card. Thicker than a playing card, it felt clumsy to a man who had once made a living playing poker.

One side of the card advertised Spalding baseball eqipment Fargo flipped it over. A linotype showed the likeness of Ned Turpine. The card said he had played professional baseball for the 1879 Chicago White Stockings, but he had lasted less than one season. He was caught drinking during a game by a teammate named Anson. Adrian "Cap" Anson was six feet two and weighed close to two hundred pounds, so at the time Turpine did nothing. But now, a year had passed, and Turpine was trying to get even.

From all accounts Anson was straightlaced, almost to a fault. He played first base, and Turpine understood he would be the perfect man to shave runs during a game. A week ago, two of Turpine's henchmen had approached Anson and given him an ultimatum: cooperate with them in their betting scheme or have his baseball career come to an abrupt and painful end.

Anson was no fool. In Chicago it was common knowledge many of the politicians were crooked. Even the police could not be trusted. Instead, Anson had gone to the Pinkerton Agency for advice.

Fargo tucked the card back in his pocket and thought of his first meeting with Allan Pinkerton. A month ago, Fargo had come in on the train and went straight to the Pinkerton Agency to inquire about work. Somehow Mr. Pinkerton already knew his name and a bit about his past. Fargo learned later that the old Scotsman seemed to know a little something about everyone. The next day, Fargo was on the job at the Union Stock Yards checking for stolen cattle. But when Cap Anson engaged the agency, Fargo was immediately reassigned.

Knowing virtually nothing about the game of baseball, Fargo thought it odd he should be added to the investigation. Since the sudden reassignment, he had been uneasy. Why, he wondered, had he been put on the case so quickly? And how much did Pinkerton actually know about Conway Fargo? Did Pinkerton know what he was capable of or what he had done in the last twenty years?

Fargo was approaching the fiftieth year of what he had recently determined was a dismal and misspent life. He had come to Chicago to forget. What he did best and what he had witnessed while doing it, he no longer wanted to remember. But even in a bustling town of half a million people, he could not get the tortured faces out of his mind. Most were faces of grief. Far too many, however, were corpses with their last expression of agony frozen in a death mask.

Someone near him spoke. "You, sir, lean against a stone that once was part of a majestic range of mountains. How unfortunate for that stone it was hewn from its heights and brought here to endure such a mundane existence. Now it is but one ordinary stone in a wall that sees nothing."

Fargo took his eyes off the hotel for a moment. The beggar from the alley was standing next to him. Set deep under long white eyebrows, the old man's bloodshot eyes were penetrating. He seemed cleaner standing in the sunlight than in the stagnant air of the alley.

"You need something?" asked Fargo, returning his attention to the hotel.

"Redemption, to be sure. But we are all in need of such."

"No doubt about that, mister," said Fargo. He sighed. "I've had a hell of time finding any."

The old man gazed up at the wall for several seconds, and then his eyes settled on Fargo. "That stone that you lean upon used to watch the sun rise and set. It could see for miles where the air was pure. Without complaint it endured the heat of summer and the cold of winter's snow. Now it has been brought to this place, chiseled by the hands of men, and imprisoned in mortar. Here it is on Randolph Street. What kind of a place is this for such a noble stone?"

"It's like any other, I suppose," replied Fargo. He took a second look at the man, this time studying him before turning back to the hotel. "What about you? You sound like a poet. What kind of place is an alley for such a noble poet?"

The old man dropped his eyes.

"Did you get something to eat with that dollar I gave you, or did you drink it up?"

"Your charity was not in vain, kind sir. God suffers fools to reap what they have sown, yet even fools require sustenance."

"So you didn't buy a bottle?"

A moment passed. The beggar did not answer. Fargo glanced in his direction and then back into the alley, searching the shadows. He scanned the crowded boardwalk, but the drunken poet had somehow vanished.

A glint of light caught his attention. Turpine exited the hotel through a pair of ornate glass doors framed in polished brass. He stood on the boardwalk shading his eyes and searching the opposite side of Randolph Street. Turpine nodded at someone in the crowd and then headed toward Lake Front Park.

The Chicago White Stockings were playing the Louisville Grays at the ballpark. According to information gathered by the Pinkertons, Turpine was to meet with the first baseman after the game. One way or the other, he intended to persuade Anson to cooperate with his betting operation. Cap Anson had been instructed to play along with the scheme until the agency had enough evidence to crack the case wide open. Allen Pinkerton believed Turpine was working for someone else, someone called the "Big Fish."

Easily concealed in the crowded boardwalk, Fargo followed Turpine at a short distance. Soon, two men joined him. Their rough clothes and heavy shoulders were those of day laborers. Each carried an ax handle.

After five blocks, the trio came to the ticket window for the ballpark. Turpine bought himself a ticket. The other two men walked east toward the railroad tracks that ran behind the park and along the shore of Lake Michigan.

Fargo waited a half minute before approaching the ticket window. Whatever was going on in the ballpark had the people in an uproar. He had never seen a professional baseball game or a stadium built for grown men to play in. He was told that those who followed the game were more than spectators. At times, crowds would go wild. At first they were called "fanatics" by the press, but now some newspaper reporters had shortened the word to "fans." It was a phenomenon he didn't understand.

Fargo had seen professional boxing matches and even fought in a few himself. There, the crowds cheered to see which man was the strongest and most skillful. He had been to horse races where hundreds, and even thousands, anxiously watched to see which horse and rider had the strength and stamina to win. But baseball was different. Here, grown men dressed in children's knickers and tried to hit a leather ball with a stick of wood.

When Fargo paid the fifty-cent admission, he was told the game was almost over, but as these were professional teams, he would still have to pay. Fargo shrugged and walked past the gate and into the noisy stadium.

Bleachers encircled a grass-covered field of several acres. The seats were packed, elbow to elbow, with angry men and women. They were dressed in their Sunday best, but this was anything but a church picnic. Fists were waving, men were swearing, and threats were flying in every direction. Some were even calling for the death of the umpire.

Midway down the bleachers, on the east side, a blanket-sized American flag waved in a steady breeze. A few feet from the flagpole, a large board had an array of numbers fastened to it. One of them was the score. The Chicago White Stockings were ahead by one.

On the field, a dozen men wearing striped caps, knickers, and knee-high socks were scattered around four white squares. All but one player stood at ease. Standing in front of the batter and catcher, Adrian "Cap" Anson was kicking tufts of grass into the air and yelling at the umpire. He threw his hat to the ground, exposing his blond hair and red face. The crowd was going wild.

Fargo shook his head and looked for Turpine. He stood only ten steps away. His arms were crossed, and his eyes locked on Anson. He was smiling.

Anson finally picked up his hat and stormed back to first base. The roar of the fans began to subside. The players took their positions. The pitcher threw, the batter swung and missed. The mass of spectators, who seconds before had thirsted for blood, erupted into ecstatic celebration. The game was over. The crisis had been averted. Chicago had won.

For several minutes, the fans congratulated themselves. A few moments later, as if being herded by invisible hands, they began funneling toward the front gate exit. Turpine stood to the side and let them pass until Anson started off the field.

With Fargo following, Turpine threaded his way through the crowd until Anson looked up and saw him. Their eyes met. Turpine stopped and pointed to the left field fence. Anson nodded.

With the crowd thinning rapidly, Fargo ducked behind a set of bleachers. In ten minutes the stadium was empty, and Anson stood alone on the grass. Turpine had not moved from where he stood. He was waiting for something or someone.

Movement caught Fargo's eye. Coming in from the entrance, the two men with ax handles started across the grass toward Anson. Turpine hopped down from the stands and joined them. They swaggered with confidence as they closed in on Anson.

Fargo waited until they were well past him and then quietly followed. He was in full view of Anson but behind the three men. He was gambling that Anson would assume he was with the other three, at least until the time was right.

Anson stood tall, waiting. He was brave, if not foolish. As big as he was, he did not stand a chance if they attacked.

Stopping an arm's length from Anson, Turpine grinned. "Nice game, Cap."

"Could have been better."

Turpine sneered, "Never satisfied, are you?"

Anson did not answer.

"Well, what's it going to be, Anson? You in or out?"

Glancing at the ax handles, Anson's confidence weakened.

"No deal."

"Now, boys," said Turpine, "didn't I tell you he'd say that?"

The two thugs started toward Anson. The ballplayer took a step back and put up his fists.

Fargo felt his blood begin to heat. His eyes hardened. Closing to within thirty feet of them, he stopped.

"What did he say?" asked Fargo.

All three men turned to see who had spoken. Anson appeared startled.

Fargo slowly repeated his question: "What was it Cap said?"

"Who the hell are you?" demanded Turpine.

Fargo smiled, but there was no humor in it. "Just a fan."

"Get out of here!" bellowed Turpine. "Get out, if you know what's good for you!"

Pinkerton had instructed Fargo just to follow and observe. But it was too late for that. One of the thugs had a pistol grip sticking out of his pants pocket.

The smile left Fargo's face. His eyes narrowed into a wolfish glare. Time was slowing down. The ritual was beginning.

"I know damn well what's good for me," said Fargo. "And I know what's good for you, too. You got a choice to make."

The bigger of the two men raised his ax handle and rested it on his shoulder. The move revealed a pistol tucked behind his belt. "My friend said beat it, mister. Now git!"

"Your first choice is to leave now," said Fargo evenly. "The second is to start praying. Two of you are about to die."

For a moment, there was silence. Turpine stared incredulously and then shook his head.

"Take care of him, boys!"

Before the men took a step, their ax handles shifted slightly, their big fists taking a tighter grip.

Fargo palmed the Colt from his shoulder holster and fired twice in less than a heartbeat. Both men flinched, then crumpled, each with a bullet hole in the center of his chest.

A cloud of gun smoke drifted between Fargo and Turpine. The odor of sulfur blended with the fragrance of freshly cut grass. Turpine's eyes were wide with shock and horror. "You killed them," gasped Turpine. "You shot them both!"

"Are you heeled, Turpine? If you are, skin it!"

Turpine threw both his hands in the air and shouted, "I'm not armed! I'm not armed! Don't shoot!"

Fargo thumbed back the hammer of his pistol. "Well, Turpine, I'll ask you what you asked this ballplayer. Are *you* in or out?"

"I'm out! I'm out!"

"Then go," said Fargo, nodding and easing the pistol's hammer down. "I don't want to ever see or hear of you again."

For several seconds, Turpine stared down at the lifeless bodies at his feet. He glanced one last time at Fargo, then made a wide circle around him and never looked back.

Anson still had his guard up.

"What do you want?" demanded Anson, trying to muster as much defiance as he could. "What do want with me?"

Fargo eased the Colt back into its holster. "I'm a Pinkerton."

"Pinkerton? You're a Pinkerton?"

"Yes."

Lowering his arms and unclenching his fists, Anson looked at the two corpses. "But you shot them. I just asked for an investigation. They're…they're dead!"

"Their choice," said Fargo. "A man lives or dies by the choices he makes."

***

Clarissa LaFarge glanced at the clock on the wall. It was almost three. As if on cue, Bell's oak telephony box began to thump. The theater company had installed one of the new devices for such occasions, but speaking into a box was crude. It lacked the charm and persuasive power of personal conversation.

She would again be late for rehearsal. It did not matter. Fame had its rewards, as did beauty. They would wait for her at the theater, as they had before. Later, others, just as accommodating, would happily wait on her as well.

She had power. What she lacked, at the moment, was money. There was never enough of it, at least not yet.

LaFarge had a modest estate in the North Division district on the edge of Chicago but preferred her luxury apartment in the center of town. Purchasing a second residence, closer to the theater district, would help her be on time for rehearsal. Or so she said.

The afternoon sun beamed through her bedroom window. LaFarge stepped into its light and took one last look in her full-length mirror. The newest fashion in women's dresses featured a long bodice that hugged her natural curves. Sliding her lace-gloved hands along her waist and hips, she turned side to side, admiring her reflection. She smiled approvingly and adjusted her feathered touring bonnet.

She took a small handbag and went to the polished teak and leaded-glass front door. She grasped the brass knob and swung it open. With practiced grace, Clarissa LaFarge descended the stairs to the boardwalk. Men's heads turned in admiration as she passed by. Without shifting her eyes, LaFarge counted the smiles. Hats tipped, but she took great pleasure in ignoring the gestures. Her talent made her a celebrity in Chicago, but in a man's world, possessing femininity and beauty was raw power.

Alongside the boardwalk, a white carriage with blue pinstripes and tan leather seats was ready and waiting. A single black horse in a polished harness stood ready for service, as did a large, blond-haired driver who appeared to be in his early thirties. He wore a neatly pressed plum-colored cutaway jacket that accented a pair of powerful shoulders.

The driver stepped toward LaFarge and extended his hand.

"Thank you, Reed," offered LaFarge as she daintily stepped into the seat and pulled in the train of her dress.

Before Reed Treadway closed the door, another man stepped up within a few feet of the carriage. He halted suddenly and removed his hat.

"Miss LaFarge," said the man, with a heavy cockney accent. "If I may have a word with ya? A word of great importance indeed, miss."

LaFarge held up her hand, signaling Treadway to hold his position. She took a moment, sizing up the intruder. Few men would attempt to approach Clarissa LaFarge unsolicited. She was amused and somewhat intrigued by his boldness.

He wore a long overcoat. His clothes were rough cut but clean. A patch covered his left eye, and he stood on a peg leg. He held his battered hat with both hands, exposing a thatch of tangled hair. A short beard covered his jaws and chin.

"What could you have to say that is of such great importance, sir?" asked LaFarge, with a hint of mockery in her voice.

The stranger hobbled a step closer and stopped. He lowered his head. He looked to the right and left. Then he spoke softly. "Beggin' your pardon, miss, but a friend of a friend, you might say, told me you just might be interested in what I've got to say."

LaFarge tolerated the public when she couldn't avoid them. This man was pathetic enough to be entertaining. The theater troupe could wait. "And who might this 'friend of a friend' be, sir? And for that matter, who are you?"

"Wheeler's me name, miss," said the man. And then, again lowering his voice, he added, "And the friend of a friend told me to mention the name of…Treadway."

Clarissa's eye's flickered at the mention of her driver's name. So did Treadway's. Both tried to appear unimpressed.

"So you know this Mr. Treadway?"

"No, miss, only the name. It was a name given to me that I might gain your ear."

LaFarge motioned for Wheeler to come closer. When he was within an arm's reach of the driver, he stopped.

"Well? Be quick about it, I'm late for rehearsal."

Wheeler reached inside his coat. "I have a map, Miss LaFarge."

"A map?" snickered LaFarge. "A treasure map, no doubt."

Bringing out a rolled-up piece of leather, Wheeler answered humbly, "I don't know for certain, miss, what it is."

Wheeler hurriedly unrolled the map, revealing a small silver coin that had been rolled inside it. It was tarnished with age. "This coin was with the map, miss. They say it is Spanish. They say it is old, very old."

Treadway took the coin and handed it to LaFarge. She turned it in her hand. "Is that it, Mr. Wheeler? A piece of leather and a coin?"

"No, miss," replied Wheeler, a smile growing under his whiskers. "There was also this."

Wheeler again reached into the inside pocket of his overcoat and began trying to wrestle an object out. For a moment, it snagged on a thread. Then he pulled out a dented metal helmet. It was pointed on both ends and riveted at the base.

"The man they say wore this helmet was a conquistador. That's Spanish for conqueror. Them three things—the map, the coin, and the helmet—was all got together, miss. They was all found at the same place. The helmet was dug up with the map and coin inside of it."

LaFarge glanced curiously at the helmet. She had seen one like it before. It was in the collection of a wealthy friend. Her interest was aroused, but she feigned boredom.

LaFarge sighed. "Very well then, let me see your map."

This time, without waiting for the driver to intercede, she took the map from Wheeler's hand. He seemed especially pleased, but Clarissa LaFarge did not notice.

She looked the map over carefully and then laid it on her lap. Again she looked at the coin.

"These items are somewhat interesting, Mr. Wheeler. Curiosities at best. What price are you seeking?"

Wheeler rolled his hat and looked down at his peg leg. "I was thinkin' one hundred dollars, miss."

LaFarge laughed. "Surely your…*friend*…told you I was no fool, Mr. Wheeler. The silver coin may have some value, but this thing you call a map is most likely is a ruse. And the helmet is of little use to me."

"But if they was all real, miss," protested Wheeler, "they could be worth a lot of money."

"If that is the case, why not keep the map? And if this *is* a treasure map, why not search for it yourself?"

Shrugging uneasily, Wheeler replied, "I can't cipher the meaning of the map….It might be a treasure map and might not, miss. Even if it was, I would need two good legs to hunt for it. What I know for certain is that them three things come from a long ways from here, way out in the desert."

"And where, pray tell, was that?"

"A place called Hawikuh."

"Hawikuh?"

"Yes, miss. I was told it was out in the New Mexico Territory or maybe Arizona Territory. Them that found it didn't know for certain. All that country is desert, and it all looks the same."

LaFarge opened her handbag and took out two coins. "I will give you forty dollars. That's a month's wages for a man with two good legs. That is the best I will offer, and I consider it quite generous."

For a moment, Wheeler hesitated. Then he held out the helmet. LaFarge took the helmet and dropped the coins into his open hand.

Placing the map and coin inside the helmet, she turned her attention forward.

"Good day, Mr. Wheeler."

Slowly closing the carriage door, Treadway watched Wheeler make his way down the boardwalk. After securing the latch, he looked at Clarissa LaFarge.

"Forty dollars?"

"And a good price," said LaFarge. "I've seen one other helmet like this one, and it was considered a prize possession."

"Wellington's?"

LaFarge nodded, a cunning smile curving her lips. "He'll know what this one is worth, and the coin, too. It is very likely he will want to buy them both."

"What about the map? Can we get anything for that?"

"It doesn't look like a map to me. But that remains to be seen. Miles will know about that as well. If he doesn't, he'll know someone who does.

"He'll want the coin and the helmet for his collection. I'll offer to give them to him, and he'll refuse, of course. He'll insist on paying. And just as he is with his horses, the more he pays for something, the more he thinks it's worth."

***

Wheeler turned into the first alley he came to and leaned over to rub the knee of his peg leg. It was sore from all the walking. He rested only a few seconds and then continued deeper into the shadows. Standing close to a wall, he unbuttoned his trousers and let them fall to his ankles.

After unbuckling two of four straps that encircled his thigh, he removed the peg leg and tossed it behind a pile of rubbish. He fumbled at the third and fourth buckles then let them drop. Slowly, painfully, his leg straightened. He massaged it for several minutes to get the blood flowing so he could stand again on his own two feet.

Looking up and down the alley, Wheeler pulled his pants up and removed the patch over his eye and the partial set of false teeth. A deep scar creased his eyebrow and his lid lagged, but the partially hidden eye danced with a devilish light.

He blinked a few times and then reached down and flipped over a crate, uncovering a shoe and derby hat. He put them on and removed his overcoat. As he walked out of the alley and back to the boardwalk, he folded the coat and hung it over his arm.

A quick glance back to where the carriage once stood told him he was safe. He turned and walked into the afternoon sun. Two of his lower front teeth were missing. One of his upper incisors was black and broken in half, but he smiled at everyone. It had been a perfect afternoon.

***

When Conway Fargo walked into the busy Pinkerton Detective Agency, a hush spread across the entire second floor. Some glanced uneasily at Fargo; others stared in admiration. They were, for the most part, investigators. The agent crossing to the main office was rumored to be a gunman of some skill. Some said he was a professional gunfighter from the West.

Fargo approached the office of Allan Pinkerton. Before he could knock on the door, the old man waved him in. The Scotchman sat behind a desk. His face was flushed red, but not with anger.

"Have a seat, Mr. Fargo," said Pinkerton. "We have trouble."

Fargo eased himself into an oak captain's chair and rested his eyes on Pinkerton. The man was a legend. He had worked with Lincoln during the late war, creating a secret network of Union spies. Since then, along with his agency, he was responsible for catching more criminals than any man alive.

"What kind of trouble?"

"The men you shot. And, mind you, I don't doubt they needed to be shot, but Anson was rattled. He's a good man, but he can be a bit simpleminded about some things. He went to the police.

"The men you shot worked for someone who has connections in Chicago. From what I gather, those connections include some of the police. They're calling for an investigation, and I don't like the bloody tone of it."

Showing little concern, Fargo said, "They came at me with clubs, and they both had pistols."

"So it was reported. But you gave them no warning. That's the rub."

"I warned them. I gave them a choice: leave and live or stay and die."

Pinkerton shook his head. "Damn it, man! This isn't Dodge City. This is Chicago!"

"Yes. And it's worse off than Dodge, I'd say. There we got law and we got order. There's not much gray in between."

Shaking his head, Pinkerton removed a pair of wire-rimmed glasses and glared across the room at Fargo. Then his expression calmed.

"You've got a point there, Mr. Fargo. In Chicago and in other eastern cities, criminals are starting to organize. That's something new. And that's why I hired you and assigned you to this case. This new breed of criminal has friends in high places, and they're ruthless. They must be handled in the same manner. Fight the devil with fire, I say. And you, sir, were to be my fire.

"For now, however, it's best you pack your bags at once. I'll find another assignment for you, but nowhere near Chicago. Until I discover who I can trust, it'll be better for you if the authorities can't find you. Stay in your hotel until you hear from the agency. Be ready to leave in the morning. I can stall them until then."

Fargo slowly came to his feet. "Suits me. I've seen enough of Chicago."

***

Mahra Brooks quietly entered the ladies' room at Hooley's Theater. She walked across the polished marble floor and placed her handbag on the counter. Slipping off her white crocheted gloves, she laid them neatly one on top of the other. From her handbag, she removed a small silver cup and a corked glass bottle. Using both thumbs, she eased the cork free and then carefully poured a measured amount of Mother Bailey's Quieting Syrup into the cup. She felt a headache coming on, and the syrup would do nicely to ease her pain.

Mahra carefully replaced the cork in her medicine bottle. Her doctor had prescribed either Godfrey's Cordial or Syndenham's Laudanum, but she liked the taste of the syrup better. It worked to ease her headaches and also cured her lack of energy. And thanks to Mother Bailey's gentle tonic, she had not endured a sleepless night in months.

After placing the bottle back in her purse, she slid her delicate fingers back into her gloves. She looked in the mirror across from her. With one hand she picked up the silver cup and with the other replaced a strand of hair that had fallen across her forehead. Raising the cup to her lips, she tilted it and swallowed. For a moment she held the cup steady, just long enough to catch the last drop of syrup on her outstretched tongue.

Feeling better already, Mahra stepped through the heavy velvet curtain of the darkened theater to rejoin Edward Davis and Miles Wellington. The three of them were the only visitors allowed in the auditorium, which held fourteen hundred seats. They were watching the rehearsal of *The Farmer's Daughter*. Davis and Wellington were seated in the front row, just behind the orchestra pit and a row of gas lights that lit up the stage. Clarissa LaFarge was finishing the last act.

Mahra took her seat next to Davis and put her arm through his. Kind and gentle, he was well educated and of the most refined breeding. He took care of everything for Mahra Brooks. With the blessings of both families, they had been engaged for six months.

LaFarge gazed into an imaginary sunset, placed the back of her hand on her forehead, and dramatically delivered her last line. It was an inspiring ending to a mediocre play. Her name and widely acclaimed talent promised to be the main attractions.

"Bravo," shouted Wellington. Coming to his feet, he began to clap his hands. "Bravo, Clarissa!"

Davis followed Wellington. With Brooks hanging on his arm, he rose and joined in the applause. "Well done! Well done!"

Mahra clapped daintily, her gloved hands making dull puffing sounds. She smiled adoringly at her best friend. "Very touching, Clarissa, very touching indeed!"

LaFarge went to the edge of the stage. Smiling at her friends, she took a graceful bow.

"Thank you, devoted followers of the stage," she said facetiously while batting her eyes. "But please do not clap. Just throw money."

Everyone laughed as LaFarge made her way off the stage and down to the front row. She hugged Wellington and placed her arm in his.

Wellington patted her hand. "That was a wonderful performance, my dear, truly wonderful."

"Yes," agreed Davis. "And the opening is still a month away. Why, you are ready to perform this very instant."

"Thank you, both," returned LaFarge with just the right amount of humility. "I thought it a fair performance."

"Oh no, Clarissa," added Brooks. "You truly could open tomorrow."

"Such flattery deserves reward," smiled LaFarge. "Let us leave my humble work behind and venture into the wonders of the evening."

Wellington nodded. "What did you have in mind? The night is young, and so are we."

"But first, to my dressing room."

"Here we go again," chuckled Davis. "Undoubtedly there will be another Chicago scandal for the four of us."

"Let them gossip," scoffed Wellington. "They have not stopped such nonsense since we left for Egypt last year. Is it our fault their lives are so dull and boring? I suppose it falls to the four of us to keep the timid and mundane aristocracy entertained."

Leading off with Wellington on her arm, LaFarge started backstage. When they entered her dressing room, she went behind a folding partition and began undressing. Davis shut the door. Mahra put her fingers to her lips and giggled.

LaFarge leaned her head around the partition. Exposing a bare shoulder, she pointed at something.

"Miles, look there on the dresser behind you."

Wellington smirked and glanced at the bare shoulder and white neck of Clarissa LaFarge. "I would rather look at you."

Disappearing behind the partition, she said, "I am sure that you would. Men are nothing more than boys. Now, be a dear and turn around like a gentleman, and tell me what you see on the dresser. If it is truly what I was told, then it is a gift for you."

Wellington turned to look, as did Davis and Brooks. Seeing the helmet, their eyes widened. Wellington was first to the dresser.

Carefully, he grasped the metal headpiece with both hands. He picked it up as if were a fragile piece of glass. Turning it slowly, he examined the exterior. A minute later, he rotated it to better study the inside.

Davis looked at Wellington. "Is that what I think it is, Miles?"

"It certainly looks authentic. Clarissa, how did you come by this?"

"A man—oh, did you see the coin on the dresser also? It came with the helmet. A man on the street thought I might have some interest in such things. He had an eye patch and a peg leg. I felt sorry for the poor wretch, so I bought them both."

"Good for you," said Mahra. "That was very kind."

Wellington handed the helmet to Davis and found the silver coin. He held it close to his eye. "This is Spanish…and it looks old."

"Did your one-legged man say where he obtained these items?" asked Davis, trying to suppress his excitement.

"A place called Hawikuh."

"Hawikuh? Hawikuh what? Did he say more?"

"He was not certain. He said it was somewhere in either the New Mexico or Arizona Territory."

Still holding the helmet, Wellington stared at Davis. "Are you thinking what I am, Edward?"

"Professor Morgan?" replied Davis.

"Precisely! He is lecturing at the Art Institute on State Street. And he is a guest at the hotel across the street from the institute."

"Who is Professor Morgan?" asked Brooks.

Davis responded. "He is only the most knowledgeable man in Chicago with regard to the Spanish conquest. He lectured at Harvard when we were studying there. He was so well respected that he was a guest lecturer at Yale, as well as other universities. Now he is the chairman of anthropology for the American Association for the Advancement of Science at Northeastern. Miles and I attended all of his lectures on antiquities. He should remember us. We always sat on the front row and frequently engaged him with questions."

Mahra drew a blank. "All those big words give me a headache. What does he do?"

Davis patted her hand, and with a smile he said, "He studies old things, dear, very old things. And two years ago, he conducted an expedition into the very region where these items were found."

LaFarge came out from behind her partition buttoning the high collar of her dress. "Then you like it, Miles?"

Wellington shrugged. "Professor Morgan will be able to verify its authenticity. If this is truly the helmet of a conquistador, it is very valuable. And, that being so, I could never accept it as a gift."

Waving a disregarding hand, LaFarge said, "I have no use for it unless…perhaps it could hold a nice plant or some flowers."

Wellington took a makeup towel from Clarissa's vanity and wrapped it around the helmet. He dropped the coin into his vest pocket and then asked, "Shall we go see the good professor? It is near suppertime, and we shall have to hurry. We would not want to interrupt him while he is dining."

Mahra merely smiled and shrugged.

Clarissa took Wellington's arm. She tossed her head back and said, "Lead on, sire. Our carriage awaits!"

Chapter 1

After the ladies were comfortably seated in the hotel lobby, Wellington and Davis started for the desk clerk to ask for Professor Morgan's room number. Before they reached the counter, Davis spotted two men descending the hotel stairs. One looked to be in his late thirties. The other, nearing seventy, was Professor Morgan.

Davis and Wellington hurried across the polished marble floor and met the two men as they reached the bottom of the stairs.

"Good evening, Professor Morgan!"

Somewhat startled and then surprised, Professor Morgan extended his hand. "Miles Wellington. How good to see you."

Shaking hands with Wellington, Morgan looked to Davis. "And Edward Davis. So good to see you as well. The last I heard, you all were in Egypt."

Wellington laughed. "Yes, Professor. We have only recently returned. And, I might add, it was your excellent series of lectures that inspired us to go abroad. However, we are here on a different matter this evening, one that is somewhat urgent."

Miles motioned for the ladies to join them. "But first, some introductions."

After Mahra and Clarissa were formally introduced, Morgan turned to the man next to him. "Everyone, I would like to introduce my good friend and colleague, Adolph Bandelier. He and I have been discussing the discoveries I made during my latest expedition."

"And where was that?" asked Davis.

"Our own Southwest," smiled Morgan. "Nothing so exotic as Egypt."

"By no means, Professor," said Wellington. "That is precisely why we have come to see you. Is there someplace we could talk?"

"Certainly. The hotel has a small library. Come this way."

The group followed the professor into a small room where shelves of books covered the walls. A small sofa and two leather chairs formed a half circle in front of a stone fireplace. Clarissa and Mahra took a seat on the sofa, but the men stood.

Wellington removed the makeup towel from the helmet, and held the helmet out.

"Gentlemen," said Wellington, "for your inspection …and possible amusement."

Morgan took out a pair of spectacles and wedged them on the bridge of his nose. He bent over for a closer look. He paused, then took the helmet and held it closer. His brow wrinkled. As he turned it slowly to study the rivets, his bushy eyebrows rose.

"Take a look, Adolph," said Morgan, giving the helmet to Bandelier.

Bandelier immediately flipped the helmet over and looked inside. With his fingernail, he scratched at the metal. Taking out a pocket-knife, he asked Wellington, "May I?"

"By all means, do."

Bandelier scraped the corrosion away and stared at the shiny scratch he had made. He gathered some of the particles from the knife blade and rubbed them between his thumb and finger.

"I would say this is authentic, Mr. Wellington. Do you know its history?"

Wellington turned to LaFarge. "Miss LaFarge purchased it from… what would you call him, dear?"

"A beggar," answered LaFarge. "He was a mudsill, a laborer at best."

"Did he happen to say how he came by it?"

"No. Only that it was from either the New Mexico or Arizona Territory. He said it was found at a place called…what did I say it was, Miles?"

"Hawikuh. That was it: Hawikuh."

Morgan and Bandelier looked at each other.

"What is it?" asked Davis. "Is there such a place?"

"Please, please," said Morgan, excitedly indicating some chairs. "Let us sit. This will take some time to explain."

Before taking a seat, Bandelier asked Wellington for the towel. He began polishing a small mark on the side of the helmet.

Morgan looked first to Wellington then to Davis. He took off his glasses and dropped them in his coat pocket. Leaning forward, he rested his palms on his knees.

"You were both good students, and very inquisitive, as I recall. But the lectures you attended covered only Mediterranean antiquities. Have either of you studied the conquistadors or the Spanish Conquest?"

"Not at all," admitted Davis.

"I have a few pieces of armor in my collection," said Wellington. "But I must say I have not researched their history in any detail."

Bandelier continued to rub. He licked the tip of the towel from time to time to wet it.

"Well, are the two of you prepared to hear another of my lectures?" asked Morgan, smiling.

"Indeed, we are." answered Wellington as Davis nodded in agreement.

"Very well," began Morgan. "I will begin at the beginning and be as brief as possible." Morgan turned to Bandelier and added, "And I would invite Adolf to add any information he considers helpful to my explanation.

"Our story begins in 1528, when a Spaniard named Narvaez sailed to America. Soon after landing in Florida, his expedition fell apart. Most of his men died of disease or were killed by hostile Indians. To survive, four men managed to sail from Florida to Mexico on makeshift rafts. Then the foursome traveled west across the northeastern part of Mexico and possibly into our own Southwest. They wandered throughout that region until 1536—eight long years!

"Of the four men, two recorded their extraordinary adventure. The most detailed account was written by Cabeza de Vaca. From his record, we know that one of the four was a black slave named Estevan. And of the four men, it is the slave who became most important.

"He was from Morocco. If you will recall from your studies of Mediterranean antiquities, Morocco had been conquered by the Arabs. Estevan's native language was Arabic, but, out of necessity, he had also learned to speak Spanish."

Bandelier broke in as he continued to polish the helmet. "Estevan apparently was an exceptionally intelligent man. His ability to learn other languages and dialects was a very valuable asset as he and his companions made their way through Mexico."

"Yes," agreed Morgan. "It was mainly through Estevan that the other three communicated with the Mexican Indians. However, when the men first came in contact with them, they were held as captives in a small village. But by some twist of fate, the prisoners were able to use their basic knowledge of medicine to heal some of the sick in the village. Word of their abilities quickly spread, and other sick were brought to them. Those who could not be helped with their medical skills were merely prayed over."

"Not merely," said Bandelier. "According to both written accounts, there were many miraculous healings, healings none of them could explain."

"Miracles?" questioned Wellington.

Morgan smiled. "That is what is reported. And it is a fact that their success and fame won their freedom. They gained such respect that they were accepted as shamans. Eventually they were allowed to leave the village and continue their journey west toward the Pacific Ocean.

"Upon leaving, however, the men discovered they were followed by almost everyone in the village."

LaFarge blinked. "If the Indians let them go free, why were they followed?"

Nodding, Morgan said, "Apparently, it was due to a strange custom of the region. The inhabitants continued following them until reaching the next village."

Morgan paused and shook his head.

"What then, Professor?" asked Mahra.

"As hard as it is to believe, the inhabitants of the second village stepped aside and allowed their village to be pillaged by those of the first village. They took whatever they pleased while the owners watched."

"They just stood by and watched?" asked Wellington.

"Yes, indeed. Perhaps it was a type of passive warfare. At any rate, when the four men moved on to the third village, the inhabitants of the second village followed them and pillaged it while the first village went back home. This custom was repeated, village by village, all across Mexico, each village in turn pillaging the next.

"I must add that toward the end, near the Pacific coast, some of the villagers, knowing they were about to be pillaged, did begin to hide some of their belongings. It seems the custom faded the farther west they traveled."

"What were the Spaniards and the slave doing while all of this was taking place?" asked Davis.

Bandelier cleared his throat and continued to polish the helmet.

Morgan glanced at Brooks and LaFarge. "This gets a bit delicate."

"Please continue, Professor," urged LaFarge. "Mahra and I are women of the world. We will not be offended."

"Good," said Morgan. "I shall continue.

"As for the three Spaniards, they continued to heal and pray as they went. Perhaps, because he was treated differently, Estevan took another path.

"He was tall and very muscular, and he had black skin, something the Indians had never seen. They began to bring him gifts of food, then objects they valued. When they started giving him turquoise, their most prized jewelry, he understood what it meant.

"He took it upon himself to take their generosity one step further. He asked for and received a woman. After that, everywhere he went, he asked for women, and they were given to him. He became like a god."

"My heavens," exclaimed Brooks.

"Finally," continued Morgan, changing the subject, "all four men made it back to Spain. We don't know the details of their report to the Spanish, but at least one of the four claimed to have heard the Indians referring to cities of gold—seven of them, in fact.

"Since it was Estevan who understood the Indians' language best, it is likely the story came through him. The cities were said to lie just north of where the four wanderers had passed on their journey to the Pacific coast of Mexico.

"Upon their return to Spain, Estevan, who was still a slave, became the property of another Spaniard.

"When the viceroy of Spain heard the rumors of golden cities, he sponsored a return expedition. He appointed a priest by the name of Fray Marcos de Niza as leader. However, Fray Marcos was no ordinary priest. He had been with Pizarro in Peru during the conquest of the Incas. He was a skilled navigator and map maker.

"The viceroy also arranged for Estevan to return to Mexico in order to serve Marcos as guide. In 1539 they landed at a Spanish settlement on the west coast of Mexico. With three hundred domesticated Indians, they proceeded north toward what are now called the Arizona and New Mexico Territories.

"Again, Estevan began to play his former role as a god. This time, however, he was more flamboyant and dramatic. He carried a gourd of some sort and claimed it had magical powers. He also had two greyhounds with him wherever he went. At his insistence, he was fed his meals on two green dishes made of glass. He wore a buffalo cape draped across his shoulders and adorned himself with feathers on his arms and bells on his ankles."

Mahra shook her head. "My goodness, this story is so complicated. My head is beginning to spin."

Morgan hesitated. Bandelier looked up for a moment and then went back to work.

"Do not be concerned, Mahra," smiled Davis. "I will explain everything later. Please continue, Professor."

"Yes, Miss Brooks," said Morgan, "it is confusing, but please bear with me. I believe you will find my story most interesting.

"As I was saying, Estevan led the way northward over country that had become familiar to him during his years of wandering. Being accustomed to traveling on foot, he and his Indian followers quickly moved ahead of Marcos.

"In the event they might become separated, Marcos had instructed Estevan to send back a white cross if he found anything that might lead them to the Seven Cities of Gold. The size of the cross was to be determined by the significance of the discovery.

"Several weeks passed before the first runner was sent back to Marcos. He delivered a small cross about the size of a man's hand. It was followed by a larger cross and then a larger one. The last cross Estevan sent back was the size of a grown man."

"A man?" questioned Wellington.

"Yes. And with it was a message to make haste to join the advance party."

Morgan paused.

"What did the last cross mean?" Davis asked.

Shaking his head, Morgan sighed. "That, we do not know, Edward."

LaFarge shifted uneasily. Her eyes narrowed with intensity. "And what happened to this Estevan, Professor? What of the Cities of Gold?"

"Quite right," smiled the professor. "Back to the story."

"Before Fray Marcos could rejoin Estevan, another runner arrived. He had no cross and was covered with blood. He said they had found a large walled city with very tall stone buildings. It was inhabited by the Zuni Indians, who called the city Hawikuh.

"The messenger reported that the Zunis had captured Estevan and imprisoned him in a round building outside the walls for three days. The Indians then killed Estevan and attacked their camp, killing all but a few who managed to escape.

Bandelier joined in. "What actually led the Zunis to kill Estevan is not completely clear. Estevan had reinstituted the practice of pillaging and demanding women. He met no resistance until he came to Hawikuh. But not only were the Zunis ready to fight for their village, they were outraged when Estevan demanded their women."

"Quite right," agreed Morgan. "Estevan then tried to frighten the Zuni into submission by telling them fierce, ironclad warriors would soon arrive. The Spanish warriors, he said, would come with sticks of fire to destroy them if they did not submit to him. The Zunis not only refused his demands, they killed him and almost all three hundred Indians with him."

"Historians disagree on whether Marcos ever reached this walled city. Some believe he turned back after the massacre of Estevan. However, once back in Spain, Marcos is said to have confided in another priest that he did in fact reach the city. He said he had seen walls encrusted with jewels. That the temples contained golden idols. And that the inhabitants wore belts of gold and fine jewelry."

"Rightly or wrongly, in Spain the Zuni city of Hawikuh came to be known as Cibola, one of the Seven Cities of Gold. The Spanish were so convinced these cities existed that the following year—that would be 1540—the Spanish viceroy commissioned another expedition. This time he was determined to conquer the Zuni and return with the treasures of Cibola. Naturally, he employed Fray Marcos as guide. And to lead the expedition, he appointed the explorer and conquistador Francisco Vasquez de Coronado."

"Now, Coronado we have heard of," said Davis.

Morgan nodded. "Yes. The first conquistador in the Southwest."

"Marcos led Coronado directly to Cibola," added Bandelier. "Coronado and his soldiers easily took the city, but after an extensive search, found no gold. Today Cibola, or rather Hawikuh, is an uninhabited city in ruins. Or, should I say, it is uninhabited by the living. There is an Indian superstition that their dead, along with Estevan, walk the ruins to this day."

"My word!" exclaimed Wellington. "What an amazing story. Simply fascinating. Would it not be wonderful if that helmet was a relic of the Coronado expedition?"

"It is possible," offered Bandelier. "I will say it is very likely."

Turning to his friend, Morgan asked, "Why do you say that, Adolph?"

Bandelier handed the helmet to Morgan. He pointed to an area that had been polished to a shine. "Look closely."

Morgan replaced his glasses and inspected the helmet for several seconds.

"Feathers and bells?" questioned Morgan, now staring at Bandelier.

"That is my conclusion as well," confirmed Bandelier.

"Feathers and bells?" asked Wellington.

Offering the helmet to Wellington, Morgan said, "Look at the figure scratched on the side of the helmet. It appears to be that of a man. His arms definitely have feathers on them, and those objects on his ankles could easily be interpreted as bells."

"Your helmet," said Bandelier, "could be the first authenticated artifact belonging to the Coronado expedition."

"There was also this," said Wellington, retrieving the silver coin from his pocket. "The man who sold it to Clarissa said it was found with the helmet."

Wellington handed the coin to Morgan. Morgan briefly examined it and then passed it to Bandelier.

"Very worn, but definitely Spanish," said Bandelier, inspecting its tarnished surface. "This is a *macuquinas*, a crude hammered coin. They are also known as *cobs*, which is an abbreviation for *cabo de barra*, or end of the bar.

"The early Spanish mints in the New World cut pieces of silver from bars and handstamped them. They were so crudely made that no two coins were exactly the same. During that period, all of them bore the same stamped image, but their shapes varied greatly. The largest of these weighed approximately one ounce, and its denomination was eight *reales*. A single coin was called a piece of eight. I estimate this coin to weigh roughly one quarter ounce; thus, it is two reales.

"Its most intriguing feature, however, is that there is no date on the coin."

"What does that mean?" asked Wellington.

Bandelier paused and glanced at Morgan. "It means, Mr. Wellington, this coin was stamped somewhere between 1536 and 1572 at one of those early New World mints!"

Morgan leaned forward, suddenly very excited. "Did you acquire anything else, Miss LaFarge? This is most encouraging. Did the man have additional relics to sell? Can you recall him saying anything more of Hawikuh?"

LaFarge hesitated. Normally, she could lie with a straight face. This time she blinked. "No. No, that was all."

"If at all possible, Miss LaFarge," said Bandelier, "I would very much like to speak with the man who sold you these items. This could be one of the most significant discoveries of the century."

"My goodness, I don't know how to contact him!" exclaimed LaFarge. "If I had only known....I feel terrible."

Wellington went to Clarissa and sat down beside her. "Now, let us have none of that. You had no way of knowing. We will search for this man tomorrow, and with luck, will find him."

Everyone in the room nodded in agreement.

Looking sorrowfully at Morgan and Bandelier, LaFarge subtly changed the subject. "Very well, then. But I am so confused. Was there, or was there not, any gold at Cibola? And were the other six Cities of Gold ever found?"

Bandelier sat back in his chair and thoughtfully folded his arms. "Five of the six cities were found. But none contained any gold. The seventh so-called City of Gold is yet to be discovered."

"So there was no gold or jewels?" asked Davis. "Nothing?"

Morgan knowingly smiled at Bandelier and then chuckled.

For a moment, the room fell silent.

"Go ahead and tell them," encouraged Bandelier. "I do not agree with your thesis, but it is a plausible theory."

"A theory?" questioned Wellington.

Morgan shrugged. "Over the years, I have given the subject of Cibola a great deal of thought. In Spain, the stories of seven Cities of Gold existed hundreds of years before Coronado set sail. As for Hawikuh, our Cibola if you will, I have a number of unanswered questions. That is all. As yet, it is not a formal theory."

"Please, tell us, Professor," said LaFarge. "It will make the helmet all the more mysterious."

The charm of Clarissa LaFarge was impossible to resist. Morgan grinned and placed his hands back on his knees.

"Well, when I first studied this incident, I found myself asking where the Zuni warriors were when Coronado arrived at Cibola. May I remind you that when Estevan traveled to Cibola the previous year, he was accompanied by three hundred Indians. It would have taken a sizeable Zuni army to wipe out that many so easily. When Coronado arrived a year later, he met no such army, only weak resistance.

"Then I started thinking why Marcos would say he had seen a city of jewels and people laden with gold if he had not? He was a devout priest, an experienced explorer, and a map maker. I concluded that a man like that would hardly be prone to exaggeration.

"Add to this, without hesitation Marcos led Coronado directly to Cibola. I wondered why he would do that knowing the expedition would find only a poorly defended stone village with nothing of value within its walls. Would any man in his right mind do such a thing when the expedition was financed by the viceroy of Spain himself?

"There was also an Indian slave named Tejo in Spain during the same time period as Marcos. He claimed to have seen large cities in the same region, where silver was in such abundance that silversmiths literally lined the city streets. What if this Tejo also told the truth?

"And finally, there is the curious fact that after conquering Cibola, Coronado sent a message to the viceroy in which he stated his belief that the Zunis had a quantity of turquoise that they had removed, along with the rest of their goods, *prior* to his attack."

Morgan leaned back and folded his arms. "Now, ladies and gentlemen, given these questions and observations, do any theories come to mind?"

Wide-eyed, Mahra looked around. She smiled sheepishly, as if having missed the point of a joke. "What? I do not understand. So, was there gold or was there not?"

No one bothered to answer her question.

"Are you saying," Davis asked, "that the Zunis may have *hidden* their gold before Coronado got there, that Cibola may actually have been a City of Gold?"

"I believe it is possible," answered Morgan. "If the Zunis believed Estevan's threatening description of ironclad warriors, they might have assumed they would eventually be attacked by an army they could not defeat. So when word of Coronado's advancing forces reached them, they simply removed the treasure and sent the warriors into hiding. That would also explain why there was so little resistance to

Coronado's attack on the city. And recall, the Indian villages near the Pacific side of Mexico began hiding their valuables when Estevan approached them from the east."

For several moments, the room was silent. LaFarge's eyes moved slowly from person to person. Her mind raced, but her face betrayed nothing of her growing excitement.

"So if the gold was never discovered," asked LaFarge innocently, "wouldn't it still be out there somewhere near Hawikuh? Do you suppose the Zuni Indians know its hiding place?"

Morgan shrugged. "To answer your questions, I can only speculate. If it does exist, then it should be somewhere near Hawikuh. Coronado and his successors lived up to the name conquistador. They were ruthless and brutal conquerors. The Pueblo Indians were forced into subjugation to the Spanish for generations. If the Zunis hid their most valued possessions from them, then it is very probable that they would have kept them hidden as long as the Spanish ruled. Perhaps even the Zunis who knew where their treasure was concealed died before they could pass on the location of the gold to succeeding generations. If that is the case, then the Zuni treasure is lost and may never be found."

Raising a hand, Morgan indicated Bandelier. "Perhaps Adolph will be able to uncover some additional clues to help answer our questions. He is planning an excursion to this same region the first week of August. I believe it his intention to research the ancient pueblo cultures."

As Bandelier handed the Spanish coin back to Wellington, he offered, "That is correct, but I plan to be a bit north of Hawikuh. Perhaps I will have time to visit there. It is hard to say.

"When I return, perhaps we can meet again. I may be able to shed more light on the history of your artifacts."

"Wonderful idea," said Wellington. "And I can show you my humble collection of Spanish relics."

Mahra smiled again, dimples adorning both rosy cheeks. "I love tales of buried treasure. And to think that old hat could be a clue. This is so exciting!"

Davis turned to her and said softly, "It is a helmet, dear, not a hat."
Everyone, including Mahra, broke out in laughter.

As her smile faded, LaFarge stood. She had heard enough. The men followed her lead, as did Brooks. "Thank you, Professor, for your time and your intriguing stories. Mr. Bandelier, I thank you as well. We will detain you no longer. It has been most interesting."

Morgan went to LaFarge and took her hand. "Will you stay and dine with us? It would be our pleasure."

Before anyone could voice an opinion, LaFarge replied smoothly, "Unfortunately, no. We have another engagement. Perhaps another time."

Wellington glanced curiously at LaFarge and then turned to Morgan and Bandelier. Shaking their hands, he thanked them, as did Davis and Brooks.

It wasn't until they exited the hotel and were seated in their carriage that Wellington asked the question that was on everyone's mind.

"Clarissa, what, pray tell, is this *prior* engagement you spoke of? I would have enjoyed dining with the professor and Mr. Bandelier."

"And I am getting hungry," said Davis, placing his arm around Mahra to keep her warm.

"I fear I may become light-headed," added Mahra.

LaFarge looked at her companions. Wellington would do as she wished, and Davis always followed the lead of his cousin. Brooks was a harmless fool. They all served their purpose from time to time. And they could again.

"I must confess to a white lie, one I told the professor."

Wellington stiffened slightly. He raised an eyebrow.

"A white lie? What on earth for? Are you referring to the engagement this evening?"

"No. Not the engagement. That, I will explain."

"What, then?"

The carriage began moving, the horse's hooves clopping methodically over the pavement. The air was cooling. A breeze churned the stale city air.

LaFarge motioned for all to lean forward. When their heads were close together, she whispered, "In addition to the helmet and coin... there was also a map."

Brooks gasped but quickly put both hands over her mouth. Davis and Wellington stared at each other for several seconds.

"What kind of map?" asked Davis in a hushed yet skeptical tone.

Shrugging, LaFarge answered quietly, "I will show it to you at my apartment. That is our 'engagement.' I thought the map was nothing, a fake. But now...I am not so sure."

Wellington sat up. "Reed, take us to Miss LaFarge's residence, and quickly!"

***

Davis closed the door to the apartment while Wellington turned up the gaslights. LaFarge went straight to her bedroom.

Brooks crossed the floor and settled into a stuffed leather sofa. There was tension in her face as she poured a measure of Mother Bailey's into her silver cup. The cool evening air, she said, had settled in her neck.

Wellington cleared a writing table and slid it to the center of the room. Davis lit a kerosene lamp and brought it to the table. He turned up the wick just as LaFarge returned with a small bundle in her hand.

"It's not much," said LaFarge. She placed the map on the table, gently unrolled it, and stepped back.

Davis and Wellington leaned in for a closer look. Various images had been painted on a cured animal skin. Most of the figures were black; some were red and a few a faded green.

After several minutes of silence, Brooks wandered over to the table. The smile on her face signaled that the Mother Bailey's had taken effect, and once again, all was well.

"You three are so quiet," said Mahra. "You were chattering like songbirds on the ride over."

Davis looked up at his fiancée. He smiled patiently and then again focused his attention on the map.

"So, is it buffalo hide?" asked Mahra.

Davis again looked up. This time his smile was more forced. "What, dear?"

Flicking her wrist as if shooing away a fly, she indicated the map. "That awful thing, is it buffalo skin?"

"Why do you ask?"

Brooks shrugged. "The professor said that black man wore a buffalo cape. Maybe the map was made from his cape."

LaFarge, Wellington, and Davis stood suddenly. They glanced at Mahra, then at each other.

"I'll be damned," blurted Wellington. "I had forgotten that bit of information."

Shaking her head in amazement, LaFarge agreed. "And so had I. Mahra, you never cease to amaze me. Well done. Well done, indeed!"

Davis was stunned. "And I thought you were not listening, dear. And yet you recalled something none of us remembered!"

Fluttering her eyes, Mahra giggled. "I was not listening to most of it. I just remembered that part, I suppose."

"Do you think it could be buffalo hide, Miles?" Davis asked.

"I have no idea. There are some hairs remaining, but they could be anything. We will have to ask someone who knows about such things. If it *is* buffalo, we could be on to something, something big!"

Mahra waved a hand. Dimples framed a wide smile. "I am happy to be of service. My work here is done. Now I will sit and rest."

Davis watched Mahra turn gracefully and walk back to the sofa. Glancing at LaFarge and Wellington, he shrugged then leaned back over the table. Pointing to several figures, he drew their attention back to the map. "These markings are clearly men. Stick figures, but men all the same. These must be spears they are holding."

"Agreed," said Wellington.

LaFarge pointed next. "All these small curved lines here…some could be…they look a bit like snakes."

Mahra closed her eyes as if she were shutting out an unpleasant thought. "Snakes! Oh, I have heard enough. Must we talk of such things? I am getting goose flesh."

"They are only paintings of snakes, sweetheart," comforted Davis. "You need not worry your pretty head over them."

"I shall not," pouted Brooks. She reached inside her purse for the bottle of Mother Bailey's but recalling she had just taken a dose, slid her hand back out. Glancing uneasily at Davis, she laid her head back, sighed, and folded her hands in her lap.

"This appears to be some kind of lizard," offered Wellington. "I count at least thirty images. None seem to be in any pattern that I can see."

"These dots," offered LaFarge. "They could be stars."

Davis nodded. He squinted and turned his head. "I think you are right. Look at the pattern. It appears to be the Big Dipper."

Wellington took a match from his pocket. Holding the head between his fingers, he used the wooden end as a miniature pointer. "Yes, Miles, I believe it may be. Look at this one, its location."

Simultaneously LaFarge and Davis chimed, "The North Star."

Hovering closer to the map and tapping his finger on the table, Davis said, "If that represents north, then this might indeed be a map."

There was another long moment of silence as each of the three studied the map's every detail. LaFarge moved the lamp closer and turned the wick still higher.

Taking the match from Wellington, she pointed to a line and a half circle on top left side of the map. "Is it possible this could be the setting sun?"

"Possibly," said Wellington.

"Do either of you notice anything about the stick figures?" asked LaFarge.

"What, in particular?" Wellington asked.

"This one," said LaFarge, outlining the figure. "This one is quite different from the rest. It is humpbacked. And the head is different."

"No," Davis disagreed. "Look, here is another. It appears to be stepping on one of those snakelike objects."

"You are right," replied LaFarge. "Are there any others like it? Do you think these things on the head could be feathers, perhaps indicating a chief, a walking chief?"

Wellington said nothing. He seemed to be deep in thought.

"It is certainly walking," said Davis. "See how the foot is up on both figures. But it seems to have something in its mouth…possibly a horn."

"Or a flute," offered LaFarge. "I have heard that some Indians use flutes in their ceremonies. This could be a musician and not a chief."

Davis straightened. He inhaled deeply and then exhaled slowly. With a growing smile, he said, "Well, I doubt we will ever be certain. I must say, these markings could mean just about anything. However, I have enjoyed our little adventure this evening, enjoyed it immensely. It has been very exciting, Clarissa. I have not enjoyed myself so much since we visited the mysterious pyramids."

"Pyramids!" blurted Wellington, snapping out of his deep concentration. "Arabic! By damn! It could be Arabic!"

"My word," gasped LaFarge. "Miles?"

"The snakes." said Wellington, pointing at one of the humpbacked figures. "Look at the snakes. Start with the one under the foot of this fellow. Count them."

Davis and LaFarge began to number the curved lines.

"I count six," said Davis.

"There are seven," corrected Wellington.

"Yes. And what of it?"

Wellington's eyes flickered with excitement. "When you spell Estevan, how many letters do you come up with?"

Davis thought for a moment. "If you spell it with a 'ph' as in Este*phan*, there are eight. If with a 'v' as in Estevan…then there are seven."

"And Estevan was a Moroccan," added LaFarge. "Professor Morgan said he spoke Arabic. And you just said, 'It could be Arabic.' Miles, what are you thinking?"

"Before our trip to Egypt last year, I studied up on the history of Egypt…and since Egypt and much of North Africa had been conquered by the Arabs, I also studied the Arabic language. They write their numbers left to right, just as we do, but unlike English, Arabic is written and read from right to left."

"And?" asked Davis, his brow beginning to furrow.

Wellington pointed to the snakelike lines "See these three 'snakes'?"

"Yes."

"Would you agree that each looks a bit like the number three backward?"

"Yes, they do, somewhat."

"Those three could be vowels that sound like the letter *A*, as in apple."

"Go on."

"This snake on the far left appears to be curled. But see here, there is a dot above it."

Davis shrugged. "Looks like a snake about to bite a mouse. The dot could be a rodent of some sort."

Wellington nodded patiently. "Or it could be the Arabic letter *N*."

"And this one, second from the right, it resembles a snake crawling. What might that be?" asked LaFarge.

"That could be an *S*. The Arabic *S* looks very similar."

"And this," said Davis. "It looks like one of our copperheads coiled up."

"That might be a *T*."

"And this, the snake with its tail in the air, I suppose that is a *V*."

Wellington grinned at Davis. "Clarissa, would you please bring me a pen and ink and some paper? I believe an illustration will help my cousin overcome his skepticism."

LaFarge brought the paper and pen. Wellington dipped the pen in the ink.

"I will now write, in Arabic, in the manner in which an uneducated Moroccan might write his name, likely the only thing a slave would ever learn to write."

Taking his time, Wellington drew out seven Arabic letters from right to left. When he finished, he held the paper up for Davis and LaFarge to see. Davis nearly shouted, "It looks just like the markings on the map!"

"I'll be damned," uttered LaFarge.

Both Wellington's and Davis's mouths dropped open. Mahra gasped.

LaFarge put a hand over her lips. "Pardon me," she said with an expert portrayal of timidity and embarrassment.

Wellington began to laugh, slowly at first, then with greater zeal. Davis joined him, as did LaFarge.

Brooks rose from the sofa and went to her three friends. She, too, began to laugh.

"What are we laughing about?" Mahra asked.

LaFarge took her hand. "We have a map," she said giddily. "We have a treasure map!"

Clapping her hands together as she laughed, Mahra asked, "Where does it lead us?"

Her question had a sobering effect on the celebration. Seconds later, they were back looking at the map.

Davis wiped his face and blinked his eyes. He again stared at the markings.

"It would appear we have a legitimate artifact. We know where north is, but we have little else. There must be more here. There has to be more."

All eyes turned to Wellington. He offered nothing but a smile.

After several seconds, Davis too began to smile.

"He knows something," said Davis. "I have seen that grin all my life. He has it whenever he is one step ahead of me. Every puzzle, every game, Cousin Miles always won. That is his gloating smile, my friends. Oh yes, Miles knows something."

LaFarge folded her arms. "Miles," she said, drawing his name out in mock scorn.

Wellington relented. "Very well. Look under the foot of each humpback. Tell me what you see."

Both peered at the map, looking from one figure to the next. The marks were small, almost insignificant.

Davis thought for a moment. He glanced at LaFarge. They looked at each other with calculating eyes.

"Numbers?" guessed Davis. "They could be Arabic numbers." LaFarge nodded in agreement.

Davis continued. "The humpback is walking. The numbers show how many steps are to be taken. The North Star is over one figure, and the sun is over the other. Take so many steps to the north and then so many steps west."

"Correct, my good friends," exclaimed Wellington. "To be precise, take twenty-one steps to the north and then eighteen steps to the west. And the starting point could be this circle with these ovals in the center. Once we have discovered what that is, we will be well on our way to finding what could be the lost Zuni treasure of Cibola!"

Davis looked at LaFarge. "That is, if Clarissa wishes to include us. After all, it *is her* map."

LaFarge shook her head. "Of course I include everyone. We do everything together. We will do this together or not at all."

"And what if there is a treasure?" asked Wellington. "What then, Clarissa?"

Placing her arm in Wellington's, LaFarge flashed a beautiful smile. "We are all partners. We will share equally in whatever we find."

Wellington patted her arm and gazed into the expectant eyes of Clarissa LaFarge. "Is she not a jewel, Edward?"

Placing his arm around Mahra, Edward replied, "We are fortunate men, Miles, fortunate indeed."

After a loving sigh, LaFarge spoke softly but with urgency. "We will have to leave at once."

Cocking his head, Wellington asked, "Why is that, dear?"

"Recall that Mr. Bandelier said he was soon to depart for this same region. I fear he may set out before he had originally planned. Professor Morgan's questions about the possibility of hidden Zuni treasure seemed to have piqued his interest. And having seen the helmet and the coin, he undoubtedly will assume there are other Spanish artifacts to be found at Hawikuh. He may even change his plans and head directly for Hawikuh."

"What about your play?" Mahra asked. "You are due to open in a few weeks."

"I have considered that. It is my hope that we will return before the opening. I have played this role so often that I needn't worry about rehearsing. However, if we are detained, I have an understudy who will welcome the opportunity to fill my role."

Davis shrugged. "I am free. And I believe Mahra is also."

Mahra smiled and gave Davis a hug. "I just go where I am told."

"Then we are agreed," said Wellington. "When do we leave?"

"None of us have ever ventured west of the Mississippi River, so we will need a competent guide," offered LaFarge. "I will bring my driver to help with the horses, the fires, and so on. And Mahra, we will need Hialeaha."

"Of course," agreed Brooks. "We must maintain appearances. And Hialeaha can cook and clean for us, too."

"Where can we find a guide on such short notice?" asked Davis. "He should be skilled with firearms and familiar with the land, a Westerner. It could be dangerous. We need someone able to provide protection should we need it. He must be trustworthy in the event we do find treasure. The wrong man could take our gold and our lives."

"Allan Pinkerton," said Wellington firmly. "My family has done business with him for years. Three years ago, in the labor strike, Pinkerton's agents guarded our railroads. Some of them even infiltrated that horrid Socialist Labor Party. Now they help protect our trains from bandits. Mr. Pinkerton will know of someone we can hire. His detective agency has connections from coast to coast."

LaFarge took a deep, satisfying breath and let it out slowly. "Tonight we finalize our plans. Tomorrow morning the four of us will go to the Pinkerton Agency. We must not speak a word of our true intentions to anyone, not even Hialeaha. And we must hire a man capable enough to do our bidding yet one who can be easily deceived."

Wellington snickered. "From what I have heard of Western men, that part of our plan should be simplest of all."

Chapter 2

Conway Fargo sat waiting in the narrow hallway across from Allan Pinkerton's office. Pinkerton had sent for him, as he had said he would. The messenger had told him to come quickly. An assignment was waiting, an assignment that would get him out of Chicago.

Through the glass window, Fargo could see Pinkerton talking with two men and three women. Two of the women were dressed in high fashion, both unusually attractive. The third woman was dark skinned and plainly dressed. She was not beautiful but was what some called handsome.

The two men were well dressed, one much taller than the other. The taller had broad shoulders but a light build. He was doing most of the talking.

Several moments passed before Pinkerton opened the door to his office. His face seemed flushed. He closed the door behind him. Taking a seat next to Fargo, he muttered something under his breath and turned.

"I have a job for you, Mr. Fargo, should you choose to accept it. Notice I said 'a job,' not an assignment. You will no longer be a Pinkerton agent. You were officially fired yesterday. And, as I told the Chicago police, I have no idea where you are.

"Do we understand each other, Mr. Fargo?"

"We do."

"If you decide to take this job, it shouldn't last more than a few weeks." Pinkerton handed Fargo a piece of paper. "That's the name of the head of a battalion of Texas Rangers down in San Antonio. I wired him about you. When you're done with these aristocrats, he said he'd hire you on the spot."

With a nod, Fargo glanced at the handwritten name. "Captain McNeely?"

"That's correct," said Pinkerton. Fargo folded the paper and shoved into his vest pocket.

"Now, there are four fools in my office who wish to take a trip west to see some old Indian villages. It seems they do that sort of thing to pass the time, as none of them has to work for a living.

"They're offering five hundred dollars for a guide."

"You said four fools. I see five people in there."

Pinkerton nodded. "Yes. The older one is a Cherokee. She was the nanny for one of the ladies. Now she is employed as a servant and travels around with them. The five of them just got back from Egypt. And that's just one of the places they've been. The two couples are high society, but they seem to enjoy being the subject of gossip. They're not married, so when they *travel* together, if you get my meaning, they take the Indian along to maintain an air of respectability."

"So where do they want to go?"

"They said the Navajo reservation, New Mexico Territory."

"Why?"

Pausing, Pinkerton scratched his chin. "The two men say they are archeologists and want to study how the ancient Indians lived. Well now, I say Indians, but they called them aborigines. Aborigines, mind you!"

"Do you believe them?"

"Maybe," muttered Pinkerton. "You can never tell with rich folks."

"When do they want to leave?"

"Tomorrow. They are in an all-fired hurry for some reason. That's what got me wondering about their story."

"So who are these people, anyway?"

"Well, there's the Cherokee. She doesn't say much but seems level headed. Her name is Hialeaha.

"The tall one is Miles Wellington. Twenty-seven years old, son of a wealthy railroad man. Went to Harvard. Was on the rowing team and was quite a boxer. A ladies' man, too.

"The other man is Wellington's cousin, Edward Davis. Twenty-six and has a father who runs a shipping company. Went to Harvard. Not much of an athlete, though.

"The pretty little brunette is Mahra Brooks. The Indian was her nanny. She also attended Harvard. Comes from old money and is liked by everyone. From all accounts, a delightful person.

"And then there is Clarissa LaFarge. She's rich, a real beauty and a famous stage actress. Miss LaFarge is known throughout the East. She says she got her money from a deceased uncle who struck it rich in the California gold fields. Nobody knows much about her, and she seems to like it that way.

"She first showed up in Chicago after the Big Fire in seventy-one. That's when a third of the city burned to the ground."

"I heard about that. Started by a cow?"

"That's what some say, but no one really knows for certain. It was terrible. It was hell on earth. What made it even worse was the looting that went along with it. Heartless bastards! They didn't even wait for the ashes to cool. They went straight for the wealthy districts—in some cases, walking right over the dead looking for their safes, silverware, anything they could steal. Property worth millions of dollars disappeared.

"Anyway, LaFarge soon enrolled in Yale and took acting classes. Something happened there, and she left. She enrolled at Harvard. The four of them have been an item ever since they met in college."

Fargo eyed the would-be travelers through the window. "Taking three women out there is asking for trouble. And I suppose they'll be traveling in style."

"Likely. Their plan is to take the train as far as it goes and then unload the new coach and wagon they just bought."

"The tracks stop at Lamy," said Fargo. "After that, the roads are good enough, but they'll stick out like a sore thumb. They'll need more guns than mine once they leave Lamy.

"Has anyone told them what it's like out there? It's sure as hell not Egypt."

Obviously disgusted, Pinkerton shook his head. "I just tried. Told them there are bandits, horse thieves, Apaches. They would hear none of it. Cocky is what they are, rich and cocky."

"They won't be cocky for long. I doubt they'll last two days."

"Well, are you interested, Mr. Fargo? I wouldn't blame you one bit if you are not."

"It beats staying here. I don't fit in Chicago anyway."

Standing and gesturing toward his new clients, Pinkerton said, "They want to meet you to see if you're what they're looking for."

"What'd you tell them about me?"

"Only that you know the country. And I told them about how you could be trusted. I vouched for that myself."

Fargo stood. Pinkerton led the way into his office. Five sets of eyes locked onto Fargo. He took them in with one sweeping glance. For a moment, his eyes held on Hialeaha.

"Ladies, gentlemen, this is Mr. Conway Fargo. He is the gentleman I have been telling you about."

The men were standing beside the women, who were seated in uncomfortable-looking wooden chairs. Fargo kept his distance, and neither man offered to shake his hand.

Wellington spoke first.

"Mr. Pinkerton, I assumed he was a younger man."

Fargo's gaze slid from the Indian to Wellington. He was taller than Fargo by two inches but light through the body. His hands were thin and pale. Likely they had never seen a hard day's work.

Pinkerton responded sharply, "You wanted experienced. Experience comes with the price of years."

Wellington coolly turned to Fargo. "No offense intended, Mr. Fargo."

Fargo responded impassively, "None taken." For several seconds, no one spoke. Then LaFarge broke the silence. Her tone was sultry. "Oh, I like him, Miles," she said with a hint of flirtation. "He seems to be a man of few words. And you know what I always say. The less a man says, the more sense he makes."

Brooks placed the tips of her white-gloved fingers on her lips and giggled softly.

Taking an immediate dislike to LaFarge, Fargo merely looked at her. He knew he was expected to respond to her charm and beauty, but instead, he turned his attention to the one called Hialeaha.

A woman in her early forties, the Cherokee sat erect. She held her head high, but her eyes had dropped to the floor. If the comment by LaFarge was meant to be an insult, the Indian was taking no part in it.

"Sometimes," said Fargo, "a person can talk too much."

LaFarge bristled at his comment. Her cheeks flushed.

"Have you ever…?" asked Davis. "Well…are you prepared to defend us if the need arises, to use a firearm against another man?"

"Not if you're not," answered Fargo.

"What?"

"Where you're going, you'll need more than one gun. All of you better be ready to defend yourselves. If you're not, you'd best just stay put."

LaFarge gasped, but it was clearly not sincere. "Stay put, Mr. Fargo. Is your speech always so vulgar?"

"I suppose."

Reaching up, LaFarge put her hand on Wellington's arm. "Is he not wonderful, Miles? Vulgar, rude…and a gunman.

"What do you think, Mahra?"

Mahra smiled. Looking at the penetrating, dark-brown eyes of Conway Fargo, she spoke timidly. "I think he is quite dashing."

Davis and Wellington shook their heads. LaFarge chuckled derisively, but Hialeaha raised her head. Her eyes met Fargo's. He saw in them a message of concern that bordered on hopelessness.

According to Pinkerton, the Indian had practically raised Mahra Brooks. She would be like a mother to her, and Hialeaha was Cherokee. The Cherokee were called the Civilized Tribe, but an Indian was an Indian. They knew things. How they communicated between tribes and over long distances, no white man understood. Did this Indian know what went on beyond the borders of civilization, of the extreme danger Mahra Brooks would face?

"We plan to take a private train as far as the tracks go," said Wellington. "From there we have a coach and Studebaker supply wagon for the rest of the journey. Can you leave in the morning, Mr. Fargo?"

Fargo turned his attention from Hialeaha to Wellington. "Could be. Who all's coming along? You'll need drivers, a horse wrangler, and a cook to make it work."

"Hialeaha will be our cook. Miss LaFarge will provide the horse wrangler. We can hire another driver at the end of the rails. I am told there are plenty of teamsters at the railheads."

"And weapons?"

"The latest rifles by Winchester. We will have two .45–75s. Edward and I will each carry .45 pistols by Colt. We also have a double-barreled shotgun and more than adequate ammunition."

"You two ever shot anything?"

Wellington sneered, as did Davis.

"Edward and I have killed big game throughout Africa, Mr. Fargo. That includes lions."

"Yes," added Davis pompously. "They were man-eaters."

Fargo's face was unreadable. "How are you with a shotgun?"

"We've hunted fowl of all sorts here in the States," answered Wellington.

"How about water and food?"

Wellington put his hand up and sighed. "Mr. Fargo. We have traveled the world over. Far more, I daresay, than you ever will. The last thing we need is your advice on how to travel. All we want from you is to be our guide until we reach our destination. After that, if you do not wish to accompany us back to Lamy, you may leave us, if you wish. We are quite capable of returning on our own.

"Now, if I have cleared that up for you, do you want the job or not?"

Fargo understood now why Pinkerton called them fools. He was about to walk out and leave them to their folly when he glanced one last time at Hialeaha. What he saw caused him to pause and then swear under his breath.

Why was she looking at him that way? It was as if she knew who he was. But how could she? He had been careful. No one knew him in

Chicago. Not even Allan Pinkerton knew many details about where he had been and what he had done. Yet her eyes were begging him to stay, pleading for him to take the job.

It was a look Fargo had seen too many times on too many faces. This, however, was the first time he had seen it on an Indian. And why on earth should he give a damn about an Indian woman, even one as handsome as this one?

Fargo swallowed hard. Why couldn't he say no to such people? Time and time again, he wanted to turn his back on them and walk away. But it was no use. He couldn't ignore their pleas for help, not even when he knew their hope was in vain. He was a prisoner of his past, of mistakes made but not forgotten. It was his destiny and his curse.

Watching Hialeaha closely, Fargo answered Wellington's question. "You've made yourself clear enough. I'll take the job."

Hialeaha closed her eyes and breathed a sigh of relief. As if a burden had been lifted, her shoulders slumped.

"I'll need a rail car for my horses and me," said Fargo. "You'll have to cover my expenses on top of the five hundred."

"Of course," snipped Wellington.

"When do we leave?"

"Six o'clock tomorrow morning. We will taking a private train of the Atchison, Topeka and Santa Fe. We must leave on schedule in order to stay ahead of other trains. We will be boarding at daybreak at Central Station. We will have our own engine and tender followed by four cars. You will see our coach and wagon loaded on a flat car. Our supplies will be stored in the wagon. Next will be a Pullman Palace car followed by a horse express car and then a drovers' car. The cars have interconnecting doors. If there is need, we can walk from car to car while the train is in motion. You will find your accommodations in the drovers' car.

"We have the horse express car reserved for our mounts. How many will you be bringing?"

"Two."

"In that case, there will be room in our express car for yours. A man named Reed Treadway will be caring for the horses as well as driving our coach after we reach Lamy."

Wellington was a rich fool, but Fargo knew there was no need to make unnecessary trouble. He would tolerate the man's arrogance long enough to get out of Chicago. When they were in the territories, things would be different.

"I'll care for my own horses, if it's all the same to you," Fargo said evenly.

"If you prefer," agreed Wellington.

"Mr. Fargo," offered LaFarge, "I may as well tell you, Reed is a trifle simple minded. He is a big man but easy going. He knows horses but little else. So do not expect too much from him."

"Have you known him long?" asked Fargo.

"Many, many years. And to answer your next question, I have found him to be dependable and hard working. He is loyal to me, loyal enough that I can go anywhere in Chicago without fear for my safety."

"So he's a fighter, then," returned Fargo.

LaFarge smiled, but her eyes narrowed slightly. "Only if there is need, Mr. Fargo. When I am threatened…or insulted, he will fight."

The change in LaFarge's expression was almost imperceptible, but Fargo had played too many hands of poker to miss it. There was more to Reed Treadway than LaFarge was admitting.

"Can he shoot?" asked Fargo.

"He shot a few skunks and rats around the stables," answered LaFarge. She continued to smile, but there was a predatory glint in her eyes. "If he takes his time and has a solid rest for his rifle, he can shoot quite well. Of course, he has had no need to learn how to shoot a pistol."

"And one more item, Mr. Fargo," added Wellington. "We wish to keep our destination and the nature of our expedition a secret. There are other archeologists about who would leap at this opportunity. We want to be the first to study the ruins we seek. And we would prefer to do it without interference from late arrivers. Do you understand?"

"Clear enough." Fargo nodded. "I'll be at the station at sunrise."

Chapter 3

A dingy glow brightened the eastern horizon as Fargo rode up to the rear of the train. He was astride a black gelding, leading a bay. Instead of his suit, he was wearing trail clothes and a brace of pistols.

Fargo's saddle was Spanish, as were his large roweled spurs. Weathered saddlebags hung behind a high cantle. Above them, a bedroll held a slicker and a hidden sawed-off shotgun.

Pulling up a short distance from the Palace car, Fargo looked it over. From his saddle, he could see twelve brightly illuminated windows. All were bordered with fancy curtains. The light in the windows came from two gaslit chandeliers that hung from a ceiling covered with a hand-painted mural. The passenger seats appeared to be covered with red velvet.

Fargo shook his head and turned his horses. A moment later, he dismounted and led them to the stock car. The wooden ramp was down. A dim light glowed inside. When he started up the planks, someone emerged from the shadows and stood blocking the way. For a man as big as this one, his steps were light, his movements agile.

Without hesitating, Fargo continued up the ramp. "I'm Fargo."

The man stepped aside, allowing just enough room for passage. He was at least three inches taller than Fargo and heavier in build. His hair was blond and shaggy but not so long as to hide a bull neck.

Seeing two horses already tethered and stalled, Fargo went to the empty stalls beside them. After tying the bay, he removed the bridle from the black and slipped on a halter and lead rope. He looped the free end of the rope through an ornate iron ring and tied a slipknot. He was loosening the latigo when the big man spoke.

"Where's your other gear, mister?" he asked. "The train's about to leave."

Continuing to work the latigo, Fargo answered, "This is it."

Taking a closer look at the other two horses, Fargo noticed the manes had been cut to a short stub. "Why are the manes cut off those two?"

The big fellow grunted. After thinking for a slow count of ten, he said, "Those are polo ponies."

"What's polo?"

Another long pause followed. "They hit a ball with a stick while they ride. It's a new game rich folks are playing. The stick gets caught in a long mane, so they took to cutting it off."

"Them two are thoroughbred and quarter horse cross."

"They look sound enough."

"I'm Reed, Reed Treadway."

Treadway's voice was a soft baritone. His words methodically rolled over a pair of thick lips. "Hialeaha will have breakfast if you want it," he said, starting down the loading ramp. "I'm closing this up. You can go through the passenger door if you want to eat."

The ramp began to rise. Fargo jerked his saddle from the black and forked it on a nearby rack. He glanced at Treadway, studied him for a moment, and then turned to look around.

A single lantern, with its wick turned low, hung on the far wall. Each stall was padded and had its own water trough and grain bin. Saddle racks were built in at regular intervals. Pegs along one of the walls held silver bridles, ropes, and several ivory-handled brushes and combs. Fargo had never seen anything like it.

The ramp sealed with a thud. A metal latch slammed shut. A horse blew and stomped. A moment later, the car jerked slightly. The train moved a few feet then stopped. He could hear the pulsing, heavy snorts of the steam engine, but something was holding up the departure.

Fargo took a piece of jerked beef from his saddlebags and sat down on a bale of pressed hay. He felt the train begin to move again. He could hear the steel wheels grinding on the rails and the strain of the steam engine as it picked up speed. In less than a minute, the coal burner found an easy rhythm. Now they were gliding westward at twenty miles to the hour.

Listening to the comforting cadence of the hum and click of iron rolling on iron, Fargo pushed his hat back and bit off a piece of jerky. He inhaled as he chewed and then let his breath out slowly. He was leaving town. Whatever trouble he may have caused was to be worked out by the Pinkerton Agency.

For a long while, he had been convinced he needed a change, to wear different clothes and maybe even change his name. Finally, he decided to go east, vowing never to return to his former life. Shortly after arriving in Chicago, however, Fargo discovered that staring at four walls was far worse than incessantly searching a skyline or checking a back trail. Danger was a constant concern in the west, but in the city, boredom was a form of torture.

Like other remedies he tried, city life was a dead end. No matter what name he used or what clothes he wore, Con Fargo knew he would never amount to much. It was better he go back where he came from and do what he did best.

Fargo glanced at the rear passenger door of the stock car. Treadway had said breakfast was waiting in the drovers' car, but Fargo wasn't particularly hungry. Most of the time, he preferred his own company anyway. In his line of work, it was better to stay detached and friendless. Some called him cold hearted. But one thing was for certain: it was a way to increase a man's chances of survival and a sure-fire method of preserving his sanity.

Time might heal all wounds, but it erased none of the scars. The more attachments a person had, the more pain would he would have to endure when the whims of life and death tore them away. It was better to be alone. Most days, at least, he could sleep without nightmares. On the darkest nights, however, he needed whiskey.

Fargo was reaching for his canteen when the rear door of the horse car opened. Hialeaha appeared. She carried a steaming coffee pot and cup. Without a word, she approached Fargo and handed him the cup. She filled it and then set the pot down next to him.

"Thanks," said Fargo. He did not expect her to respond. Most Indians were tight lipped around whites.

Hialeaha said nothing. Stoically, she stood for several moments studying Fargo as he drank his coffee. He studied her in return.

"Good coffee," offered Fargo. He knew Indians. When she was ready, she would speak. Unlike whites, Indians tended to think long and hard before opening their mouths.

"We almost left without a brakeman," Hialeaha finally offered. "He was late."

As the woman spoke, her eyes took in every detail and line of Fargo's face. She noticed a scar above his eye, then the fine streaks of gray in his hair. Next she measured the width of his shoulders and the pistols around his waist. Finally, she turned toward his horses, paying particular attention to the brands on the flanks.

Fargo topped off his cup with more coffee. He studied Hialeaha from the corner of his eyes. This Cherokee was searching for something. Or she knew something.

"Then it is true," said Hialeaha.

"What is?" asked Fargo, taking a bite of jerky.

"You are Far-go."

The name was right, but it was how she pronounced it that caused Fargo to raise an eyebrow.

"Yep."

"Far-go," repeated Hialeaha.

Staring now at the Indian, Fargo said nothing. His eyes hardened.

"You are the one," said Hialeaha.

Fargo snorted. "The one what?"

"The one the Apaches call…Tats-a-das-ago."

Fargo stopped chewing. This was a city-dwelling Cherokee. More than likely, this particular one had never even seen an Apache, much less talked to one. And even if she had, Fargo's hair was short now and his face shaved. Yesterday, he was wearing a three-piece suit and lace-up shoes. He looked no different from any man in Chicago. How could she possibly link him to Tats-a-das-ago?

"You sure about that?" asked Fargo, hoping to shake her confidence. "Must be you're thinking of somebody else. Maybe I just look like this Tatsa fella."

"Mexicans say you are a priest. Some whites call you Parson."

"Hell, I'm no priest, lady," sneered Fargo. The realization that he had just referred to an Indian as "lady" flashed through his mind, but he let the thought go. It only added to his growing irritation. "And I sure as hell am no parson."

"Indians say you have medicine. It watches over you."

"You must be thinking of somebody else." Fargo shrugged. "Who listens to Mexicans and Indians, anyhow?"

"The whites say you enjoy killing."

For several seconds, except for the hum and click of the wheels, the train car was silent.

Fargo took a deep breath and wiped his lips with the back of his hand. He began to chew. What did it matter if she knew? He was going back to what he had been anyway. There was no escaping it. He was the same man, the same Tats-a-das-ago, even in a city the size of Chicago.

"They'd be wrong on that account."

"I will tell no one who you are," offered Hialeaha. "It is better for us both."

The last comment begged for elaboration, but Fargo let it slide. He was more intrigued with how a citified Cherokee Indian, living in Chicago, had discovered who and what he was.

The train slowed for a moment. The stock car rolled slightly from side to side. The whistle blew, and then the train accelerated and quickly regained full speed.

Fargo ran his eyes over Hialeaha. She wore a traveling dress gathered tightly around a small waist. If her hair had been put up and pinned, she could almost pass for white. It was because of her pleading eyes that he had accepted the job. Had she been concerned for her own safety or for the safety of the others? Could she have known who he was from the beginning?

What did any of them know? They were leaving Chicago, gliding smoothly away from its paved streets, gas lights, and professional baseball games. Where these Easterners were going, there would be no more high-rise hotels, no marble floors, velvet curtains, or running water. They were bound for a primitive land as foreign to them as they could possibly imagine. It would be wild and untamed country, a place where hardship and sacrifice was a way of life. They were going west.

"How is it," asked Fargo, "a Cherokee in Chicago hears such stories about a man from so far away?"

"Far-go can come to Chicago. Word can come also. There are many Delaware in the West who scout for the army and some Cherokee as well. They hear stories. My people's stories travel like the winds. They spread quickly."

Fargo shrugged and took a sip of coffee.

"So if I am who you think, if I deserve the name the Apaches have given me, why would you keep something like that to yourself?"

Hialeaha stiffened. "It is said that Far-go speaks only truth. His words are like iron. Such a warrior, even a white warrior, is respected. It is out of this respect that I say nothing."

"On the frontier, a man is no better than his word. It's not like it is here in the East," said Fargo.

"Then will you also keep to yourself the words I speak to you now? I have much I want to say to you, much that troubles me."

Fargo's eyes narrowed. There was something about this Cherokee woman, something he could not put his finger on. She dressed in white-man's clothes, spoke almost perfect English, and had skin on the lighter side of brown. But there was more to this woman than outward trappings.

She was Indian in her mannerisms. No doubt she still thought like one, yet she seemed to be reaching out to Far-go, a white man with a reputation for killing Indians. He had sensed the same thing when they were in Pinkerton's office. But even then, he guessed that whatever she wanted was not for herself but for Mahra Brooks.

"I will repeat nothing, if that's what you want."

Turning slightly, Hialeaha glanced at the door that led to the Palace car, then at the one that led to the drovers' car. She took a step and sat down beside Fargo.

"I have cared for Mahra Brooks since she was one year of age. I swore to her mother I would care for her until she wed."

Fargo listened carefully. He had never known an Indian to waste words.

"Her mother has been dead for many years. Mahra's father is always away on business. He spoils her when he is home. His money spoils her when he is away."

Pointing toward the Palace car with his cup, Fargo muttered, "Seems like all four of them were raised with silver spoons in their mouths."

This time it was Hialeaha's eyes that narrowed. "Three of them, yes. Of the fourth, I am not so sure."

Setting his cup down for a moment, Fargo began unbuckling his spurs. "You'd be talking about Miss LaFarge, I suppose?"

Hialeaha seemed to stop breathing. "Then you know?"

Fargo removed one spur and then the other. He buckled them together and set them aside. Picking up his coffee, he continued. "I only know she's different from the other three. Just how, I can't say."

Staring in the direction of the Palace car, Hialeaha spoke in a near whisper. "I fear for Mahra. I fear for her in many ways, but now there is more that keeps my eyes open in the black of night."

Swirling his coffee, Fargo stared into the cup. How many times had he sat next to total strangers as they bared their souls to him, telling him, in grizzly detail, what horrors they had seen or how much they had suffered. He always listened quietly. It was better to let them say their piece. More often than not, just having someone listen brought some semblance of peace. In the end, if he could, he would offer them what they desperately sought.

"Go on."

"Mahra...Mahra is little more than a child. It is because she has been protected all her life. She has never followed a difficult path, never overcome a hardship. Her life has been one of comfort, of playthings.

"None of them know what lies west, yet there is suddenly a great desire to go to the territories. Mahra only follows the others. The men do not know it, but they always follow Miss LaFarge. She leads them where she wants. They are like blind men. They do not see. But I see."

Fargo thought of his first encounter with Clarissa LaFarge in Pinkerton's office. She was self-assured and arrogant. That was nothing unusual for an aristocrat, but it was the cat-and-mouse smile that did not fit. He saw it first when she delivered her thinly veiled insults. Then he noticed her eyes. He had seen the same expression in poker players who held a royal flush. She had power, and she knew it all too well.

"A pretty woman," Fargo casually offered, "can get a man mighty confused sometimes."

Hialeaha grunted. "Women can do this only to white men. Indian men are not such fools."

Chuckling softly, Fargo admitted, "It is the curse of our race."

"There is also Reed Treadway," Hialeaha continued, "the one who works for Miss LaFarge as her coachman."

"What about him?"

"It is said that he has no interest in women, that when he was a boy there was an accident or a sickness that caused it. This is why he can work for Miss LaFarge in the way that he does and there is no talk, no scandal."

"I've heard of such. We call them eunuchs."

Hialeaha shook her head. "He is no eunuch."

Fargo glanced at Hialeaha. She was a woman, but she was Indian. They did not share the same timidity as whites when it came to such matters.

"Are you sure?"

"I see how he looks at Mahra. I have seen him staring at Miss LaFarge. I see even how he looks at me. I am sure."

Fargo thought while he took a sip of his cooling coffee and then said, "If Treadway is like you say, you have to consider the fact Miss LaFarge may not know. But if she does, both of them are living a lie. You have to consider all the angles."

For the first time since sitting, Hialeaha looked directly at Fargo. "But that would mean…that would…"

"Should I," interrupted Fargo, "call you Miss Hialeaha or just Hialeaha?"

Her train of thought broken, Hialeaha blinked. "To everyone I am Hialeaha…but thank you. It is kind of you to ask."

A faint smile turned one corner of Fargo's lips. "Your name's got a nice ring to it. What does it mean?"

The Indian hesitated for several seconds. "Beautiful Meadow."

"Beautiful Meadow," repeated Fargo, noticing the fine lines at the corner of her eyes. She had to be over forty, but for those minor imperfections, her skin was smooth. At first glance, she would appear to anyone to be years younger. "That's a good name."

Hialeaha blushed and looked away.

"As for Miss LaFarge and Treadway," continued Fargo, "what's between them is none of my business."

With her brow furrowing with worry, Hialeaha said, "But that would change everything. Mahra is in bad company, worse than I thought."

"Now, hold on," cautioned Fargo. "Maybe it is only Treadway that isn't telling the whole truth. I only meant for you to consider they could both be lying."

Staring at the rear wall of the horse car, as if watching her thoughts play out before her, Hialeaha nodded slowly. "But it would explain much. I have never liked Miss LaFarge, but I could not say to myself why this was. Some things I could understand, but not all."

Fargo thought of his own first impression of LaFarge. He didn't like her either, but his reasons had to be different from Hialeaha's. Or did they?

"What can you tell me about her?"

"It is a long story."

For a moment, Fargo listened to the clickety-clack coming from the rails. The air in the stock car was cool. The light was soft, and he found himself liking Hialeaha's company. "We've got a long trip ahead of us. Go ahead."

Hialeaha gathered her thoughts.

"Four years ago, Miss LaFarge was not with Mahra and the others. She was with another man at a college called Yale. The other man's name was Bryce Stewart. They were in theater classes together. They both wanted to be actors.

"Mr. Stewart's father was very wealthy, but then he made a big mistake. He built a bad sailing ship or something. He lost all his money. It was only then that Miss LaFarge began to notice Mr. Wellington. He was at the college called Harvard with Mahra and Mr. Davis.

"Because of Miss LaFarge, there was much bad talk between the men of the two colleges. They were like young warriors from different tribes. Bryce Stewart became very jealous. Soon there was much trouble between those of Yale and those of Harvard. Finally, there was a challenge. There was to be a fight between the two lovers of Miss LaFarge. It was to be inside a square made of ropes."

"You mean a boxing match? This Stewart fella and Wellington put on a boxing match?"

"Yes. They called it a match. But it was a fight."

"So how big was this Stewart?"

Hialeaha shrugged. "Not as big as Mr. Wellington, maybe not as big as you."

Fargo nodded but said nothing.

"Why do you ask how big?"

Leaning forward, Fargo held his cup with both hands and glared thoughtfully into the blackness of the coffee.

"When I was younger, I fought professionally for a few months. We worked up and down the Mississippi. At times it was brutal. Usually the bigger man won…unless the smaller man was especially skillful."

"Is that how you got the scar above your eye?" asked Hialeaha.

Fargo sat up and smiled. "No. That came much later."

"It was as you said," continued Hialeaha. "Mr. Wellington was bigger, but Mr. Stewart was not more skillful than Mr. Wellington.

"Before the fight, some told Mr. Stewart not to do it. But he was too proud and too jealous. The jealousy of both men was made to burn by Miss LaFarge. I believe it was on purpose she did this. There was a big crowd, but Mahra left before the fight started. I stayed to watch, to see what Miss LaFarge had done."

"So I gather Wellington won the match and Miss LaFarge to boot."

There was a long silence. Hialeaha closed her eyes. "Mr. Wellington hit Mr. Stewart over and over. But Mr. Stewart could not hit Mr. Wellington. Mr. Stewart would not give up, even though his friends begged him. His love, his jealousy, and his hate drove him to madness. Mr. Wellington was like a rooster…strutting, always strutting. The crowd was screaming as if they were going to war.

"There was blood…little at first. Then it was everywhere. It was all Mr. Stewart's blood. His face was like the mask of a demon. I do not think he could see at all out of his swollen eyes.

"Finally, his friends pulled him through the ropes to stop the fighting. Some say after the fight, his mind failed him. His family fortune was gone, and his friends left him. They say one day he just wandered away. He has never been seen since that time. Some say he is dead."

Hialeaha opened her eyes. Fargo let her regain her composure before he spoke. These days the Cherokees were a civilized tribe. She had likely never seen such raw brutality in her life.

"The wrong kind of woman can turn a man into a fool," said Fargo. "And it looks like Miss LaFarge was on the money trail. I've seen it before."

"I was at the fight to see what Miss LaFarge would do with her power, and I saw it. But after the fight, I stayed in the shadows long after the others had left.

"I saw her with Mr. Wellington, her arm now in his…laughing as they walked. She had been at the slaughter of her onetime lover, and she was laughing with the man who had done it. And now this same woman, this heartless woman, is Mahra's friend?"

Fargo huffed. "I see your point."

"If she is lying about Treadway, she could be more evil than I thought. Now she is taking my innocent Mahra far out into a land full of savage Indians and bandits. But why does she do this? Why must she bring Mahra?"

"Didn't they all go to Egypt together? That's a long ways from Chicago, too."

"We all went. But that was different. There was no danger, at least none that I knew of. This is different. I know many Apaches have left their reservations. So have many Navajo and Ute."

"Easterners don't know any better," Fargo said disgustedly. "They think all Indians are the same. They want even the worst of them treated as government pets.

"Did you try explaining all of this to Miss Brooks to discourage her?"

"She would not listen. None of them will listen. They are young. They have yet to face regret, to grieve over what life is sure to bring. Mahra never wants to hear bad things. She lives in the clouds with her eyes closed to what is real.

"She is very excited. She speaks of 'adventure' and 'mystery' as if she were in a fairy tale. Mahra does not usually get so excited about traveling, especially over rough roads.

"In Egypt it was but a few hours from the ship to the great pointed tombs. How long will it take to get to the Zuni reservation?"

"Maybe a week or ten days after we get off the train. It depends."

"That is far too long. None of them knows hardship, especially Mahra."

Scratching the side of his neck, Fargo thought out loud. "Well now, if what you say about Miss LaFarge is true, she's got something in mind that works to her advantage. Most people like her are easy to figure. They're either after money, or they're after power—both if they can get them in the same deal.

"Now, there's no power that I can think of where she's headed, so that leaves money. I'd wager she's looking to get rich somehow."

Hialeaha glanced skeptically at Fargo. "She has money. And she has Mr. Wellington. He is rich, very rich."

"Maybe he's not rich enough. Some folks never seem to have enough money. They're as bad as a drunk is with whiskey. And besides, Wellington's not a sure bet, at least not yet. She's got no ring on her finger that I can see.

"That old beau she had, Stewart, lost his fortune. Maybe she's hedging her bets thinking it could happen again with Wellington."

"What you say would answer many questions," agreed Hialeaha. "I never thought of the rich seeking more money. If they have more than enough, how much more can they want?"

Fargo thought for a moment. "Do you know of the Pinkertons?"

"Yes."

"The chief of the Pinkertons knows something about everyone that's important. Yesterday he told me he could find out very little about Miss LaFarge. He said she came to Chicago after the Great Fire in seventy-one. She already had money when she arrived. It seems she got it from an uncle, but no one really knows. She's tight lipped about her past."

Hialeaha took the empty cup from Fargo. "Do you want me to make more?"

"Don't go to the trouble on my account."

Holding the cup in her lap, Hialeaha's eyes narrowed in thought. "I once heard Miss LaFarge say she had known Treadway since they were children. I know he worked for her when she was with Mr. Stewart."

Fargo was about to say something when the rear door of the horse car opened. Treadway stuck his head in.

"We could use some more of your coffee, Hialeaha," said Treadway in his easy, methodical voice. "That brakeman that we had to wait for said he could use some, too. And some breakfast."

Picking up the empty coffee pot, Hialeaha came to her feet. "I will be right there. I was inviting Mr. Fa-rgo to join us."

Treadway nodded. "We expected he would."

When the door shut, she said softly. "We speak of these things to no one. There would be trouble."

"I don't see that it makes much difference to me. They're rich and, likely as not, are looking for some way to get richer. My job is to point the way and make sure they don't get in too much trouble."

"Please, Far-go. Say nothing to anyone."

Fargo looked into the eyes of the Indian. He paused and then nodded. "Count on it, Miss Hialeaha. You have my word."

Hialeaha turned to leave, but Fargo stopped her.

"A while ago you asked me how far to the Zuni reservation."

"Yes."

"Didn't you mean the Navajo reservation?"

"No, to the Zuni. This Mahra told me. They go to a place called Hawikuh."

Chapter 4

Fargo glared at the dry stick of beef in his hand. When on the trail of renegades and bandits, he was thankful to have a piece of jerky. But he wasn't on the trail now, and jerky didn't compare to a hot breakfast.

Talking with Hialeaha had given him an appetite. But sitting elbow to elbow with a bunch of strangers in the drovers' car was something he would rather avoid. And he hated idle talk.

However, they would be expecting him, and it would give him a second look at Reed Treadway. He would eat, make his observations, and then explain he had to get back to the horses. That should satisfy everyone.

Stuffing the jerky into his pants pocket, Fargo reluctantly came to his feet. He tugged on the brim of his hat and then adjusted his pistols.

Fargo opened the rear door of the horse car and stepped out onto the iron deck. He closed the door behind him and paused. The sun was rising, and it was good to be in fresh air. They were well beyond the foul odor and smoke that continuously engulfed Chicago. Instead, the smell of hot biscuits and frying bacon drifted from the drovers' car. His mouth began to water.

Fargo swore then spat. "May as well get it over with," he muttered, then opened the door and stepped inside.

Closing the door, Fargo heard bacon frying and saw coffee steaming. Hialeaha was working at a cast-iron stove. He had not noticed before, but her hair was woven in a silky black braid that ran down the middle of her back. It stopped just above her waist. Her skirt hung a few inches short of the floor. Beneath the hem he saw moccasins.

Four men sat at a long table made of whipsawed planks eating a batch of gravy-covered biscuits. All but Hialeaha looked up. Treadway quickly lost interest and went back to eating. The other three sized up the newcomer, their eyes resting on his pistols.

Hialeaha turned. With both hands she held a heavy skillet of sputtering-hot bacon. Going to the table, she said, "Gentlemen, this is Mr. Far-go." She set the skillet on the table. "Have a seat, Mr. Far-go."

Sitting across the table from Treadway, two men in coal-smudged overalls and short-billed hats nodded. One waved a fork and grunted a friendly hello. On Treadway's right, a third man sat grinning. A few teeth were missing from his smile, but his overalls were spotless, apparently new.

The man in the new clothes stood. Leaning backward, he extended his hand behind Treadway. "I'm Smitty, the brakeman," he said boisterously while shaking hands with Fargo. "Set yourself down. You ain't never had such good biscuits and gravy in your life!"

Fargo sat down to the left of Treadway but kept his distance. He liked his elbowroom, partly for comfort and partly from habit. Sitting too close to someone made it hard to draw a gun.

Reaching soiled and calloused hands across the table, the other two men introduced themselves to Fargo as Hialeaha handed him a tin plate, knife, and fork. The engineer was named Gordon, the fireman Todd.

"We're the second crew," said Todd after swallowing a wad of bacon. "We need two sets of engineers, firemen, and brakemen to keep up the pace. That Wellington is in an all-fired hurry to get to end of tracks."

"Sure is," agreed Gordon, talking with a mouthful of biscuit. "He was offered a wood-burner engine, but he turned it down. Wanted a coal-burner. Nothing but the best for him."

Fargo took a biscuit and sliced it open. Watching the steam escape, he swabbed it with butter. "What's the difference?"

"Coal burns hotter," answered Todd. "You have to make fewer stops for fuel and water. The only real stop we have will be in Dodge City, Kansas. We sidetrack there for a while to let another train pass going east. Other'n that, we're going to make near record time all the way to Galisteo Junction."

"They don't call it that no more," rebuked Gordon. "I told you, it's called Lamy, now. Lamy! They named it after that Padre, that Catholic fella."

Todd snorted. "Lamy, as you call it, ought not to be named after a priest. It's full of saloons, card sharks, and whores. Like they say, end-of-track towns are Hell on Wheels."

"How long do you think it'll take to get to Lamy?" asked Fargo.

"A little more'n a day and a half to get to Dodge, if all goes well," answered Todd. "And another day and a half to reach Lamy. We left at six this morning, so we should get to Dodge by four in the afternoon tomorrow."

"Well, we almost didn't leave at six, though," chided Gordon. "Our extra brakeman was late. We was expecting McCoy, but he didn't show. We almost left without Smitty here. It's a good thing he showed up. That other brakeman would'a got awful tired working two straight shifts with no rest."

Using his fork, Smitty scratched the overnight growth of stubble on his jaw. He had a drooping mustache. A band of pale skin on the rest of his face and neck indicated a recent shave and haircut. He was several years younger than Treadway and the others. His hands were small, but the muscles on his arms had been built up by years of hard work. He was talkative, wiry, and high-strung, constantly tapping his heel.

"Wull, I weren't going to work today," returned Smitty, with his mouth still full of food. "I was going to see my girl, but McCoy come and got me last night and asked would I do his job for him. His wife done took sick from a rat bite, and he was in a fix. So I come in his stead. But just a tad late, I suppose. Never figured a body to be in such a hurry as this here Wellington."

Smitty wiped his lips with the back of his sleeve. "Makes me wish I was still a mule skinner. Them mules was never in a hurry, I can tell you that."

"Mule skinner," barked Gordon. "How long have you been a brakeman? You don't look that old to have done both."

Smitty wagged his head. "Well, bein' a brakeman don't take that long to learn. I just do what I'm told. I just turn that brake wheel like they tell me. That's all there is to it. That ain't near as hard as learnin' to handle the ribbons on a bunch of ornery mules.

"Besides, I left home when I was still wet 'hind the ears. I been around plenty long."

Studying Smitty, Fargo asked, "Where'd you do your teamstering?"

"All around. Mostly up north, Minnesota mostly."

Treadway's head tuned slowly toward Smitty. "Mr. Wellington says we'll need another driver for the hoodlum wagon. He was going to hire one where the tracks run out."

"What's he payin'?"

"I don't know."

"Well, what's he payin' you, Reed?"

Treadway shrugged. "He doesn't pay me anything. Miss LaFarge pays me. I work for her, not Mr. Wellington."

Fargo took a casual glance at Treadway. His shoulders were heavily muscled, as was his bull neck. If Fargo had to bet, he would say Treadway was no less a man than anyone at the table. But even if there was more to his relationship with LaFarge than anyone suspected, it was none of his business.

Smitty took a slice of bacon and bit off a piece. He chewed while he thought.

"LaFarge, you say? That's a familiar sound'n name."

"You never heard of Clarissa LaFarge?" asked Todd.

Smitty shrugged. "Maybe yes, maybe no. Who is she?"

"Why, next to Sarah Bernhardt, Clarissa LaFarge is just about the most famous actress around!"

"Oh, that Clarissa LaFarge," said Smitty. "I heard of her."

"She's that well known?" asked Fargo.

Gordon, Todd, and even Treadway agreed in unison.

Fargo merely shook his head. If she was that famous, she was going to be trouble.

"Where you all goin' after you get off the train?" asked Smitty. "She got an acting job somewhere out there? Santa Fe, maybe?"

"We're going to some place I don't know," said Treadway, as if his answer were explanation enough.

"If we're lucky," said Fargo, "we'll be ten days to two weeks going there. Likely the same coming back…if we're lucky."

Smitty leaned forward to look around the hulking Treadway. "What do you mean lucky? Where you off to, anyhow?"

Fargo ignored the question. He took another biscuit and then cut a slice of butter. He held it out on the tip of his knife. "Where we're going there'll be precious little of this. That much I can tell you."

Hialeaha set down a large bowl of scrambled eggs and a jug of milk.

Fargo pointed at the eggs and milk with his buttered knife. "Not much of this or that either. But we could have our hands full of Indians or bandits. If that happens, these rich folks won't be much help. And traveling in this country with a bunch of women is asking for trouble."

"Well, we ain't no Injuns or bandits," said Smitty. "How come you to be heeled with them two smoke wagons?"

Smiling flatly, Fargo muttered, "Habit."

Hialeaha took a step toward the table. "I go now to cook for the others. There is more coffee on the stove."

Turning smoothly, she left the drover's car.

Everyone but Treadway watched her go. He continued to eat, his head low over the plate to shorten the distance his fork had to travel.

"That's one good-looking Indian," confessed Gordon.

"Uh huh," agreed Todd. "And she's not fat like most of them her age."

"She can damn well cook, too," added Smitty, giving Treadway a good-natured elbow in the ribs. "Don't you think so?"

Treadway looked up. He stopped chewing for a moment. He shrugged. "I suppose."

Unsatisfied, Smitty leaned back, looking at Fargo. "What do you say there, Mr. Fargo? She a better looker or a better cooker?"

Fargo thought for a full count of ten. Hialeaha knew who he was, at least in part, yet she had approached him privately. She cared enough for Mahra Brooks, a white woman, to ask Tats-a-das-ago, a killer of Indians, for help. His hatred of Indians ran deep, wide, and long, but this particular Indian might be different.

"She's an Indian. I don't care either way."

"You don't?" asked Smitty.

"I make it a rule to never turn my back on any of the red devils," replied Fargo, yet knowing what he said was not entirely true. He had met a few Indians he did not want to kill outright. And, unexplainably, he found himself trusting Hialeaha.

"Oh, she ain't like no real Indian," offered Smitty. "She's one of them city-livin' Cherokee."

Fargo's response was ingrained; it had become almost instinctive. "They're all the same," he snapped, but again realized what he said was not entirely true. Hadn't he known some Indians before the war, long ago in Tennessee, who were good people?

He had not thought of them in what seemed like a lifetime. Twenty years of being witness to unspeakable atrocities inflicted on men, women, and children left little room for distant recollections.

Smitty shrugged. "A man's entitled to his own opinion, I always say. Anyway, who are these rich folks we're hauling? What're they up to?"

"I don't know exactly," answered Gordon. "But I saw them loading a mighty fancy new coach. And they like to eat good, let me tell you. I saw all sorts of canned goods. They got oysters by the crate. And there was every kind beef—Armour, Libby, and Wilson. They got fruit, fish, cherries, peaches, and even lobsters. They got something called pineapples, too. I didn't even know they canned some of those things."

Leaning forward to see past Treadway, Smitty glanced down at Fargo. "Ain't you the pilot? You ought'a know somethin' about these folks."

Fargo filled his coffee cup. "They're rich. They're paying. I'm guiding. And if you're interested in driving, I wouldn't be asking too many questions."

"Wul, I'm like that cat they talk about. You know, curious like."

Fargo took a sip of coffee and set his cup down. "West of the Mississippi, asking too many questions can get a man in trouble. You know what happened to that cat."

"Wul then, how 'bout them Indians and bandits you mentioned? You think them rich folks will pay me extry if we run into any?"

"I wouldn't know."

"I run into my share of 'em up on the plains, Sioux mostly. I know how to fight 'em."

"The ones we could run into are nothing like the plains Indians," said Fargo. "The Sioux and Cheyenne like to fight from horseback. They like to shoot you from a distance. The Apache and their kind sneak in close. Sometimes you never even catch sight of them."

"Up close is good. I ain't such a good shot, you see. I 'magine they die just the same as a them Sioux."

Fargo took another drink of coffee but this time held the cup close to his lips. He savored the aroma. "None of them die easy."

Smitty looked at Gordon and Todd. They were obviously interested in the subject of Indian fighting. Even Treadway had stopped eating.

"Oh, they're tough, all right," admitted Smitty. "Them Sioux can go a hundred miles on foot in one day. They been known to run down a man on horseback."

Easing his coffee cup to the table, Fargo was suddenly wary. Anyone familiar with plains Indians knew they were horse warriors. So were the Comanche. It was the Apaches who were known for their incredible feats of endurance on foot.

Smitty was wrong about the tactics of the Plains Indians. It was a mistake no true Indian fighter would make. Was he merely a blowhard, or was he outright lying about fighting Indians?

As Smitty continued his yarn, Fargo thought of the Apaches. He had been away from their depredations for little over a month and was already going back. When he left Arizona Territory, he swore he would get as far from marauding renegades as possible and never look back. He was going to sleep in a bed, bathe every night, and sleep through the night without listening for a twig to snap or the crunch of sand underfoot.

Living in Chicago, however, was nothing like he had imagined. He spent most of his time in a haze of indifference and boredom. It was a world of luxurious high-rise hotels, fancy restaurants, and opulent opera houses, all of them backed up to garbage-filled alleys and draining sewers.

Every building had a number, and every street corner a sign. By night, the walkways were lit. It was a realm where the pampered rich, the corrupt, and even the completely inept could not only survive but thrive. They needed no courage to stand alone, no stamina to endure the elements, and no skill to stay alive.

Every day thousands of them safely scurried up, down, and across the endless maze of streets. Their greatest concern seemed to be European fashion and baseball scores. How long could a country survive breeding so many spoon-fed fools?

Fargo thoughtfully turned the coffee cup with his fingers. The mirage he had coveted for so long was sand after all. Now he knew it. For better or worse, he was going back to what he did best. He was known to whites as deputy marshal, Indian fighter, and US Army scout. To the Indians, he was Tats-a-das-ago.

Smitty had been talking nonstop for close to a half hour when Hialeaha opened the drovers' car door. She held on to the door handle as the wind whipped about her skirt and blew a few strands of black hair across her high cheekbones. She spoke above the rattle of the train linkage and the rhythmic clanking of iron on iron. "Mr. Far-go, Mr. Wellington and the others would like to speak with you if you are finished."

Fargo studied Hialeaha, allowing his eyes to roam for a few seconds. The men were right. She was indeed an attractive woman, even if she was an Indian.

Sensing that Hialeaha wanted to speak to him privately, Fargo stood. "Now's fine," he said and followed her back into the stock car.

Closing the door behind him, he paused. She turned to face him.

"Do you know much of the Zuni tribe?" asked Hialeaha.

"Some. Why?"

"I believe their final destination may not be the Pueblo of Zuni. They may want to go farther."

"Mr. Pinkerton told me only that we're headed for some Navajo ruins," said Fargo. "Or at least he said they were headed for the reservation. And that was my understanding until earlier, when you mentioned the Zuni."

"What of the Zuni?" asked Hialeaha. "Are they dangerous?"

"Not to whites. They've been friendly for years. But they can hold their own against their enemies, the Apaches and Navajo."

"Are they a rich tribe?"

"No. They raise wheat for the army and get paid a fair amount. And Beale's wagon road runs right past the old Zuni pueblo. There're a lot of wagons going through there on their way to California. They trade with the whites, but they're not rich at all."

Hialeaha was puzzled. "So why does Miss LaFarge go there? Is the pueblo so grand?"

Fargo scratched his jaw and thought. "No, it's nothing to write home about. There's an old church there, built by the Spaniards, but it's been abandoned for years. The Zuni have their own religion, and the padres couldn't wean them off of it. They've got a god for just about everything under the sun…and under the ground, for that matter. My guess is, they didn't see the point in having just one."

"So the church is not magnificent?"

"It's empty and run down, just a lot of adobe bricks and a couple of bells."

"Then it is something else. They have a secret, as I suspected. I do not like how it makes me feel."

"What is it you're feeling?"

Hialeaha folded her arms. Her brow furrowed. "It is the presence of evil."

Shrugging, Fargo smiled and looked into her dark brown eyes. "There's no shortage of that anywhere. You find people, and you'll find sinners."

"You think like a white man," scoffed Hialeaha. "I am Christian, but I am Indian, still. I speak of more than sin."

The smile vanished. Fargo winced at the thought of having offended the woman. She was sincere, and he was acting the fool.

Fargo cleared his throat. "You'll have to excuse me. I've been too long in Chicago for my own good.

"I don't dismiss your feelings or your ways. And I won't pretend to understand all of them. But I have learned to respect them. I'll take what you're feeling to be a warning. I'll be especially vigilant."

Slowly unfolding her arms, Hialeaha stared at Fargo. She paused for half a minute then said, "You are an unusual man, Far-go."

Fargo lowered his eyes. "That's a polite way of putting it. Please accept my apology."

The faintest of smiles turned Hialeaha's full lips. "You are forgiven," she said, and then she turned. "They are expecting us."

Before knocking on the Palace car door, Hialeaha glanced uneasily at Fargo. "Wait here."

Hialeaha knocked, then stepped through the door and closed it behind her. She approached the dining area. The couples had finished eating and were now enjoying their morning tea.

Hialeaha lowered her eyes. "Mr. Far-go is here."

"Good," chimed LaFarge, taking a slow sip of her tea.

Several seconds passed. Hialeaha looked up. LaFarge was gazing at her.

"Shall I see him in, miss?" asked Hialeaha.

LaFarge raised an eyebrow. "We think he should wait outside for a while, don't we, Miles?"

Miles grinned. "If you say so, my dear."

Again Hialeaha lowered her eyes. "I do not think Mr. Far-go is one who likes to wait."

"Then he should learn," quipped Wellington. "He is in our employ. The sooner he accepts that fact, the better."

"Yes," agreed LaFarge. "It is enough that we are called to endure his boorish behavior. And we must get rid of that ghastly black suit he wore yesterday. Simply dreadful, even for a Pinkerton man. Is he wearing it again today?"

"No," returned Hialeaha. Her eyes flickered back at LaFarge. "I think you will see no more of the black suit."

Rolling her eyes, LaFarge covered her mouth with her napkin and chuckled. "They should have jailed his tailor."

Hialeaha stole a glance at Mahra, but her back was turned. Mahra had no concept of arrogance, but she habitually went along with the others. LaFarge, on the other hand, was a she wolf in sheep's clothing. But she was about to meet a man who would as soon kill a wolf as a sheep.

For two minutes the foursome chatted about a number of trivial matters. Another minute passed while they discussed the scenery. Finally, LaFarge turned and smiled at Hialeaha. Her painted lips colored an artificial smile. Her eyes were hard.

"You may invite Mr. Fargo in now."

Saying nothing, Hialeaha turned and went to the door. She opened it and then suppressed a smile.

Closing the door, she returned to the breakfast nook. "He is gone."

"He is what?" demanded LaFarge. Her face flushed red. "You don't mean…what do you mean?"

"I left him standing at the door. He is no longer there."

Wellington tossed his napkin on the table and stood. "I'll have a word with this Mr. Fargo. This is intolerable. Dash him, I say. He needs to know his place!"

Raising her eyes, Hialeaha looked directly into Wellington's. "He is armed, Mr. Wellington."

Wellington was about to take a step. His weight shifted forward, but his feet did not move. He studied Hialeaha for a moment, and then his face began to twist with mounting rage.

"What are you saying, woman? Do not think for a moment that I will be insulted by a hired servant without consequence! Am I to fear this impudent old man wearing a cheap suit?"

"No, not at all, Mr. Wellington."

Wellington's nostrils flared. "Armed, you say? Why, I could disarm him before he knew what was happening. Armed? Rubbish!"

Hialeaha thought of Fargo's Apache name, Tats-a-das-ago. It meant "quick killer." Wellington would swiftly learn the ways of hardened men. Or he would soon be dead.

"I know something of the man called Far-go," cautioned Hialeaha. "He is of the West. Men there are not like...they are different from men of the East. You would call them rough, unrefined. Men such as Far-go are not accustomed to waiting...nor do they hold to many other Eastern customs. Perhaps, though, it is just such a rough and unrefined man you will need where you are going."

Davis put out a hand and grasped Wellington's arm. Davis had always been more cool headed than his cousin. "I think she is right, Miles. No doubt the man is a rube, but unless we can find another with his qualifications, we do need him."

"What do you think, Clarissa?" asked Wellington. "Perhaps he needs a good thrashing to remove his insolence."

"I do not think he looks that old," interjected Brooks. She looked thoughtfully at Davis. "Do you think he's old, Edward?"

Brooks's innocent comment and off-the-wall question immediately cooled the rising tension. And she did have a point. Fargo had a bit of gray in his hair, but most would agree he appeared anything but feeble.

LaFarge thought for a moment. Davis was right, but Hialeaha had overstepped her position. No one had asked her for advice. LaFarge tapped her chin with a finger. "Miles, I believe we should trust Hialeaha's judgment. After all, I should think she has been with many men like Mr. Fargo in her time."

Clinching her jaw, Hialeaha glanced at Mahra and said nothing. In time, Clarissa LaFarge would be humbled. Like the grass of spring, she would soon wither.

"I am in agreement with Clarissa, Miles," offered Davis. "What do you say? Let's give the old man another chance, shall we?"

Slowly, Wellington took his seat. "Very well, then. Hialeaha, will you please escort Mr. Fargo into our quarters? And this time, do not announce him. Just bring him in. We would not want to keep him waiting."

Without so much as a nod, Hialeaha left the Palace car. As expected, she found Fargo in the stock car alone. He was brushing down his horses. He did not look up when she entered.

"They ready now?" asked Fargo as he continued brushing.

"When you are, Far-go."

After patting the black with the palm of his hand, Fargo hung the brush on a peg and then looked at Hialeaha. "Miss Brooks is like a daughter to you, isn't she?"

"She is."

"Thought so."

"Beware of Miss LaFarge, Far-go."

"She's not as slick as she thinks. You know, the eyes are the light of the soul."

"You quote the Bible?"

"Sometimes," answered Fargo. "My version of it, anyway." Extending his hand, he said, "After you."

Hialeaha led the way into the Palace car, but a few feet from the dining table, she stepped aside and allowed Fargo to go ahead. He stopped a step away. Davis and Brooks turned to look as Wellington and LaFarge glanced up. What they saw stunned them.

The day before, they had seen an old man with a tint of gray in his hair. He was a Chicago Pinkerton agent with no hat, a poorly fitting suit, and street shoes that needed polish. Standing before them now was someone else.

He wore a broad-brimmed hat with trail dust engrained in the sweat-stained crown. His shirt was sun-bleached gray. His pants were faded pinstripe, and his boots brown and scarred. On his hips hung a fully loaded cartridge belt and two pistols. One of the pistol butts faced forward, the other backward. Both grips were burnished with heavy use.

Fargo ignored their stares and glanced around the Palace car. Two crystal chandeliers hung from an artistically painted ceiling. Lamps with silk shades sat in the middle of two mahogany reading tables. The seats with them were plush and covered in leather. Drapes adorned the windows, and carpet blanketed the floor. The Easterners sat around a dining table draped with a white linen cloth. The teapot on it as well as the utensils were polished silver.

"You wanted to see me?"

Brooks was the first to speak. She often did so without much fore-thought. "Why, you have changed, Mr. Fargo. What happened to your suit?"

Her question was sincere. Mahra Brooks was hard not to like. Her smile was as genuine as her childlike charm. She had a way of brightening everyone's day.

"Well, Miss Brooks, I left it in Chicago. I didn't fit the suit or the town, so I hung them both up for good."

Pointing to the pistols, Brooks asked, "Are those loaded?"

"Yes they are, Miss Brooks. They're not much good if they're not."

"But we're on a train," protested Brooks.

Fargo merely smiled. Charm only went so far. After a while, it served no purpose.

With Brooks staring at the pistols and Wellington as well as LaFarge dumbfounded, Davis broke the silence. "We wanted to ask you a few questions, Mr. Fargo, about the road we'll be taking. And what might be the estimated distance to the Navajo reservation."

Fargo hesitated just long enough to generate a glint of irritation in the eyes of Clarissa LaFarge. "The road we'll take is called Beale's Wagon Road. It's well traveled and in good condition, as roads go. It's about two hundred fifty miles from Lamy to Zuni. From there, it's not too far to Navajo country."

"Then would we be able to travel the distance to Zuni in a week?" asked Wellington, his voice lacking the bravado it had possessed moments before.

"If all goes well. Ten days at most."

"Splendid," said Wellington. "We will need to purchase horses for the coach and wagon in Lamy. We will also require another coachman."

"There's a man in the drovers' car," offered Fargo. "Says he's a driver. He seems interested. Name's Smitty."

Davis looked at Wellington. "It would save some time if he's qualified."

LaFarge had not taken her eyes off Fargo. Clearly, he was not impressed by her beauty, nor was he responding to anything she said or did. In fact, he had virtually ignored her. Even worse, he was a vision of raw power and recklessness. He would be difficult to manipulate and impossible to dominate. Fargo would have to be handled another way.

"Mr. Fargo," said LaFarge, "I see that you have dark skin and very dark eyes. Are you part Indian or perhaps Mexican?"

Fargo looked impassively around the Palace car. He had inherited his dark skin from his grandfather, a Portuguese sea captain. But that was none of anyone's business. He understood that among genteel Southerners and aristocrats in the East, sun-darkened skin was attributed to the lower classes and those with mixed breeding. Her question was meant to be an insult.

"No," returned Fargo. With a faint note of sarcasm he added, "But folks that don't know much about Mexicans or Indians often make that assumption."

Wellington glanced questioningly at LaFarge. His eyes held on her for a moment and then went back to Fargo. "Do you think this Smitty fellow will do?"

"He seems capable."

"Good. Then all we will need is horses and a few supplies."

"Mules would be better," offered Fargo.

Still staring at Fargo, LaFarge protested, "Mules? Does not the word 'mulatto' come from mule? I believe it means mixed breed. Oh, how ghastly to be a half-breed, Miles. Please let us stay with horses. Mules are so hideous looking."

If the others understood LaFarge's insinuation, there was no outward sign. What Hialeaha thought about the half-breed comment was anyone's guess. Fargo spoke Portuguese and fluent Spanish and, in fact, often passed for Mexican, but he was no half-breed. He ignored LaFarge's barbs as he would threats from a dying man.

"Then we'll use horses," agreed Wellington, apparently oblivious to LaFarge's insults. "I have no experience with mules anyway."

"What is the climate like in the territories?" asked Davis. "I have heard that it can be quite hot."

"It's high desert country. Likely it'll be around ninety at the hottest part of the day."

"Will we be near water?" asked Brooks. "After a warm day, a cool bath is so delicious."

"Two to three days west of Lamy, we'll come to the Rio Grande. There'll be plenty of good water there. After that, it'll be a few days until we hit another stream. You'll have to make do with what we have in the water barrel."

"What of the dangers after leaving Lamy?" asked Wellington. "What mishaps might we expect along the way?"

Fargo glared at Wellington and then indicated the two women with a nod of his head. "Maybe we should talk about that another time."

Wellington flinched. One eyebrow arched disdainfully. His courage had returned. "I'll be the judge of that, Mr. Fargo. And I would like that information…not another time, but now."

LaFarge smirked triumphantly. Brooks looked down. Davis fidgeted. Only Fargo was unmoved.

"All right, Mr. Wellington. For starters, you'll be traveling across desert most of the way. If you run out of water or get cut off from it, you're going to get real thirsty. Then, if you don't find water in a day or so, your lips are going to start cracking. Your eyes will get so blurry you can't see. About day three, your tongue will turn black and swell so big you'll choke on it.

"Or you could get stung by a scorpion or bitten by a rattler and die of gangrene. Then there are road agents. The white ones will steal everything you've got, and if they're of a mind, they'll kill all the men. But white men won't harm the women. Women are safe enough around them.

"The Mexican bandits are the same as the whites except the women won't be safe. They might be taken to Mexico and sold, or they could be traded to the Indians as slaves.

"And then there are the Indians, especially the Apaches. They usually kill everybody, including the women…after they've finished with them. And that's the sugar-coated version of what happens. If you want the details, I'll give them to you…now…if you want."

Brooks put her hands over her ears and closed her eyes. "I do not want to hear about this. I do *not* want to know this. It's giving me a headache."

Davis put his arm around Brooks and patted her shoulder. "Perhaps, Miles," Davis said softly, "we can forgo the details for Mahra's sake."

Assuming an air of condescension, Wellington ignored his cousin's request.

"Perhaps the Indians were a problem in times past, Mr. Fargo. But I have it on good authority the Indians you speak of are presently confined on reservations. Our government has assigned Indian agents to see to it the aborigines are properly cared for and protected from white aggression. Surely an old Indian fighter like you should know we solved the Indian Question long ago. Or have you forgotten?"

Fargo stared at Wellington and slowly shook his head. "Reservations?" he repeated slowly. He paused. "You mean sanctuaries. There are no fences on these reservations. The Indians I'm talking about come and go as they please, and the agents are none the wiser. The braves travel hundreds of miles on raids and return with their loot to the protection of the reservation boundaries.

"Time after time the guilty ones have been trailed right back to the reservation, and the agent swears they never left. And that same agent likely never traveled so much as a mile from his house to check on his thousands of government pets.

"And then there are the renegades who refuse to hide under the government's nose, the ones like Victorio. He and his entire band jumped the reservation about two years back. Three months ago, he massacred eighteen whites and thirty-six sheepherders near Alma. That's only one hundred miles south of where you're headed, just a good day's ride for an Apache. And it's been just two weeks since his bunch massacred some folks on the road to Lordsburg.

"And either the Navajo or Utes just killed two men a few miles west of Zuni. And these killings are just the ones I know about."

For a moment, Wellington was speechless. He had been outmaneuvered. Fargo had exposed his ignorance in front of everyone. He thought quickly.

"Well," said Wellington, casually clearing his throat, "we should not be discussing such matters in front of the ladies. We will continue this another time, Mr. Fargo."

Wellington composed himself. "Now, what can you tell us about the countryside, the terrain we will be traversing?"

LaFarge put out a hand and touched Wellington's arm. "Oh, dear, since our guide is such an expert on all things Western, can we ask him about Dodge City?"

Flashing an insolent smile, LaFarge did not wait for Wellington to respond. "Mr. Fargo, the newspapers say Dodge City is the 'wickedest city in America.' They also claim the town is full of cutthroats and every house is a brothel. Do you have many friends there, Mr. Fargo? Surely you must."

LaFarge was spoiling for a fight, but Fargo wasn't in the mood to waste his breath. Her wealth and fame made her important in Chicago, but in the West, Clarissa LaFarge would soon discover a different world. There, a person's caliber, the very core of his or her being, would eventually be put to the test. And that person's worth would be judged by how he or she handled themselves. LaFarge would be tested soon enough. Until then, the actress could spit venom all she wanted.

"I know a few folks in Dodge," replied Fargo.

"Oh, do tell, Mr. Fargo," taunted LaFarge.

If he wanted, Fargo could have made a living playing poker. His face was unreadable. He would play LaFarge for the fool she was.

"Well, there's Dog Kelley. He used to scout for General Custer. After the Little Big Horn, he took the general's greyhounds to race them. That's how he got his name. Now he's the mayor. He owns a restaurant and a saloon. The last I heard, he also ran an opera house.

"I'm sure he'd be honored, Miss LaFarge, if you would perform there after we arrive."

Unable to control herself, LaFarge burst into laughter. "Oh, certainly, Mr. Fargo. I would be delighted. I cannot wait to be introduced to...Mr. Dog Kelley.

"And who else do you know in this 'Bibulous Babylon of the Frontier,' as it is so often called?"

"Oh, there's Chalk Beeson. He owns the Long Branch Saloon and conducts a cowboy band. And then there's Ham Bell. He's the new deputy US marshal."

LaFarge bit her lip. "Oh, Miles, I do so look forward to meeting his friends. All three gentlemen. Dog, Chalk, and Ham."

Mahra laughed, as did Davis. Studying the face of the former Pinkerton, Wellington did not even smile. Instead, his eyes narrowed suspiciously.

"Is Dodge City safe?" asked Wellington.

Fargo thought of the two men he had shot dead on the Chicago baseball field. According to Allan Pinkerton, criminal activity was rampant throughout the city, and no one living in Chicago was truly safe.

Fargo eyed Wellington. Unlike the others, the young man wasn't laughing. His question was a serious one. Perhaps there was some hope for him.

"Dodge is not all that different from Chicago. Stay north of what they call the 'deadline,' and you'll be fine. The deadline is Front Street. Go south of it, toward the Arkansas River, and you'll be where the gamblers and cowboys spend most of their time and money. That's where you'll find the majority of trouble."

"I've heard," continued Wellington, "of a Sheriff Bat Masterson. I was informed that he was a good officer. Is he still the sheriff?"

"No. He lost the last election to a man named Hinkle. The Earp brothers were good lawmen, too, but they left for Tombstone a while back."

Wellington thought for a moment. "Well, we should not be in Dodge City for more than a few hours. We want nothing to delay our departure. We must stay on schedule."

LaFarge grew more serious. She softened her tone. "Mr. Fargo, are there many buffalo herds near Dodge City?"

"Not anymore. Most all the buffalo have been killed off. I haven't seen any in years. This time of year, though, the cattle herds are coming in from Texas. There'll be close to seventy thousand grazing around Dodge."

"So, would you be able to identify a buffalo skin if you saw one?"

"I'd say so."

Taking out a linen bundle, LaFarge removed the leather map and handed it to Fargo. "What do you make of this?"

Fargo unrolled the supple hide. Holding it with two hands, he looked at the paintings and then flipped it over. Seeing a few fine hairs on the backside of the skin, he rubbed them through his fingers. They were light brown, silky, and soft.

"It's buffalo hide. An old one. Painted up by Indians but not Plains Indians. This is from somewhere in the Southwest."

"Why not Plains Indians?" asked Davis. "How can you tell so quickly?"

Pointing to a single humpbacked figure, Fargo answered, "Because this is Kokopeli. You only see him in the Southwest. He's seen all over, especially on rocks where the Indians carved it. Most likely, you'll see quite a few where we're going."

"And how do you know this Kokopeli is a 'he'?" asked LaFarge.

Fargo sighed. This was no time for a lesson in primitive art or basic anatomy. "Because that's what the Indians tell me."

"And what else do the Indians tell of this Kokopeli?" asked Davis. "You say the hide is old. How old are the stories about him?"

Thinking for a moment, Fargo stalled. Glancing from face to face, he could see the sudden interest in Kokopeli. Even Mahra was attentive. But why Kokopeli? Was it the Indian myth or the hide it was painted on?

"Well, Kokopeli's a character who's generally up to no good, a troublemaker of sorts. He was a chaser of women, you might say. But the tales about him are so old that none of the Indians know for sure where he came from. They say he was around before their ancestors took over the land from 'the ones who came before.' I've heard some call those first Indians the Anasazi."

"So," continued Davis, "could this Kokopeli character be, say, several hundred years old?"

"Don't know." Fargo shrugged. "It may be that old. Indians don't count time like we do. Could be a thousand years old. There's no way of knowing."

"Thank you, Mr. Fargo," said Wellington. Then he politely took the skin. Rolling it back up, he attempted a smile. "We were just curious as to whether this was an authentic artifact. I am a collector, you know. I have come across counterfeits and forgeries from time to time.

"Hialeaha, please show Mr. Fargo out. We have no more questions."

After opening the Palace car door, Hialeaha waited for Fargo to pass through. Following him into the stock car, she closed the door behind her and stopped.

"You know something, Far-go. Do you not?"

Fargo turned. Hialeaha was as perceptive as she was beautiful. Her brown eyes met his. She seemed to read his thoughts.

"What does it matter?" protested Fargo. "It's none of my business,"

Hialeaha waited. For several seconds their eyes held, each studying the other.

"Perhaps," replied Hialeaha. "But Mahra is *my* business."

Fargo exhaled slowly and shoved his hat back with the tip of his thumb. Every man had a weakness. In his younger years, it was women. At that time, he was a fool known as Caleb Felton. He was nearly fifty now and for the last fifteen years had been Conway Fargo. Women were still his weakness, but now for an entirely different reason.

"She's a grown woman."

"Mahra," Hialeaha said firmly, "will never be a grown woman. She is like a child. I tried to teach her as she grew. Her life was too easy. I could not change her, could not help her, yet she is still like a daughter to me."

"Then she should've stayed home," snapped Fargo. "Where they're headed isn't for her kind."

"She is here, and she will go with them."

Fargo bristled for a moment and then frowned and shrugged dismissively.

Hialeaha spoke solemnly. "And you will be with us, also…Far-go. You will also be there for Mahra."

"What's that supposed to mean?" demanded Fargo, knowing all too well the answer to his own question.

Hialeaha's face was devoid of emotion, but her eyes were locked on his. "You are Far-go, are you not?"

Fargo swore under his breath. When he had ridden East, he had intended to reinvent himself and leave his past behind. But he should have gone farther than Chicago or at least changed his name. Now he was going back to where he had started and was already in deeper than he wanted. It was starting all over.

Fargo said nothing for several seconds. He muttered a few more curse words then said reluctantly, "I caught wind of a little here and there. For one thing, I noticed all of them are much too interested in that painted skin. I suspect it's got something to do with why they're headed to Zuni.

"You said that's where they want to go, not to the Navajos. If that's so, whatever it is they're after, it's in or near the Zuni pueblo. Maybe it's in one of the pueblo houses or hidden underground in a secret kiva."

"It must be of great value," said Hialeaha. "But you said the Zuni are not a wealthy tribe."

"Not that you can notice. They do some silver work here and there. That could be what they're looking for—a deposit of silver."

"But why is the skin of any importance?" questioned Hialeaha.

Fargo thought for a moment. "The way they're acting makes me think it's likely a map of some sort. The Zuni wouldn't need a map to find anything, so they wouldn't make one. If that hide was made by the Zuni, it would have some other meaning. And you're right about what you said."

"About what?"

"About them looking for something of great value. Whatever is out there, the four of them believe it's worth a lot of money. Clarissa LaFarge wouldn't be going to a place like Zuni unless she stood to profit from it. You can bet your last dollar on that."

Hialeaha frowned. "Others will think the same way as you. They will follow to see where we go."

"I thought about that, too. Those four will stick out like a sore thumb. Even if they convince folks they're just a pack of Eastern fools looking over the country, they'll still be rich Eastern fools. That alone will invite trouble."

"My only concern is for Mahra," Hialeaha said coldly. She paused. "She is the only innocent one. And she is so young."

Fargo flinched. He peered at the Indian. How much did she know? He had fiercely guarded his most loathsome secret for nearly twenty years, at least from whites. Until this moment, what stories might be told around Indian campfires had never crossed his mind.

Maybe Mahra Brooks was innocent and maybe not. It did not matter. Because of a woman like her, he had become what he was: a hunter of men.

As a Confederate prisoner, he was offered his freedom on the condition he would become a galvanized Yankee and pursue Apaches across the Southwest. After the war, as a deputy marshal, he trailed Comanche, Mexicans, and whites deep into Mexico. Killing was the only craft he was good at and the only worthwhile profession he had in three decades. Perhaps there was no end to it, no final payment after all.

Fargo swore again, but this time the epithets were more audible. A man might be forgiven of an evil deed, but the guilt of it never washed off. It was always there, always haunting the nights. Some were driven to drink by its grip, others to despair. Conway Fargo's price of redemption was a life of killing.

"Can you shoot?" asked Fargo, feeling the heat rise under his collar.

"Yes. I did not always wear white-man's clothes."

"Have you said anything to them about me," inquired Fargo, "or about my past? You seem to know more than you let on."

"I have heard things about you. What is true and what is not, I cannot say. I have said nothing to anyone."

"Good!" said Fargo. Wondering just how much the woman knew about him, he added, "Keep it that way."

Fargo ran a hand over his face. He took a deep breath and cleared his mind. Hialeaha was only concerned with Mahra Brooks and how to protect her. The Indian needed his help, and he might need hers before long. The road to Zuni would be a long one.

"Will they know you in Dodge City?" asked Hialeaha.

Fargo shook his head, and his brow wrinkled. "It's a cow town, the end of the Chisholm Trail. The cowhands come up from Texas with the herds and leave as soon as they're broke. The cattlemen stay to themselves. The saloons…maybe some there might know me. I know three or four men who live in Dodge. But we won't be in town long enough to do any socializing. It's a busy town. If we're lucky, we can get in and out before anyone notices we're there."

Chapter 5

B y half past three the following afternoon, the temperature in the Palace car was over ninety. The windows had been lowered to stir the air. The train was ten miles from Dodge City when Mahra Brooks began waving a hand in front of her lightly freckled nose.

"What on earth is that odor, Edward?"

"Oh! I smell it too," said LaFarge, who for the moment had stopped fanning herself. "How dreadful!"

Davis glanced out the window but saw nothing. He stuck his head out. Squinting his eyes as the wind whipped his hair into a tangled mat, he looked up and down the rails.

Ducking back inside, Davis flattened his hair with the palm of his hand. "I didn't see anything. I wonder what it could be?"

The front door of the Palace car opened. Miles Wellington walked in with a smile on his face. He shut the door. "We are nearing the stockyards," he offered, brushing a layer of fine dust from his jacket and pants.

"Stockyards!" exclaimed Davis. "I just looked out the window, and I did not see any stockyards."

"I was talking with the men in the drovers' car," said Wellington, taking a seat next to LaFarge. "They said you can smell the cattle for miles, especially when the wind is right. There are thousands of cattle in holding pens and tens of thousands more surrounding the town waiting to be driven in and shipped. Several southern routes, called cattle trails, end at Dodge City. The cattle are driven there by herders on horseback called 'cow boys.'"

"I am getting a headache from that awful smell," said Brooks. She reached for her tonic. "Cow boys?"

"Yes, cow boys. The men tell me once the herders bathe and discard their motley trail raiment, they buy new clothes and strut about the town with their pockets full of money. Their attire, though considered high fashion in Dodge City, sounds most comical. They wear large, wide-brimmed hats and neck scarves made of brightly colored silk. Their pants are tucked into boots that have high heels with large musical spurs attached. And most interesting, every last one of the jolly fellows buckles on a belt full of cartridges and a loaded pistol!"

Wellington smirked. "It is said that Dodge City stands on the extreme border of civilization. Or to put it in delightfully vulgar terms, it is a wide-open town. They have a saying that 'anything goes in Dodge'!"

Davis glanced uneasily at Brooks, who was swallowing a dose of Mother Bailey's syrup from her silver cup. "But will we...Will Mahra and Clarissa be safe there?"

"We will all be safe as long as we avoid those areas of the city that Mr. Fargo mentioned earlier. We shall stay just long enough to see the sights and refuel with coal. In any event, I have been assured that women are never harmed in Dodge City, not even the 'scarlet ladies of the evening.' I have also been informed that women of all varieties are practically worshiped on the frontier. There are so many men and so few women, you see."

A hint of red colored Davis's cheeks. "All the same, I think Mr. Treadway should be close at hand. With so many guns about, perhaps Mr. Fargo should accompany us as well."

"That sounds wise, Miles," agreed LaFarge. "And it would do no harm to observe Mr. Fargo's behavior, should any trouble arise. We have nothing but a recommendation from Mr. Pinkerton that he is the right man for our purposes. I would like to see something of his capabilities before we leave the train in Lamy. At this point, I am not certain we can rely on him. If he should prove unworthy to the task, I am certain we can hire a younger, more virile man when we reach Lamy."

Wellington shrugged. "I have already spoken to Reed and Mr. Fargo," he conceded and then began to grin at LaFarge.

"What is it, Miles?"

"Oh, I simply cannot wait. I must tell you, Clarissa. I telegraphed ahead that you were coming to Dodge City. They have never had a person of your celebrity visit them. They will be waiting at the station to greet us."

"Who is 'they'?" asked LaFarge.

"Do you remember Eddie Foy from Chicago?"

"Yes. I believe we met briefly. He was a vaudevillian, was he not, a clown and dancer? Certainly he was not in theater."

"Foy is a comedic performer and quite well known in Dodge City. He is arranging everything. The mayor and the sheriff will be on hand. Wait until you hear the band. Oh, it will be grand!"

LaFarge produced a practiced smile, a stage façade. "Well then, we shall make our grand entrance in style. And we would not want to disappoint Mayor Dog Kelley. Perhaps he will even bring his namesakes with him."

Davis began to relax. "They will likely give us the keys to the city."

"They would," blurted Wellington, as he began to laugh, "if they had any keys."

"You mean," joined in Davis, "if they had a city!"

"Oh it gets better, Edward," roared Wellington. "They have two streets where all the businesses are located. And the city rubes named both of them Front Street!"

Listening to the laughter, Mahra Brooks ran a dainty finger around the inside of her cup and then sucked it clean. She squinted thoughtfully at the bottle of elixir. Licking her lips, she said quietly, "I thought Dodge City *was* a city."

LaFarge stood and adjusted the high collar of her royal purple satin day suit. "What do think, Mahra? Sunbonnets or touring hats?"

Brooks smiled, showing her dimples. She always enjoyed dressing in the latest fashion. "Oh, touring hats. The ones with the feathers, I should think. And I will take my white lace parasol and matching fan."

The rancid odor of urine and cow manure wafted through the Palace car. LaFarge wrinkled her nose and took down a hatbox.

"I shall take my fringed parasol and my ivory lace fan," said LaFarge, trying on the hat. "What do you think, Miles?"

Wellington looked at Clarissa LaFarge. He shook his head in awe. "You are a goddess, Clarissa. Dodge City will never be the same."

Brooks had not moved. She still wore her childlike smile. She looked first at Wellington and then at LaFarge. "Oh, you are beautiful, Clarissa."

"As are you, Mahra," returned LaFarge, taking down another hatbox and handing it to Brooks. "We must not dally. The menials await."

"Dare we paint our lips, Clarissa?" asked Brooks. "Dare we have red lips?"

"I almost forgot. Guerlain's Lip Pomade, our latest addition from France. Of course, we shall wear it! As Miles said, 'anything goes in Dodge.'"

The train began to slow. Davis took two derby hats from a rack. Handing one to Wellington, he looked out the window. "Ah, yes, the small wonder of vulgar curiosity. Let us not disappoint the common herd."

Accepting the hat, Wellington carefully placed it on his greased-down hair. After brushing the sleeves of his black cutaway coat and adjusting his paisley puff tie, he reset his derby and cocked it to one side of his head.

"I have instructed Treadway and Fargo to stay near us. Not too near, of course, but close enough. Should we encounter any of the vagrant or barbarous stripe, it should prove interesting to see how they handle themselves.

"Fargo seems a bit too old, if you ask me."

Davis nodded. "He must be in his fifties. Have you noticed those wrinkles at the corners of his eyes? He looks positively devilish."

LaFarge finished applying her red lipstick. "I do not like him. I find his manners contemptible."

Brooks set her feathered hat in place. "Hialeaha says he must come with us. She told me she prayed he would come."

LaFarge, Davis, and Wellington turned in unison to look down at Mahra.

LaFarge spoke first. "Why would Hialeaha say such a thing?"

Shrugging, Brooks answered simply, "I do not know."

"Did you ask her why she feels so strongly he must come?"

"No."

Wellington thought for a moment. A faint smile twisted his lips. "Well, she is about the same age as Fargo. Perhaps Cupid is afoot."

"Never too old," snorted Davis. "Never too old, I say."

"Oh, my heavens," scolded LaFarge, "a white man, even a man like Fargo, with an Indian! Surely you do not think he would…?"

"Yes, my dear," interrupted Wellington, "from what I have learned, it is not unheard of on the frontier."

Davis had known Mahra Brooks for years. Hialeaha had always been there to care for her. Even now the Cherokee was her guardian when he was not around. He quickly glanced around the Palace car searching for Hialeaha. Seeing she was not present, he sighed with relief. Looking back at Clarissa LaFarge, his eyes twitched with uneasiness.

The express train blew its whistle and then slowed to a stop. Outside the windows, a three-hundred-foot-long platform came into view. The station itself was a wooden, two-story structure with freight offices on the top and telegraph and ticket windows on the bottom. A crowd gathered at the end of the platform. A band was playing in a fog of steam as black clouds belched skyward from the train's smokestack.

Davis listened as the train came to a halt. "The band is actually quite good."

Wellington bent and looked out a window. "My word, the conductor is leading with a pistol instead of baton!"

"Come, come, Miles," said LaFarge, holding out her hand. "The mudsills await."

Wellington took Clarissa's hand and then prepared to open the Palace car door. He glanced behind him. Arm in arm, Davis and Brooks waited eagerly.

"Shall we?" asked Wellington.

Davis grinned at Brooks. "Shall we, my dear?"

Brooks batted her eyes. "We shall."

Catching sight of LaFarge, the crowd erupted in cheers. They waved and pointed as Wellington helped LaFarge step down onto the platform. She smiled and with a flick of her wrist returned the waves. Two men approached, both dressed in starched collars and broadcloth suits.

"Welcome to Dodge City, Miss LaFarge," said a man with a waxed handlebar mustache. "I'm Mayor James Kelley." He pointed to the man next to him. "And this, here, is Eddie Foy."

LaFarge made a living being charming on cue. She offered her gloved hand. "How do you do, Mayor Kelley. This is such a wonderful surprise." She then offered her hand to Foy. "Mr. Eddie Foy, I believe we may have met, in Chicago perhaps."

Foy was in the varieties. The grin on his face was legendary in Dodge. "Why yes, Miss LaFarge. I am humbled that you would recall."

Davis and Brooks stepped down onto the platform. The eighteen-man band struck up another lively number. All the members wore hats, neckerchiefs, chaps, and spurs. A banner behind them read Dodge City Cowboy Band.

"That's Chalk Beeson conducting," said Foy, raising his voice over the music. "He owns the Long Branch Saloon."

Kelley was about to speak when he noticed several men exiting the drovers' car. One of them he recognized. After a short pause, Kelley said, "Again, welcome to Dodge, Miss LaFarge. Now, you and your party have a good time."

Tipping his hat, Kelley added, "Excuse me, but I see an old friend."

Clarissa's face flushed red as Kelley abruptly sidestepped her and went toward the rear of the train. Foy was saying something about the theaters in town, but she did not hear him. Her eyes followed Kelley until she saw him vigorously shake hands with Conway Fargo. Her jaw muscles pulsed under her creamy-white skin.

"We only have a short time, Mr. Foy," said Wellington, unaware that LaFarge had been upstaged. "We would like to see as much of Dodge City as we might."

"Would you like me to show you around? I would be more than pleased to do so."

"Thank you, Mr. Foy, but we prefer to tour on our own. We find it more adventurous."

The band was still playing as the Easterners strolled through the crowd to the end of the platform. Before following Wellington and LaFarge down the stairs, Brooks tugged on Davis's arm and stopped.

Looking dismayed, she announced, "Why, their streets are made of dirt!"

"Yes, dear," said Davis. "But it is only a short distance to the buildings, and I see they have boardwalks. We will be fine."

Wellington was helping LaFarge onto a boardwalk in front of a hardware store when he noticed the tension in her face.

"What is it, Clarissa?"

"Are Reed and Fargo behind us?"

Glancing over his shoulder, Wellington saw Treadway nearing the platform steps and caught a glimpse of Fargo coming through the crowd.

"Yes, they are coming along as instructed."

LaFarge looked at her reflection in the store window and adjusted her hat. "I am certain Mr. Fargo has friends in town he wishes to see. Reed is more than adequate as our escort. Please tell Mr. Fargo that we do not require his services at this time, that he is free until we depart. And send Reed to me. I would like a word with him."

Wellington escorted LaFarge into the shade of the store's overhang. "That is very considerate of you, Clarissa. I will relay your wishes."

Passing Davis and Brooks, Wellington first came to Treadway, who was now crossing Front Street. He delivered his message and then approached Fargo, who, along with Kelley, had stopped to shake hands with two other men. They were dressed in trail clothes.

Walking up to the men, Wellington did not interrupt. The men Fargo was speaking with wore guns and badges.

Noticing Wellington, Fargo paused. "Mr. Wellington, this is George Hinkle. He replaced Bat Masterson as sheriff of Dodge. And this is Ham Bell, the deputy US marshal I told you about."

Shaking hands with the sheriff and marshal, Wellington asked, "Is there any trouble?"

Bell laughed. "No. We're old friends, all of us. You're travelin' in good company, Mr. Wellington. Con here is one to ride the river with."

"I beg your pardon?"

"He's been known to wear a badge from time to time," said Hinkle. "He's a good man to have around."

"Oh. Quite right," agreed Wellington. "Mr. Fargo, as you seem to have many friends in Dodge City, Miss LaFarge suggested we grant you this time to visit whomever you please. We will see you back at the train shortly."

Fargo watched Wellington walk away before looking down Front Street. LaFarge was talking with Treadway while Brooks and Davis stood off at a distance. Wellington had no reason to lie, so it had to be LaFarge's idea to separate him from the group. Whatever her reason, it was not so he could visit his friends.

After saying good day to the lawmen, Dog Kelley wiped his forehead with his handkerchief and then ran a finger under his starched collar. "I got ice-cold beer at the Alhambra. I'm part owner now."

"You've come a long way since we scouted for the army," said Fargo. "Look at you in that suit. You're not only a businessman, you're mayor of Dodge. You've done well for yourself, Dog."

"And look at you, Con. I'd give my eye teeth to be traveling with Clarissa LaFarge, and all the way from Chicago. I'd say you come a good distance yourself."

Instead of LaFarge, Fargo thought of Mahra Brooks. She was naive and innocent, much like another woman he had known long ago. Brooks was the reason he had taken the job as guide. He blamed himself for what happened to the other young woman. Since then, nothing much mattered. He had not come far at all. In fact, he was right back where he had started.

"No," said Fargo. "Nothing's changed with me. I'm taking them west. Then I'm back on my own, doing what I always do."

"Well, hell!" Kelley grinned. "I'll drink to that. There ain't none better at it than you. Let's have that beer."

The men started up Front Street, passing Hoover's Cigar Store. "You remember old Hoover?" asked Kelley. "When we first came by here as scouts, he had his whiskey bar in that old sod hut. That was all there was of Dodge back then. By all rights, Dodge should be called Hooverville or Hoover City, or some such."

"I remember. So he just sells cigars now?"

"Yep. That and pouch tobacco. He's doing fine, too."

Walking farther, Fargo heard a piano playing in the Long Branch Saloon. "How's Chalk doing with his saloon?"

"Good. Dodge has sixteen saloons and a brick courthouse. This time of year, they're all doing real good. The town gets up to five thousand people through August. Chalk's usually got his five-piece band playing, but they're part of his Cowboy Band down at the station. Them boys is getting famous."

The two men came to the Alhambra. It looked like all the other wood-frame gambling houses, but this one had a balcony.

"I could use a good man, Con," said Kelley. "Business is booming, but Dodge is full of crooks and cutthroats. I'm always lookin' for men I can trust."

Fargo shook his head. "I got a job. And you know city life isn't for me. I tried it out here, and I tried it back east. Thanks all the same."

"So what are you up to with those four Yankees?"

"Don't know exactly. They say they're looking for artifacts."

"What the hell is a artyfact?"

"Old things. Things the Indians left behind."

Dog Kelley swore and spat onto the dusty street. "How old? I could show 'em a passel of graves the Indians left behind, graves you and me helped dig a few years back. There's lots of them. Maybe them four want to see that." Pointing to the saloon doors, he sneered, "To hell with 'em. Let's have that beer."

All of the tables were occupied, but there was standing room at the bar. Kelley waved at the bartender. "Two beers."

Behind the bar, rows of amber and green bottles were separated by a large mirror framed in mahogany. Above the mirror hung a large painting of a reclining nude woman. It was a saloon like dozens of others Fargo had seen. He turned to look over the crowded room. For the most part, it was full of cowboys celebrating the trail's end. No one looked familiar.

"You always busy this early in the day?" asked Fargo. "It's not even time for supper."

Kelley pointed to a large clock on the far wall. "Only half past four. Wait till tonight. We'll be runnin' full chisel then."

Fargo glanced over his shoulder at the clock and caught a glimpse of a man coming through the batwing doors. He wore no hat, nor was he armed. It was Smitty.

The brakeman nodded to Fargo but went to the far end of the bar.

"Who's that?" asked Kelley.

"Name's Smitty. He's the brakeman on our train. Says he's a mule-skinner too."

"Here you are, boss," said the bartender, setting two frosty mugs of beer on the polished wood.

Fargo and Kelley turned. Each grabbed a mug. "To General George Armstrong Custer," said Kelley.

Fargo was about to drink to the toast when a powerful shoulder bumped his right arm. The beer spilled on his shirt. Looking sharply to his right, he saw Treadway.

The big blond seemed unaware of what he had done or whom he had done it to. Fargo brushed the beer from his shirt and stepped to his left, a bit closer to Kelley.

"To Custer," repeated Fargo, and made another attempt to drink.

Treadway's elbow hit Fargo's upper arm, causing the rim of the mug to smash into his lip. This time Kelley noticed what had happened. So did the bartender and some of the cowboys nearby.

Suddenly, Fargo understood what had transpired in the short meeting between LaFarge and Treadway. He looked at Kelley, who was about to protest, and shook his head no. Watching Fargo change the mug to his other hand, Kelley acknowledged with a nod.

Raising his mug once more, Fargo said, "To a great Indian fighter."

Treadway made his move, but Fargo saw it coming in the mirror. Stepping backward, he pulled his Colt from its cross-draw holster and slammed the barrel across Treadway's temple.

Treadway staggered, and Fargo hit him again. This time he crumpled to the floor.

Most of the cowboys noticed nothing. A few saw a man hit the floor, likely drunk. But at the end of the bar, the hatless brakeman thoughtfully scratched his ear. Earlier, he had doubted that Conway Fargo knew how to handle himself. Reed Treadway, though, was a dangerous man, and he lay unconscious on the barroom floor.

Fargo was smart and surprisingly tough. If Treadway did not kill the guide for what he had done, Fargo could prove useful.

Smitty rubbed his way through the crowd until he reached Fargo. Pointing down and grinning, he said, "He's shore a big dumb ox, ain't he?"

"That's what they say," replied Fargo, then took a sip of beer and gazed at the painting.

Taking out a soiled handkerchief, Smitty leaned over the bar and held it toward the bartender. "Can I get some ice? He's gonna have a sore head when he wakes up. He'll be madder than a March hare."

"He was spoiling for a fight," said Kelley.

Smitty bent over, placing his hands on his knees. He turned his head sideways, staring at the rising welt on Treadway's head. "Well, my daddy always said, 'God suffers fools to reap what they have sown.'"

"Lucky for him," said Kelley, "he's only going to have a headache."

"Wall, you can't be shootin' no unarmed man," said Smitty, straightening. "Even one as big as him. See, he ain't got no gun on him."

"Size don't matter," muttered Kelley. He kneeled on one knee and searched Treadway. He reached into Treadway's right front pants pocket, pulled out a short-barreled pistol, and then slid it back into place. Standing again, he said, "You see he's heeled well enough. But I wasn't talking about shooting him. Conway's no stranger to fisticuffs."

The bartender took Smitty's handkerchief, loaded it with crushed ice, and handed it back. Smitty twisted the handkerchief as he squatted. Holding the icepack on Treadway's temple, he studied Fargo more closely. The bones of his hands were thick, the knuckles scarred. There was also a scar above one eye. The man had indeed seen his share of brawls.

"That's why he got buffaloed," answered Kelley.

"What?"

"That's what Wyatt Earp called it. A pistol barrel slapped across a man's skull saves a lot of fighting and a fair amount of shooting."

"Who's Wyatt Earp?"

"He was a lawman here for a while. A good man, but he moved on last year."

Kelley pointed at Treadway with his mug of beer. "You know him?"

Smitty looked confused. "We both do, me and Mr. Fargo. He's with us. We're goin' with them rich folks on the train. His name's Treadway."

"He an Easterner, too?"

"Yep, born and raised."

Glancing at Fargo, Kelley warned, "You know, he's gonna be trouble now. There'll be bad blood between the two of you."

"I sleep light," replied Fargo.

Shaking his head, Kelley frowned at Smitty. "You tell Treadway to keep his distance from Conway here. That is, if he wants to stay healthy. Tell him things are different out here. More often than not, disagreements are settled with lead, not knuckles."

"I'll tell hm. But he seems a might slow in the head. Don't know if it'll do no good."

Fargo set his beer down. It was only half empty. "I've a mind to walk my horses."

Kelley put out his hand. "Good seeing you, Con. I'm going to finish my beer and then catch up with Miss LaFarge and see how she's likin' Dodge. Maybe on her way back, she'll stay awhile longer. Be good for business."

Stepping over Treadway, Fargo disappeared out the saloon doors.

"He that dangerous?" asked Smitty, still holding the ice on Treadway's head.

"You can see he don't say much. Seems harmless enough, but the hounds of hell don't hold a candle to him." Kelley took a big gulp of beer. "Some call him the Parson. The Apaches call him Tats-a-das-ago. Means quick killer. I say he's both."

"Want to chew them words a little finer, friend?"

Kelley laughed. "Well, let's just say he don't take a long time to make up his mind to kill a man. And when he does, if he's got the chance, he'll give them time to pray before he pulls the trigger.

"Damndest thing I ever seen was the time he give an Indian time to sing his death song before he killed him. I thought Con was loco at the time, but the Indians got word of what he done. They want like hell to kill Conway Fargo, but every last warrior and man-child respects Tats-a-das-ago. And whoever kills him is gonna be big medicine."

Treadway was regaining consciousness. Smitty stood back. He thoughtfully watched the big man gather himself and gain his footing. Fargo had not sought any trouble with Treadway, so there was a reason he had come to the bar and gone straight for Fargo. His gun was hidden and difficult to get out of his pocket. His plan must have been to pummel Fargo with his fists. But why? Had there been trouble between the two of them in the horse car? Even if there had been, Treadway would not start a fight with their only guide without permission of LaFarge. More likely, what he had tried to do was at her direction.

Why then, did LaFarge want Fargo beaten? There was no profit in it, no lovers' quarrel. And if Fargo had been badly injured, he might have quit or been unable to travel. That being the case, as far as LaFarge was concerned, Fargo was expendable.

Smitty thought for a moment before it came to him. He grinned knowingly, showing his missing front teeth. Fargo had not angered Treadway. Instead, he had somehow earned the disfavor of the high-and-mighty Clarissa LaFarge! For such an offense, she had ordered the man publicly bloodied and humiliated.

Treadway's head began to clear. Unsteadily, he looked around the saloon. "Where is he?" he demanded. His defiant words came quickly, without their usual lethargy.

"Gone," said Smitty. "Take it easy."

Fingering the knot on his head, Treadway growled, "The hell I will!"

"You came in here looking for a fight," said Kelley. He finished his beer and set the mug on the bar. "You got more than you bargained for when you did that. You'd best stay clear of Fargo."

Treadway eyed Kelley for a moment.

"That's right, Reed," agreed Smitty. "Think about it, now. We got a long and dangerous trip ahead of us. We don't want no trouble out on the trail, now do we?"

A hidden thought flashed in Treadway's eyes. He hesitated and then without a word went for the saloon door.

Watching Treadway leave, Kelley asked, "Do you know where you're headed after you leave the tracks?"

"No," replied Smitty. He could lie with the best of them. "No idea at all."

"How is it traveling with her? Miss LaFarge, I mean. She as nice as she is pretty? I never seen such a pretty woman."

"She's an angel," replied Smitty, smiling. "You'd never hope to meet no one nicer."

***

Instead of walking his horses, Fargo saddled the black and, leading the bay, rode down the tracks past the stockyards. The sun was crowding the western skyline when he returned to the train. He stepped down in front of the ramp. Hialeaha and Smitty were waiting next to it. Worry darkened Hialeaha's features.

"Evening," said Fargo.

"You had trouble," returned Hialeaha. "You will have more."

Fargo dismounted and loosened the cinch of his saddle. "No more than usual. Just a little mix-up in a saloon."

"What will you do?" asked Hialeaha. "Will you leave the train?"

"No."

"I saw it all," offered Smitty. "I saw Treadway try to start somethin' for no reason. He had a bone to pick with you, and now he's got a bigger one. He don't seem too bright. I 'magine he'll be lookin' for his chance to get even."

"That's the way I figure it."

Smitty shook his head. "Well, I wouldn't wanna be in your shoes. He's a big 'un."

Fargo led his horses up the ramp and over to the tie-offs. He began unsaddling the black. Smitty spoke softly to Hialeaha then went to the drovers' car. Hialeaha waited a moment before following after Fargo.

Taking a brush from the wall near her, Hialeaha asked, "Why would Treadway do such a thing?"

Fargo hoisted his saddle onto a tree and draped his blanket over it. He turned to face Hialeaha. "Who knows?"

Hialeaha handed the brush to Fargo. "Smitty does not trust Treadway. He said not to turn your back on him."

"Venga lo que venga," said Fargo, gazing at the brush in his hand. Hialeaha had taken it from its hook and almost absent-mindedly handed it to him. Her simple gesture stirred a distant memory, a time when the presence of a woman was part of his life. Slowly, he raised his head. Hialeaha's eyes held a question. "It means 'come what may' in Spanish."

"He had a pistol in his pocket?"

"He did," answered Fargo. "And when we were in Mr. Pinkerton's office, Miss LaFarge said he had no use for pistols."

"A lie, then?"

Fargo started brushing the black. "Maybe. Likely, I'd say."

"But you will stay, even though he carries a pistol?"

"Takes a long time to get a pistol out of a pocket."

"But why? Why did it happen?"

"Why do you think it happened?"

Hialeaha thought as Fargo finished brushing the black and started on the bay. Finally, she said, "Miss LaFarge sent him. It is what she would do. You did not bow to her. You made her wait for you. For this, she wanted you to have trouble, to pay for what you had done."

Smiling, Fargo looked over the back of the bay. He nodded. "You'll do, Miss Hialeaha. You'll do."

"But this will only make it worse. She will not stop until she gets what she wants."

"Well, the way I see it, she has Treadway and I have you. I'd say the odds are in my favor."

For several seconds, Hialeaha said nothing. Her brow furrowed. "You would trust me to help you? It is said that Tats-a-das-ago hates Indians."

Resuming his brushing, Fargo said, "Not all of them."

Hialeaha studied Fargo for several seconds with unblinking eyes. "What can I do?"

"You'll know when the time comes. You're twice the woman she is."

Hialeaha blushed at the unexpected compliment, but Fargo did not notice.

"I can handle Treadway," said Fargo.

"But how? You must sleep, and when you do, he can have his revenge."

Fargo slid his hand over the rump of the bay then hung up the brush. "I've been through this before. He won't give me any trouble right away. You can count on that.

"Is there any chance you can talk Miss Brooks into turning back, and maybe Mr. Davis as well?"

"There is no chance. None."

"Then we just keep going west. Venga lo que venga."

Hialeaha was about to speak when heavy footsteps pounded up the ramp. She turned. Treadway glared at her from the edge of the horse car. She looked back at Fargo.

"I'll have my supper in here tonight," said Fargo. "The drovers' car is too crowded."

Understanding she was to leave, Hialeaha answered, "Yes, Mr. Far-go."

Ignoring Treadway, Hialeaha quickly disappeared down the ramp. When she was out of sight, Fargo approached Treadway. The big man's eyes were deep set and threatening. Gone was his portrayal of the village idiot.

Stopping two steps in front of Treadway, Fargo spoke evenly. "You'll sleep in the drovers' car tonight. And when the two of us are in this car, if you get within ten feet of me, I'll kill you. If you reach inside your pocket, I'll kill you. And when we get on the trail, you'll keep your distance and stay in front of me. If you don't...I...will...kill you."

Treadway's neck turned red under his thick blond hair. His jaw muscles pulsated.

"Or," said Fargo, his eyes flashing a deadly warning, "we can finish it now. But if you know any prayers, you best start saying them while there's still air in your lungs."

"That would be murder," sneered Treadway.

"In Chicago, maybe. If I'd known you had a pistol in your pocket back in the saloon, they'd be mopping your blood off the saloon floor right now. And nobody would have faulted me one bit for killing you. When they finished cleaning up, they'd go on about their business, as if nothing had happened. This is Dodge City, Treadway. West of here, it gets even worse.

"From now on, as far as I'm concerned, you have a pistol hidden somewhere. Make one wrong move, and I won't wait for you to pull it."

As Fargo spoke, the hatred in Treadway's eyes vanished. The threat, the assurance of victory stamped on his face seconds before melted away. His advantage of size and strength, his ability to intimidate, was gone. The man in front of him fought with a gun. And the chances were better than even that he was a stone-cold killer.

Treadway started to say something. His lips twitched, but no word formed between them. His breathing was shallow. He was used to back alleys and dark corners, where he used his fists and an occasional knife. A pistol was noisy and always a last resort.

A country where men wore pistols in plain sight and would not hesitate to use them was new to him. He had fought many men and murdered some of them, but he had never faced the certainty of his own death. Now he was staring it in the face.

"You should know something else," said Fargo. "What you and the others are up to is none of my concern. I hired on for one reason: to keep Miss Brooks and Hialeaha out of harm's way. But anything that endangers them becomes my business. If and when that happens, the rest of you can be damned."

Chapter 6

The next day, Treadway entered the horse car to feed and water the stock and then was gone. Fargo stayed with the horses and out of the drovers' car altogether. Hialeaha brought him his food and coffee, often staying a few minutes to talk.

She told him there had been no discussion in the Palace car of what had happened in the Alhambra Saloon. She also told him that no one had mentioned the incident, and this caused her to worry. She worried not only for Mahra Brooks but also, she confessed, for him. The thought of anyone caring about his safety, especially a woman, kept Fargo awake the night they left Dodge. Now those same thoughts had woken him again.

Each evening he had propped a broom against the rear door of the stock car. If anyone had tried to enter in the darkness, he would have heard them. He should have slept better. But now, the second night, thoughts of Hialeaha were again keeping him awake.

Perplexed, Fargo stared into the darkness. Hialeaha was an Indian, yet she had fair skin. Except for her moccasins, she dressed like any other white woman. Her dresses were modest but seemed to fit disturbingly well. That much had caught his eye in Pinkerton's office. In her demure, unassuming way, he found her more attractive than either Mahra Brooks or Clarissa LaFarge.

She knew he was Tats-a-das-ago, but how much had she actually heard about that name? Did she know it had started in Tucson during the war? He was a Confederate then and a spy. He was returning from a mission and stopped to rest. He fell asleep when he should have kept going. Had he continued on, he would have reached Tucson in time to stop a young woman from going to the San Xavier Mission. Her name was Bricela.

He was too late. When he found her, two Apache bucks had her on the ground. One was on top of her. The other was standing over them, waiting his turn. She was only fifteen. That was the beginning of the killing.

He left Bricela at the mission with the Papagos. Her eyes were fixed in a blank stare, her mind seeming lost in a thick fog. At San Xavier, the Yankees captured him. That day was twenty years behind him yet ever in the forefront of his thoughts. The sights, the sounds, the smells never faded.

It was his fault that Bricela had been going to the mission. She went because she was in love with him. That was also his fault. Up to that moment, his life had been a disgrace. For her, however, on that horrible day, he swore an oath. He vowed her unspeakable suffering would not go unanswered or be in vain. It would count for something.

He started with renegade Apaches. Hate knotted together with revenge and guilt drove him initially. When he had killed all the renegade Apaches he could find, he turned to lawless Mexicans and whites. There was never a shortage of evil men, each vendetta offering another chance for redemption.

The side door of the stock car was open, allowing the warm night air to circulate. Fargo sat up and worked his jaw to loosen it. He had been clinching again, the result of being cooped up too long. It was time to be out in the open where he belonged, not in a Chicago hotel room and certainly not in a wooden crate rattling along on steel rails.

Fargo came to his feet and stretched. Outside, the stars were fading. The train would be in Lamy by sunup. They needed to purchase horses. As soon as they had their stock, they should leave. The end of the tracks was no place for decent women and greenhorn Easterners.

After buckling on his pistols, Fargo lit a coal-oil lantern and hung it on the wall. Using his fingers as a comb, he straightened his hair and then put on his hat. Twisting his neck left and right, he heard it pop and grind. He felt the stiffness leave his shoulders, a stiffness that had not been there twenty years before.

As he rolled his blanket, a whiff of coffee swirled through the open door. He paused, realizing Hialeaha must be up. For a moment he imagined just the two of them were awake, that she had slept no better than he. He wondered what it would be like to walk into a kitchen and have a woman waiting with coffee, ready to share the sunrise and the day ahead.

Irritated with himself, Fargo shook off the sentimental foolishness and finished rolling his blanket. He was tying it onto his saddle when the door to the Palace car opened.

"I brought coffee," said Hialeaha.

Fargo felt his pulse jump. Only one other woman had ever had that effect on him. "You're up early."

"I had much to think about. I did not sleep well. The best way to make use of a restless night is to end it."

Fargo started to confess his own sleeplessness but decided there was no point. He said nothing.

Hialeaha went to the same hay bale they had used before. She sat and poured the coffee into two cups. Fargo took one and sat beside her. The air was cool. Steam swirled above the black coffee.

Holding the cup close to his lips, Fargo blew steam from its rim. He wanted to look at Hialeaha in the soft glow of the lantern's flame, to try to read her thoughts. Instead he looked straight ahead.

"Anything in particular ruin your sleep?"

Hialeaha hesitated. She picked up her cup and cradled it in both hands, absorbing its warmth. "Something is wrong, something new. I cannot say what it is. It whispers to me, but I cannot hear."

"Is it a good something or a bad something?" asked Fargo.

Hialeaha took a sip of coffee. "Bad."

Fargo felt a wave of disappointment. She had not slept well, but not for the reason he'd hoped. "Maybe it's just because we're about to get off the railroad and be out on our own. There's a big difference between being on a train and on the trail."

Again Hialeaha paused. "No. That troubles me, but something else keeps me from sleeping. What I feel is…It is the presence of evil."

"Are you sure that evil presence isn't me?"

With her cup halfway to her lips, Hialeaha froze. She turned toward Fargo and shook her head. "You are a dangerous man, Far-go. What makes you such a man, I do not know. But I know you are not the evil I speak of."

Fargo again resisted the impulse to look at Hialeaha. "There's good reason the Apaches call me what they do. If I told you about Tats-a-das-ago, you might think different."

"I have heard those stories," said Hialeaha. For the first time, her tone was gentle, less the voice of a worried nanny and more that of a woman. "And I have heard stories of the Parson, too. An evil man would not earn such a name as the Parson."

"Depends on how you look at it, I suppose."

With her eyes still on Fargo, Hialeaha took a sip of coffee. "How do you look at it?"

Fargo turned toward Hialeaha. His eyes meet hers. "What do you mean?"

"My father," explained Hialeaha, "died fighting the government soldiers who were forcing us off our land. He refused to give everything to the whites. He killed whites defending his land and protecting his family. He was a good warrior, not an evil man."

"That's war. It's different from what I do. I've got no land or family."

"No? My father fought for a small piece of Georgia, his wife and young daughter. You fight for families that have suffered at the hands of murderers. The Tats-a-das-ago, the Parson I have heard of, does not murder. He avenges."

Fargo's brow wrinkled. Was she comparing him to her father?

"My father wasn't a fighter," said Fargo. "Believe it or not, he was a Methodist preacher in Tennessee. I was a boy when your people were marched past our farm, on their way west to their reservation. Papa tried to help them as best he could. I remember how poor they looked, how tired and hungry.

"Were you on that march?"

"No. My father resisted to the end. He instructed my mother to do the same. Before his last battle, he told her to take me and go east to the Great Smokey Mountains. There we joined the Oconaluftee

Cherokee. Four hundred of them lived on private land and were not forced to leave. They are the Eastern Band of the Cherokee.

"I was only five then. If I would have gone on the long march, I might have died as many did."

Taking another drink from his cup, Fargo looked away. "So, then, do you hate white people?"

Hialeaha took a deep breath and let it out slowly. "The land of the Oconaluftee belonged to a white man named Thomas. He had been adopted by the Cherokee when he was a boy, so when he became a man, he provided land for them. I was too young to despise the whites for what they had done to my father and my people. My mother was bitter against the whites, but even she learned to like Mr. Thomas. And as the years passed, she learned to like other whites...and that all were not to be hated."

Her last words stung. Fargo remembered what he had said just days before in the drovers' car, that all Indians were red devils and not to be trusted. He had been thinking of renegades when he said it, but it was still a struggle not to think that way about all of them. It was simpler, and in the West, it was safer.

"Sometimes it takes a while to get over things," admitted Fargo. "Well, to get past them, anyway. Some things you never get over."

Resting her cup in her lap, Hialeaha said, "You have given your word that you will help protect Mahra. I know you will do that. I am here to protect her also. In helping her, will you not be protecting me as well...even though I am Indian?"

Fargo finished his coffee and set the cup down between them. "I've been thinking about that. Been thinking about it since you first asked me to come along."

"About me being an Indian?"

"Yeah," said Fargo, nodding. "About you being an Indian and me not caring about that so much...In fact, about not caring at all sometimes."

Hialeaha seemed to stiffen. Fargo could sense it more than see it. As he repeated the words in his head, he realized they could easily be taken the wrong way. He cleared his throat. "I won't let anything happen to you...you or Miss Brooks."

The door leading to the Palace car opened. Davis stuck his head in. "Good morning," he said cheerily. "We're early risers today, Hialeaha."

"Coming, Mr. Davis," said Hialeaha, rising to her feet. She started for the Palace car, taking a few steps before stopping. She turned and looked back at Fargo. Their eyes met. A moment later, Hialeaha cocked her head to one side. She gave an appreciative nod and then disappeared through the door.

***

Even the dim morning light could not hide the squalor that bore the name Lamy. Board shanties and dirty canvas tents with rough-sawn plank floors haphazardly surrounded a wooden saloon. Across what passed for a street, the only other structure was a low-roofed adobe mercantile.

The corners of the saloon were splintered and chipped, signs it had been disassembled and rebuilt several times. Between the saloon and mercantile, a bloated mule lay dead on a pile of empty cans. Discarded bottles and trash were everywhere.

Men who had not seen a bathhouse in months were filing out of the saloon and some of the tents. Dozens loaded into empty wagons, and others climbed on wagons stacked with railroad ties.

Three men in cheap suits leaned against the outside wall of the saloon, their inquisitive eyes roaming over the train that had just arrived. While they watched, a two-hundred-pound woman wearing undergarments came outside and stood next to them.

Wellington was glaring out the window when the train came to a stop alongside an unloading platform. "Wretched," he mumbled, "simply wretched."

"What, dear?" LaFarge asked. She was already dressed and seated at the dining table. "What do you see?"

Pulling down the window shade, Wellington went to the table. He turned up the flame on a nearby lamp and took a seat. Edward and

112

Mahra were coming out of the sleeping quarters. Hialeaha was bringing hot tea.

"I have heard of these places," said Wellington as Brooks and Davis took their seats and placed linen napkins in their laps. "It is worse than I imagined."

Davis covered his mouth and yawned. "You mean Lamy?"

Hialeaha filled four white porcelain cups with steaming tea.

"Tents, shanties, filth…vile sexual commerce. Why, I just witnessed a scarlet sobriquet walk out of a saloon. She was half dressed, mind you." Wellington shuddered, as if to dislodge the thought from his mind. "One would have to rake the bottom of hell to find worse than Lamy. No wonder they call these end-of-track towns Hell on Wheels."

Both Davis and Brooks blushed at Wellington's graphic description. LaFarge sipped her tea and stole a glance at the far window. She was disappointed to see the shade pulled down.

"We will purchase our horses and depart as soon as possible. This is no place for ladies. Compared to Lamy, Dodge City is Paris on the prairie."

"Is it that horrible, Miles?" asked LaFarge.

"It is so much so that I must insist you and Mahra remain in the Palace car until we are ready to leave."

"Oh, must we, Miles?" asked LaFarge. "I want to see the town."

Wellington looked at LaFarge, her wide eyes pleading, her lower lip protruding ever so slightly.

"Well, many of the men do seem to be leaving town, I presume to work on the rails. And I did see a mercantile as we were arriving. Perhaps, after most of the men have left town, we will escort you there, if you wish. It should be safe enough by then. But we will venture no farther.

"I also saw a corral behind some shanties. We will send Reed and Smitty to purchase the horses. Edward and I will hire some men to unload the coach and wagon from the flat car. The coach weighs one and one half tons. I think half a dozen strong backs should be able to do the job."

LaFarge perked up. "Why not instruct Mr. Fargo help them, Miles? He has not been good for anything as yet."

Without hesitation, Wellington shook his head. "No. The minute we step off the train, he will start earning his pay. I want his guns with us. Those men out there are a despicable race."

Beneath her neatly applied makeup, LaFarge felt her cheeks flush with rising anger. Twice in a matter of seconds, Miles Wellington had denied her what she wanted, something he had never done. And yesterday, she had sent Treadway to humiliate Fargo in front of his friends. Instead, it was Treadway who ended up on the floor of the saloon. Things were getting out of hand.

She could put Wellington in his place easily enough, but Fargo was another matter. It would take more effort, but, in the end, he would prove no different from any other man. They were all fools. All but Reed.

When LaFarge met Reed Treadway, she was little more than a guttersnipe in the slums of New York. He taught her how to use her natural talents, how to distract men so he could club and rob them. At first she received only a small percentage of the take. As she got older and discovered her power over men, Treadway gladly paid her half of everything.

They were in Chicago at the time of the fire. Treadway had been working the wealthy neighborhoods. He posed as a simple-minded gardener while casing the homes for future burglaries. When the fire destroyed those mansions, he knew exactly where go. In days, the two of them had stolen more valuables and money than they had ever dreamed possible. It was enough to allow them to aim higher, much higher. Soon after, Mattie O'Brian entered Yale as Clarissa LaFarge.

It was to be an old game but a tried and true one. Marry rich. When her husband died unexpectedly, marry richer. There would be no end to easy money. Men in shipping were a good bet, but her first choice lost his fortune. Then she met Wellington.

His family was in railroads, but there was always the possibility that financial disaster could strike him as well. With so much at stake, it paid to be cautious. Then the helmet and map appeared. If she and Reed could find the Zuni treasure, there would be no need for pretense. The two of them could live a life of luxury as respectable members of the Eastern aristocracy.

LaFarge calmed herself and smiled. "Of course you are right, Miles. Whatever was I thinking? I am so fortunate to have you looking out for me. What would I do without you?"

LaFarge placed her hand on Wellington's forearm. She gazed at him wistfully. "That you are my protector, Miles Wellington, is but one reason I love you so."

Wellington beamed. "Do not worry, my dear," he said, reaching over and patting her hand. "We will be on our way in less than two hours. That is a promise."

After a breakfast of poached eggs, toast, and fresh peaches, Wellington and Davis quickly finished their tea and stepped out onto the loading platform. The sun was an hour above the eastern hills. Treadway and Smitty were waiting. Fargo had his horses saddled and ready. They were tied just beyond the drovers' car. He was leaning against the hitching rail, watching those on the platform.

"We need eight horses," said Wellington. "Is that correct, Reed? Do you think eight will do?"

"Yes, sir," returned Treadway in his usual simplistic manner.

"I been thinkin' twelve," offered Smitty. "You know, with the sand and all. Might need to hitch the wagons six up instead of four."

"Wasn't thinking of sand," said Treadway.

"Perhaps twelve, then?" offered Davis. "No need to take any chances."

"Twelve it is, then," agreed Wellington. "Smitty, locate the corral and select the best horses you can find and bring them to the train. Tell the proprietor I'll settle with him when they are hitched and ready.

"Reed, find a half dozen men and hire them to help you unload the wagons and supplies."

Watching the two men go, Wellington faced the rising sun. He stretched and inhaled deeply. The sun's rays warmed his face. "Just breathe that air, Edward, simply magnificent. Dry and thin. Almost like a drink of tasty water when one is thirsty. It's desert air. That is what it is, simply wonderful."

Peering into a cloudless sky, Davis sniffed the air. "It *is* dry."

"We are here, Edward! So invigorating. The adventure is just beginning."

"While we wait, Miles, dare to test your mettle?"

Sensing a challenge, Wellington smiled. "What do you have in mind?"

"A drink of whatever is served in that humble establishment," said Davis, pointing at the saloon. "I will if you will."

"The saloon?"

"You are quite generous with your description, Miles. But yes, the saloon."

"Not one drink, but two, I say. And the devil be damned."

Davis pretended to draw a sword. "Then onward, knave. To the victor go the spoils."

Fargo waited until Wellington and Davis entered the saloon. He closed his eyes and rubbed the bridge of his nose with his thumb and fingers. He wondered for a moment if he had ever been so foolish. Knowing full well he had been, he shook his head and looked back at the saloon.

The men who had been standing in front of the saloon were going back inside, no doubt on the heels of Wellington and Davis. They were likely bunco men, card sharks, or worse.

A few minutes later, Treadway returned with a crew of rough-looking men. They began rolling the wagon and coach off the flat car onto the loading platform. The women were wisely staying out of sight.

Depending on the route they took, there might not be another mercantile until they reached the Zuni pueblo. Fargo needed a supply of jerked beef and another box of cartridges. With Treadway nearby, the women would be safe enough.

Crossing to the mercantile, Fargo went inside the adobe building. The shelves were well stocked. A fat man with a bald head greeted him. "What'll you have, sir? You name it, and I've got it. If I don't have it, you don't really need it."

Glancing around, Fargo agreed. "I believe you. Give me a sack of jerked beef that'll fit in a saddle pocket and a box of forty-fours."

The storekeeper snapped his fingers. "Got just what you need." He turned and started climbing a ladder that leaned against a wall. "You come in on the train?" he asked, reaching for a box of Colt's forty-fours.

"Yeah. Be leaving soon, though."

The storekeeper stepped down and handed Fargo the box of shells. He started for the back of the store. He spoke as he walked. "Going up to Santa Fe? If you are, it's about twenty miles to Pecos, then another twenty to Santa Fe. Good road, but steep, and it winds every which way. The railroad was going to go there, but it's too much work to lay track now. Later, maybe. A spur line, they say, but not now. Have to wait."

Fargo didn't answer, but the storekeeper didn't seem to mind. He grabbed a white cloth sack and went to a large glass jar. He took off the lid and paused. "Good town, Santa Fe. Or will be someday, now the railroad is here. Then there's Albuquerque. Nice little pueblo, too. All these little towns and villages really are about the same. Adobe houses, a plaza, a church...all adobe. All the same out here. Without the railroad bringing in lumber, there's not enough wood, I suppose."

Through the window of the mercantile, Fargo saw a man hurry into the saloon. Another was trotting toward the front door.

"Now if you're thinking of going anywhere west of Albuquerque, I'd think twice. I trapped beaver up north until thirty-six. Never seen it this dry. I hear most of the water holes are dried up."

Fargo saw no more activity in front of the saloon but kept looking out the window. Stuffing the sack with jerky, the storekeeper continued. "I been told Antelope Spring has water. That's two days south of here. From there, it's forty miles to the Rio Grande, good road all the way to Peralta. You can cross the river there, but there's not much water after that, all the way to Zuni."

Walking back to Fargo, the storekeeper noticed him looking across the street. "Two dollars, friend. Something brewing at the saloon? Nothing good, I'm thinking."

Keeping his eyes on the saloon, Fargo handed the man two silver dollars. "I got a feeling you're right."

"Can I interest you in anything else?"

Davis came halfway through the batwing doors. Glancing back into the saloon, he took a few quick steps into the street. He stopped. After looking in every direction, he ran toward the loading platform.

"Got any lineament?" asked Fargo. "For bruises and such."

"Sure do."

The storekeeper went back to his ladder, moved it a few feet, and climbed up. "Just bunco steerers over there, card sharks mostly. Sawdust Charlie, Sheeney Frank, and Winter Monkey Jack."

"Monkey Jack's over there?" asked Fargo, momentarily taking his eyes off the saloon.

"Yeah," answered the store keeper. He handed the bottle to Fargo. "He's big as a barn door but not a bad man, really. Just don't play poker with him.

"That's two bits."

Reaching in his vest pocket for a quarter, Fargo again checked the saloon. A man wearing a black suit stumbled backward through the batwing doors. He lost his balance and landed in a cloud of dust. Instantly, he was back on his feet but wobbling. He put both fists up, poised in a classic boxing stance.

The batwings again swung open, revealing a bearded, barrel-chested man weighing well over two hundred pounds. He pointed at the boxer and then back in the saloon. A heavyset woman appeared. She wore a corset and bloomers. Several men followed quickly, forming a circle around the two men.

"That's Winter Monkey Jack," said the storekeeper. He's a brawler."

Fargo nodded. "And the other one is named Wellington."

This time the storekeeper nodded. "He the one that gets the liniment?"

Walking out the door of the mercantile, Fargo muttered, "He's the one."

Fargo paused to take in the situation. He had crossed paths with Monkey Jack a few times. The card shark was big and the hairiest man he'd ever seen. He would routinely fight a man one minute and buy him a drink the next.

The men from the saloon were yelling. The woman was spewing profanities. Somehow, Wellington had made some enemies.

Monkey Jack closed the distance between himself and Wellington. Wellington attempted some textbook jabs that got past Monkey Jack's clumsy arms but did no harm.

A hairy, knuckled fist collapsed the boxer's guard and landed squarely on Wellington's temple. He spun and went down to one knee.

"Now apologize to Darla," said Jack. "Go on, now. Tell her you're a sorry, no-good son of a bitch."

Switching the bottle and sack of jerky to his left hand, Fargo started toward the saloon. He had taken only a few steps when he saw Davis and Treadway running in the same direction. Fargo stopped where he was.

Treadway shoved his way through the crowd and helped Wellington to his feet. The hulking blond was brushing the dust from Wellington's lapels when his eyes met Fargo's. Wellington and Treadway spoke to each other, but Fargo was too far away to hear what they said. Treadway then turned slowly to face Winter Monkey Jack and started for him.

Jack grinned. "Well now. Just as soon fight a real man as a snivelin' coward."

Treadway swung a roundhouse left for Jack's jaw, but it was deflected. The right that followed landed on Jack's ear. Jack swung an upper cut into Treadway's gut. He grunted with the impact but swung another left that missed. Jack was big, and he was fast.

Both men started swinging, each arm like a sledgehammer. Some of Treadway's blows landed and bloodied Jacks lips, but there was little damage otherwise. Treadway was getting the worst of it and knew it. He suddenly dove for Jack's midsection, lifting him off the ground and slamming him down on his back. Jack tried to roll, but Treadway was too quick and slid around behind him. Treadway hooked his right arm under Jack's throat and locked it on the bicep of his left. The left hand went to the back of Jack's head, driving his throat into Treadway's right forearm. It was a hold Fargo had never seen, one that could kill even a big man like Monkey Jack.

When Fargo got to the circle, Jack's face was already blue. His eyes were rolled to the top of his head as he vainly clawed at the arms strangling him. Watching in horror, the spectators were shocked onto silence.

"You made your point," said Fargo, calculating how much time Jack had left.

"He's killin' him," screamed the woman.

Treadway's face was red, his neck veins bulging with determination.

"You've won, Treadway." Fargo's voice was icy now. "Let him go."

Fargo waited for a similar order from Wellington or Davis. No command was given. An instant later Fargo's Colt .44 thundered flame and smoke. A lead slug hissed within an inch of Treadway's ear. He jerked backward, freeing Jack.

Treadway came to his knees and then stood. Focusing his attention on Monkey Jack, he avoided eye contact with Fargo.

Jack lay in the dirt. Coughing and rubbing his throat, he stared at the man who had saved his life. "Con? That you?"

"You had enough?"

Jack rolled onto his hands and knees then gained his feet. Still rubbing his throat, he turned to face Treadway. "That's some choke hold you got there. Was you tryin' to kill me?"

"He appears to be simpleminded," interrupted Fargo. He knew Treadway's portrayal of the fool was a ruse, but the railroad men stuck together. If word spread that someone tried to kill one of their own, there might be trouble. And it was best that Treadway believe his secret was still intact. "He doesn't know any better."

Treadway responded in character. "Sorry, mister," he drawled. "Didn't mean to hurt you."

Jack grunted. He pointed to Wellington, who seemed to be gaining his senses. "What about you, mister?"

Wellington stood erect. His starched collar was ripped halfway off, and his nose and mouth were dripping blood. "I meant no disrespect."

"Darla?" questioned Jack. "That even it up?"

"Damn right, it does!" jeered the whore. "But count yourself lucky Jack got to you before I did."

The crowd broke into laughter. Jack bellowed, "Drinks are on me!"

As the locals filed into the saloon, Jack shook Fargo's hand. "I owe ya, Con. He had me good."

Fargo glanced to his left. Treadway was leaving with Davis and Wellington. The big blond was powerful. He knew at least one death hold, but when he swung his fists, they went wide. It was valuable information. "Forget it."

"You workin' for them greenhorns?"

"For a week or two."

"You comin' in to splash some liquor with me?"

"I'd better get back to the train," said Fargo. He paused. The storekeeper was relying on hearsay about the water holes. It was always best to have as much information about the country as possible, and Winter Monkey Jack would most likely have firsthand knowledge. "How's the water out on the trails?"

"Dry. Dry as a powder house. Water holes is few and far between once ya leave the rivers. The Rio Grande has plenty of water, but some of the others are mighty low if there's any water in 'em at all."

"Any Indian trouble?"

"No more'n usual. A killin' here and there, but no raids lately."

"Bandits? Road agents?"

"Now that's a horse of a different color. Lots a thievin' on the road to Santa Fe. They had some holdups goin' down to Bernalillo and Albuquerque, too."

"What's the best way west?"

"I hear not many are heading south first. But it's the safest trail, and there's water to be had at Antelope Springs. Go down to the springs, then you cut through the pass to the Rio Grande. Takes an extra day to get to Albuquerque, but you'll likely get there in one piece."

"Poco still at the springs?"

Jack scratched his head. "Last I heard, he was."

Fargo nodded. Smitty and another man were leading eight horses up the street. "Take you up on that drink next time I see you."

"I'll be with the tracks," said Jack, and then he went back inside the saloon.

Seeing the gaunt stock, Fargo raised an eyebrow at Smitty.

Smitty shrugged. "These is all they had. The good stock all belongs to the railroad."

Walking along side Smitty, Fargo frowned. "We won't make good time with these. I here it's a dry year. Besides water, there won't be much feed along the way."

Smitty pointed over his shoulder with his thumb toward the man leading the second string of horses. "That's what the livery man said, too. Them rich folks best buy some grain to haul with us."

"Good idea. And make sure they have a water barrel, maybe two. You tell Wellington what he needs. They don't want to take much advice from me."

"That 'cause you coldcocked their hired hand back there in Dodge?"

"Something like that."

Smitty studied Fargo from the corner of his eye. The gunman was older than anyone on the train. He was lean, yet thick through the shoulders. He spoke very little, but his words reflected Southern upbringing and an education. It was not much to go on. It was time to stir the pot. "That big fella's been making threats against you, Mr. Fargo. I don't think he makes 'em to nobody but me, but he makes 'em just the same. I'd sure keep an eye out for 'im."

Fargo did not respond to his fabrication, but Smitty was confident he had planted a seed that would grow. The question was, who would prove to be more dangerous to his plans, Treadway or Fargo? And which would be easiest to get rid of when the time came?

Unfortunately, neither seemed the type to change his allegiance and join him in taking what was theirs by right. Like so many others, the two men were mere pawns of the rich, to be used for a short while then discarded. Even the most obvious injustices were beyond their limited grasp.

They were blind to the fact that the wealthy rode roughshod over the backs of countless underpaid workers. Without one drop of sweat, the rich acquired power and lived in undeserved luxury. Clannish and ruthless, they took whatever they wanted whenever they wanted it. They pilfered practically everything they had from the poor. It was only right he even the score and steal some of it back.

Smitty thought of Davis. He would be nothing without Wellington. But what would Wellington be without Davis? For that matter, what would LaFarge be without Treadway? Mahra Brooks and the Indian would merely be necessary casualties. Fargo, however, was the unknown, the loose end. Who was he? How good was he?

"Comin' out of the corral I heard a shot," said Smitty. "Any trouble? Seen a crowd file into the saloon. Somethin' happen in the street?"

"Wellington got into a ruckus. Then Treadway got into it. Wellington got a little taste of his own blood, but nobody got hurt."

Smitty swore. His face reddened, and he swore more bitterly.

Fargo glanced curiously at Smitty. "What's got into you?"

"I missed it!" snarled Smitty. "Damn it all! I missed it!"

"It wasn't much of a fight."

Smitty cooled quickly. "Well," he stammered, "I mean you don't see a rich man get bloodied every day."

"I didn't see that part myself. I saw him take one punch, but he was already bleeding before it landed. After that, it was Treadway who was fighting with Winter Monkey Jack. He did good. Would have killed Jack, maybe. Had him in a choke hold, one I've never seen before."

Smitty grunted and leered at Fargo. "So, maybe he ain't as stupid as he comes across?"

Fargo shrugged. "I don't know about stupid, but he learned to fight somewhere. And he's quick on his feet."

Nearing the train, Smitty began to smile. "You say that Wellington had a bloody mouth?"

"Broke his front tooth," replied Fargo. "He'll have trouble eating for a while."

Smitty let out a whoop then laughed to himself. With his free hand, he swung a few short jabs at an imaginary opponent. "Lord a'mighty, I'd loved to have seen that boxin' match! He didn't win that one, did he?"

Shaking his head, Fargo said, "Him being a college boy, it's likely he was a boxer. But Wellington was in a brawl. There's a big difference."

"Better hope that tooth he broke don't get ulcerated," offered Smitty. He spread his lips with a grimy finger showing several missing teeth. "Had my share of 'em. You get a carbuncle, and then it feels like your head's gonna blow off."

Releasing his lip, Smitty continued, but his voice began to trail off. "Had more'n my share, more'n my share of ulcerated teeth."

Fargo raised his eyes. It was his turn to swear.

The canvas tarp no longer covered Wellington's coach. It had been unloaded from the train and sat waiting in the morning sun. Its brilliant red color would be visible for fifty miles. The intricate gold scrollwork and pinstriping would proclaim to everyone the passengers inside were well-to-do. And with no rack or additional seats on top, it would be clear that this coach was private and not part of any stage line.

Hiding a smile, Smitty said, "Fancy rig, ain't it? Bet they got feathers for them horses, too—you know, them plumes and such."

"I was expecting they'd have better sense. Basic brown and canvas, maybe."

"Trail dust'll tone it down some," offered Smitty, his voice now reflecting concern. "Gonna get hot inside, too. Canvas top would'a been better."

Several men rolled up the Studebaker wagon. It, at least, was simple wood construction without gaudy paint to draw attention. It was already loaded with supplies. A water barrel was strapped on its side.

"Don't forget to tell them about that second water barrel," said Fargo, veering away from Smitty and heading for his horses, "and the grain."

Unbuckling his saddlebags, Fargo thoughtfully packed his jerky and extra cartridges. Water was going to be scarce, the coach would attract unwanted attention, and even with lots of grain, the horses weren't strong enough to make good time. They would bottom out in minutes if they had to break into a run.

It would be best to head south to Antelope Springs, then west to the Rio Grande. There was less chance of trouble and enough water. If

Poco was still at the springs, he would know if there were bandits over the pass or Apaches in the region.

Fargo untied his mounts and led them to a watering trough on the shady side of the train depot. Smitty and Treadway began hitching the wagons, four up. There was no sign of anyone from the Palace car until Hialeaha stepped down onto the platform. She immediately started for Fargo.

The horses buried their muzzles in the water, sucking it up. Fargo rubbed the black's neck, watching Hialeaha approach. She walked like a white woman, not bent by years of heavy labor living in an Indian village.

Descending the platform steps, Hialeaha walked into the shade. She stopped two steps from Fargo. Her eyes were hard and questioning, but she said nothing.

Fargo liked what he saw. Knowing what was on her mind, he suppressed a smile.

"He would have killed a man named Jack," offered Fargo. "Jack is…well, I know Jack. And I know railroad people. If Treadway killed Jack, they would have hung him and then come after us."

The lines of anger slowly faded from Hialeaha's face, leaving only concern. "Then why not tell them your reason for shooting at Treadway? They are talking of replacing you, hiring someone else as guide."

Fargo's mood darkened. "They could do that. But I'm still going along, even if they do."

Hialeaha's head drew back slightly. "What? You would come anyway?"

"I gave you my word," replied Fargo. He hesitated and then added, "That's enough by itself…but there is more to it."

"What if they will not allow you to come with us?"

Fargo's eyes hardened. They seemed to smolder with instant rage. Hialeaha watched the transformation in awe. This was the one she had heard of. This was Tats-a-das-ago. She felt a chill race across her skin. She sensed the power, the much-talked-about medicine of the white man Far-go.

"That won't happen," muttered Fargo.

Fargo was facing Hialeaha when he spoke, yet he seemed to look right through her. It was the same expression she had seen in her father's eyes the day he left for his final battle and never returned.

"I will tell them why you fired the shot. I believe they will understand."

The morning air was cool. Fargo took a few deep breaths. He slowly uncoiled. Hialeaha was about to turn and go when she saw something in Fargo that made her pause.

He spoke softly. "You are part of it."

"Part of what?"

Fargo seemed to be coming out of a fog. He blinked his eyes several times. "Part of the reason I would still go. You're part of it."

"Because you gave me your word?"

"No."

There was a long silence. The bay blew, clearing water from its nose. The voices of the men loading the wagons were garbled in the distance. Fargo had averted his eyes, now looking at nothing in particular. Hialeaha was staring at him, questioning what he meant.

"Have I done something wrong?" she asked.

Fargo forced himself to make eye contact. He gathered the reins of his horses. "You're a good woman, Hialeaha," he said, walking away from her. "I'll just leave it at that."

Watching Fargo, Hialeaha's eyes narrowed with confusion. A moment later, they opened wide.

Chapter 7

The momentary paralysis that follows shock was passing. Now, like a slow-burning grass fire, Hialeaha felt an intoxicating blend of excitement and sedation engulfing her. She had all but forgotten the pleasure a man could bring to a woman. But the man who had just expressed an interest in her was no ordinary man.

When she first heard Mr. Pinkerton mention Fargo's name, she was thinking of nothing but the dangerous trip Mahra was planning. As Pinkerton described Fargo's background and qualifications, she had paid little attention.

When she caught sight of Conway Fargo, however, it struck her how much he resembled an Indian. His skin was dark, his eyes brown and penetrating. Though he wore a suit, there was no hiding the power in his shoulders and narrow waist. When he crossed the room, his movements were those of a hunter. Smooth and catlike. His very presence commanded respect and fear. Some warriors possessed it. The Indians called it "medicine."

It was then that she began to repeat his name to herself. Fargo. It had a familiar ring. The instant their eyes met, she knew this was Far-go…the Parson…Tats-a-das-ago. The one the Delawares spoke so much of was standing in front of her!

She had heard stories, but like all Indian lore, fact was sprinkled liberally with fiction. Looking at him, being in the same room with him, however, was enough for her to know at least one part of the stories was true. She could sense that he was lethal.

Hialeaha's father had fought such men. Even though they were his bitter enemies, he respected them for their bravery and honor in battle. It was the way of all Indians. Whether it was the same with all whites she did not know.

The stories she had heard told of a man who bore scars inside and out, scars that drove him to kill all red men. Those same scars drove him to fiercely protect women and to avenge the wrongs done to them. It was this that she had counted on when she approached him for his help.

Certainly, it was out of concern for Mahra that he had taken the job. But now, what had he said? He had admitted that she, an Indian woman, had become part of something. Was she part of his determination to go on?

Hialeaha felt herself smiling. It did not seem real. How could it be that Far-go spoke such words to her, a moccasin-wearing Cherokee from Chicago? She needed to know more, to be sure.

Looking about for Fargo, she saw him leading his horses to the supply wagon. She started in his direction but caught sight of Wellington and Davis walking rapidly toward him. Wellington's upper lip was swollen. Davis's jaws were clinched tight. Hialeaha could see what was coming. She hurried toward them to explain, to defend Fargo.

Three steps from Fargo, Davis pointed a finger. "A word with you!"

The two men stopped less than an arm's length in front of Fargo.

"You barely missed poor Treadway," bellowed Davis. "And he was only doing his job—unlike you, sir."

"As I see it," added Wellington, the words slurring past his swollen lips and broken tooth, "he was doing what you were hired to do. What you failed to do!"

"Can you give us one reason not to terminate your employment?" demanded Davis.

Fargo impassively looked from Davis to Wellington. "I can give you one, maybe two."

Wellington sneered, "By all means, do tell."

"He was only trying to help," said Hialeaha, coming to a halt beside but slightly behind Fargo.

Glaring at Hialeaha, Wellington snipped, "If I want the opinion of a nanny, I will summon you."

Separado

Fargo's eyes flashed at the insult. Now he spoke bluntly. "That was Winter Monkey Jack you were fighting. You let Treadway finish your fight. He had Jack in a choke hold. A few more seconds and Jack would have been dead. He's a well-liked man along the tracks. There are no lawmen here. These men act as judge, jury, and executioner when they think their version of the law has been broken. And they don't waste time doing it.

"If Treadway had killed Jack, that mob would have strung him up. And you two would likely have been next. Even if the law did finally show up, there'd be no witnesses to say what happened. You'd be dead, and it would be over and done with."

"That is preposterous," returned Davis.

Wellington was suddenly quiet. Fargo's words were sinking in.

Fargo continued. "This isn't Chicago. Who you were back there means nothing here in Lamy. And the farther west we go, the less it will mean. If you don't like what I'm telling you or the way I get things done, my advice to you is to turn around and go back home."

"Smitty said he could find the way without you," spouted Davis, but now with less fervor. "There is a road we can take that goes to a place called Bernalillo. From there, he said it was about fifteen or twenty miles to Albuquerque."

Smitty? Fargo recalled him saying he had never been to the Southwest. How would he know about the roads? He had just purchased the horses and could have talked to the livery man. But did he ask about water, bandits, or renegades?

Smitty was a brakeman yet claimed he was also a teamster. If he drove wagons for any length of time on the frontier, he would know roads were often in poor condition and hard to follow. Sometimes they stretched for miles over packed ground or gravel. They could easily disappear in windstorms or wash away in floods. Getting from one place to another took more skill and knowledge than following a well-worn wagon road.

"What else did Smitty say?"

Davis was still defiant. "He said we could hire gunmen to protect us in Albuquerque, and if not there, in Santa Fe."

"For someone who's never been in this country, he seems to be full of ideas. Ideas like his can get you all killed."

Breaking his silence, Wellington said, "Perhaps, Edward, we have been too hasty. This all appears to have been a simple misunderstanding."

Davis glanced questioningly at Wellington. Several seconds passed. When Wellington spoke again, his tone was curiously subdued.

"We shall continue to trust Mr. Pinkerton's recommendation. How should we proceed from here, Mr. Fargo?"

Davis dropped his eyes. The steam was gone. His chest deflated.

Fargo studied Wellington. What he saw in the rich man's eyes was anything but trust. It was unlike him to change his tone so quickly.

Fargo pointed to the west. "There's little or no water from here to Bernalillo, and there've been several robberies on the road that leads there. With that coach, every bandit within twenty miles will know you've got money. We need to skirt trouble the best we can. First we'll go south to Antelope Springs. There's water there and a man I can count on. He'll keep his mouth shut about us coming through. Then we head west to the Rio Grande. We avoid Albuquerque. It's full of bandits. It's only a small village anyway, a few adobes and a church."

"Will we lose time going that route?" asked Wellington.

"No. It's about the same distance even though we go south first. This route has more water and fewer people."

"Good," said Wellington. "As soon as we are ready, we will be on our way."

With that, Wellington and Davis walked past the wagons and then disappeared into the Palace car. Fargo turned to Hialeaha.

"Did you know Smitty offered to take over as guide?"

"Yes. I overheard them talking about it when Smitty came to ask about buying another water barrel."

"Did he volunteer to guide them, or did they ask him to do it?"

"I do not know. I did not hear that part. I only heard him boasting about his experience as a teamster. He said he handled the reins of teams all over the west."

Fargo looked at Hialeaha. "Are you sure that's what he said? 'Handled the reins'?"

Hialeaha thought for a moment. She shrugged. "Yes. He said 'handled the reins.' Why?"

"Just curious," answered Fargo. For now, there was no reason to divulge his growing suspicions concerning Smitty. It was a small thing, but teamsters and stage drives did not refer to the long leather straps as reins, as Smitty had. They called them lines.

"Smitty did tell them he had not been in this country before. But he seemed sure he could find his way to Albuquerque without your help. I did not like what he said. I was…was afraid they would agree to leave you behind."

"How sure was he that he could find his way?"

"Too sure, I thought. Almost eager."

Fargo considered how Smitty had unexpectedly showed up at the train station to replace the regular brakeman. He had also mixed up his facts about the plains Indians and the Apaches. And he had called lines reins. Mistakes, to be sure, but easy to explain if any of them were questioned.

Fargo also recalled how Smitty had warned him to watch out for Treadway. Just what had Smitty said? That Treadway was making threats, and that the threats were only made in front of Smitty. No one else heard them, just Smitty.

"Do they talk to you like that very much?"

"What do you mean?"

"Like how Wellington insulted you, referring to you as just a nanny, that sort of thing."

Hialeaha paused. She gazed at the train car. "No. This was the first time. Usually they are very polite to me. I think it is out of respect for Mahra, but still, they are polite. I believe Mr. Wellington was just angry. I doubt he has ever been beaten at anything."

"I didn't like it."

Shifting her brown eyes to Fargo, Hialeaha studied him intently. "Thank you. I hope we have some time to talk, time alone."

Through the years, Fargo had met a few women who caught his eye. Before it went very far, he was usually called away. Sometimes he chose to ride away.

He told himself it was best to keep his life simple. But he knew it was partly out of guilt. Now there was no escape. With Hialeaha, he couldn't just ride away. There was too much at stake.

"Sometimes it's better not to talk. Sometimes a person learns more than they want to know. This would be one of those times."

"Perhaps yes, perhaps no," said Hialeaha. "Does it not depend on what we talk about?"

"I suppose. But I've been down this trail before. Believe me. It doesn't work out."

Hialeaha sighed. "You are not the only one with scars. I have many of my own. Sometimes we have to bury our past. Then we have to place rocks on the grave. Then more rocks, and more. What lies there must stay buried, or the ghosts will rise and take our lives while we still live.

"I do not want to know about your ghosts, Far-go. You can tell me of them if you wish, but I will not ask. I would expect the same of you."

Fargo felt uneasy with Hialeaha so close. He allowed himself a long look at her. "Then we'll find time to talk."

"Good," agreed Hialeaha. She attempted a smile. "We will do that."

Glancing at the supply wagon, Fargo saw it was nearly loaded. A second water barrel was being hoisted into the back. Treadway was attaching red feathers to the headstalls of the two lead horses on the coach. Plumes—just what Smitty had predicted.

"One more thing," said Fargo. "Keep an eye on Smitty for me. Don't tell him anything you don't have to about where we're going. And don't tell him anything about me, or yourself…nothing. In fact, the less we're seen together, the better."

"You do not trust him?"

"I usually don't trust anybody. It's a habit. No offense."

"I am not offended. I will watch and listen for you."

"Do you still have that feeling you were having, the bad one?"

Hialeaha nodded. "It is the same. Maybe a little worse today."

"I'm starting to get it too."

As Hialeaha started for the coach, the door to the Palace car opened. Davis stepped out. He wore a white cotton shirt, brown riding pants, and black knee-high boots. On his head was a tan pith helmet. Around his waist was a new cartridge belt and pistol. He extended his hand to Brooks and helped her onto the platform. She was dressed in a trim gray traveling suit. For shade, she wore a wide-brimmed straw hat with a veil that covered her entire head and neck.

Next came Wellington, dressed and armed the same as Davis. From the back of his helmet, however, a white cloth hung to the top of his shoulders. He took out a pair of green-tinted glasses and covered his eyes. Turning from the glare, he offered his hand to LaFarge.

She wore white lace gloves. Her hat and traveling suit were pale blue. She squinted for a moment looking to her left and right. The platform was empty. There was no crowd, no welcoming committee, and no band.

Fargo hitched his bay to the back of the supply wagon and then swung onto the black. He eased the gelding forward. A knot in his gut told him something was wrong, out of place.

Smitty was climbing up and onto the wagon seat. Fargo paused next to him, looking back at the second water barrel. It was tied securely. Smitty knew his knots.

"You get that extra grain?" asked Fargo.

"Hunderd fifty pounds. Figured we could stock up again at Rancho Bernalillo or Albuquerque."

"Could be," said Fargo. Albuquerque was a known destination, but the small rancho was something only locals would know of. "Think the rancho will have grain?"

Smitty adjusted his hat, a narrow-brimmed derby. "The livery man said they growed it along the *rio*. Good land for crops, I s'pose. Must be a sight better ground than this here place."

It made sense that Smitty would have asked at the livery where to get grain for the stock. But he referred to the Rio Grande as the *rio*. Did he intend to shorten the name of the river, or did he know that *rio* meant river in Spanish? Mixing Spanish and English in the same sentence was common practice in the Southwest. But Smitty claimed he had never been in New Mexico Territory or anywhere near the Mexican border.

Finished with the plumes, Treadway went up the ramp of the stock car and returned leading the two polo ponies rigged with what looked like McClellan saddles. Wellington mounted his horse smoothly, but Davis was awkward, bumping his knee on the cantle as he swung his leg over.

Both horses pranced nervously, straining at the bit. Fargo rode to the front of the coach. Treadway helped the three women inside and then climbed up and took the lines.

The road out of Lamy to Antelope Springs headed southwest. Fargo hesitated, taking one last look at the tent city, the iron rails, and the Palace car. From here on, they were on their own.

Hialeaha had her own reasons for worrying. She said it felt as if something evil lay ahead. His reasons for concern were more concrete. The renegades in the vicinity were quiet, but never for long, and there was no shortage of bandits and cutthroats. Water and feed would be scarce. If they were lucky, there would be few accidents. But there would be some.

Smitty was an unknown, but sooner or later, Treadway would have to be dealt with. Wellington and Davis could prove competent. Brooks would be harmless but helpless, in need of constant care. LaFarge, on the other hand, was capable of anything. She was the one to watch. Whether the others knew it or not, she was in charge. If Hialeaha was sensing evil, it had to be the presence of Clarissa LaFarge.

Squinting, Fargo checked the sun. It was not yet noon, but he guessed it to be over eighty degrees. It would get close to one hundred. He nudged his horse. They would have a good eight hours of daylight before making dry camp. Before dark, they would be halfway to Antelope Springs.

Leather lines snapped. Smitty bellowed a "git up." Treadway clucked twice. Hooves churned, then thudded on the hard-packed dirt in front of the depot. Mahra began to giggle excitedly. Davis responded with a timid whoop and holler. LaFarge laughed and held her gloved hand out the window for Wellington. He rode next to her. Leaning in his saddle, he took her hand and kissed it.

Wellington winked at LaFarge and released her hand. "Soon, my dear," he promised. "Very soon."

***

For the first hour, Fargo stayed on the primitive road that led southwest through a low range of juniper-dotted hills. Fifty yards behind him, Wellington and Davis rode side by side. Behind them came the coach, followed by the supply wagon.

Just ahead, a cluster of squat, flat-roofed adobes marked a junction in the road. One trailed to the north, the other to the south. Passing by a dozen curious Mexicans, Fargo took the southern fork. A half mile beyond the adobes, he played a hunch.

Fargo rode back to Wellington and explained that he needed to speak to Smitty and then rode to the supply wagon and wheeled his horse.

"Just so you know," said Fargo, keeping pace with the wagon. "That pueblo we passed back there was Galisteo."

Smitty seemed unmoved. He thumbed back over his shoulder. "Shouldn't we oughta have took that north fork and headed up to Santa Fe?"

In the deserts of New Mexico Territory, roads seldom could be built on a direct route. One often had to go south in order to navigate around a mountain or canyon before going north again. There was a fork to the north out of Galisteo, but how could someone new to the Territory know it led to Santa Fe? In a few miles, it could have turned and gone east.

Smitty had told Wellington he could find his way to the Rio Grande by heading first to Santa Fe and then to Bernalillo. If he had asked at the livery how to get to Albuquerque, he would likely have been told to go that way. But Bernalillo was nowhere near Galisteo, and the liveryman would have had no reason to mention the village or the roads near it.

"More water this way and safer," said Fargo. "We're going by way of Antelope Springs, then west."

Shrugging indifferently, Smitty grinned. "Makes me no nevermind. You're the pilot. I get paid no matter which way we go."

Fargo could read men. Either Smitty did not care which route they took, or he was an exceptional liar. Just how was it he knew the country? Something did not add up.

Still wearing her hat and veil, Mahra stuck her head out of the coach. "Mr. Fargo," she called. Inhaling a bit of dust, she coughed. "Oh, Mr. Fargo."

Cantering to the coach, Fargo slowed. "What is it, Miss Brooks?"

"When do we get to a town? Or some trees? This is too big."

"What's too big?"

Brooks raised the veil over the brim of her hat. She pointed out the window. "That. There is nothing out there. We are in nothing. Not even trees. It is all too big."

Following her finger, Fargo looked at the bleak horizon and then peered into the coach. Hialeaha sat next to Brooks. LaFarge sat across and facing them, fanning herself and wearing a faint smile.

"There won't be any towns, Miss Brooks, just villages and pueblos. We'll see some bigger trees in a couple of days."

Brooks slumped back in the leather seat, leaving her veil up. Taking off her gloves, she reached into her handbag and brought out a small bottle. Leaning forward and searching down by her feet, she grumbled, "Where is that cup?"

"When can we bathe, Mr. Fargo?" asked LaFarge. "It is dreadfully hot."

"Tomorrow night, if Antelope Springs has enough water to spare. If not, the next chance will be in the Rio Grande. That's two more days."

"Two days from the springs?" protested LaFarge.

"Could be."

"That is barbaric," whimpered Brooks.

Fargo shrugged. "It's a dry year."

"Then will the Rio Grande be easy to cross?" asked LaFarge.

"Maybe, maybe not. That water comes from a long way off. Never can tell."

LaFarge stopped fanning. She seemed agitated. "But none of us can swim. What if we capsize? Can you swim, Mr. Fargo? Not even poor Treadway can swim."

"We won't capsize," said Fargo. "But yes, I can swim."

"Well enough to rescue one of us if we go into the current?"

"I grew up on the Mississippi. And my grandfather was a Portuguese sea captain. He made sure I could swim."

"A sea captain?" repeated LaFarge, laughing. She began to fan herself again. Under her breath, but just loud enough, she uttered, "And your grandmother was queen of England."

Fargo felt the sting of her insult. She was as good as any bunco artist. He had fallen into her trap, and she sprung it. He would be smarter next time.

Unable to find her cup, Mahra took a drink of Mother Bailey's directly from the bottle.

"Mahra!" gasped Hialeaha.

"Well, I have a headache, and I *cannot* find that silly cup. And what difference does it make out here?"

"Better take it easy on that, Miss Brooks," cautioned Fargo. "This heat and altitude can play tricks on you."

"Altitude?" questioned LaFarge. "This looks like desert to me."

"We're over a mile high right now."

"And I suppose," quipped LaFarge, "you do not take a drink of something from time to time?"

"Not under these conditions. I'd recommend none of the men drink under these conditions."

"Oh," returned LaFarge. "And just what conditions are you referring to?"

Fargo looked into the cunning eyes of Clarissa LaFarge. It was his turn. "Whiskey can make a fool of a man. The wrong kind of woman can make him a full-fledged idiot. The two combined would be Armageddon. And I assume the men brought whiskey."

Before LaFarge could respond, Fargo spurred his horse. He waved as he galloped past Wellington and Davis. He rode a half mile before reining in the black. It felt good to put some distance between him and the others. He had grown accustomed to keeping his distance from people. More than that, he preferred it.

***

An hour before sundown, Fargo waved to those behind him. He veered off the road, angling for a patch of sand surrounded by a half acre of sagebrush and a few tufts of dry grass. Bordered on three sides by low hills, it would be a fairly safe place for a small fire, and the ground was level enough to pitch a tent.

Fargo waited as Wellington and Davis dismounted.

"It would be best," said Fargo, "if you cook now and have no fires after dark. But if you're going to have one, pull the wagons in to block the sight of it as much as possible."

Wellington cocked his head. "Are you going somewhere?"

"To scout around. I'll be back near dark and bed down just outside of camp."

"Your supper will be cold if we have no fire," said Davis. "And we have not seen a soul all afternoon. We can see for miles out here. I hardly believe there is reason to worry about intruders, Mr. Fargo."

"It's my nature to worry, Mr. Davis."

The coach pulled into the sandy clearing followed by the supply wagon.

"And you're right. You can see a long way in this country. At night a big campfire can be seen for fifty miles."

Wellington smirked. "We will keep that in mind. Anything else we should know?"

"You said you had two rifles. They should be on your horses from now on."

"A rifle is so dreadfully uncomfortable to straddle on a long, hot ride," protested Davis. "And I see you do not carry one."

"Sold mine when I left for Chicago. Didn't see the need for it."

"Then, Mr. Fargo," said Davis, "if you feel they are so necessary, I insist you use mine."

"Fair enough. I'll pick it up in the morning."

Fargo rode to the supply wagon. Smitty was stepping off the box and stretching his back. "Made good time today. I figure twenty mile 'r more."

"I'm checking our back trail. I need you to grain and water my bay, but leave him hitched. When I get back, I'll need water and grain for this one, so leave it out where I can find it in the dark.

"Another thing. Davis said I could use his Winchester rifle. I'd appreciate it if you'd have it here, too, with the scabbard and a box of shells."

Pointing at the front wheel of his wagon, Smitty nodded. "I'll be sleepin' under the wagon, but I'll put the rifle right yonder, along with a bucket of water and nose bag. And there's a cup on the water barrel for you.

"How do you think them greenhorns is gonna hold up? Mighty hot today. By and by, them women'll wilt sure 'nuff."

Fargo shook his head. "Only Miss Brooks. She's the weak one."

Smitty grinned. "Weak and sickly, I'd say. She finished off a bottle of her medicine today. She dropped it out of the coach window, secret like. But I seen it when I rode past. Musta had one of her headaches."

"Maybe," said Fargo, changing the subject. "You've lived in Indian country. Try to get them to keep their fires small and hidden."

"Why me?"

"I've already warned them. I won't be in camp tonight."

"You ain't staying out all night long?"

"I'll be close enough."

"Oh," replied Smitty, his voice almost a whisper. "I get it. Like a lookout or sentry."

Reining his horse around, Fargo galloped back to the road. Watching Fargo head north, Smitty scratched his chin, speaking softly to himself.

"You're a cautious man Mr. Fargo. Could be you're a might suspicious, too. Hard to sneak up on a man like that. Old Smitty'll have to be more careful where he steps from now on."

Turning back to the wagon, Smitty took out a coiled rope. He tied one end to the top of the rear wagon wheel and ran the other to a nearby juniper. Stretching it tight, he secured a guy line to tether the horses.

Gazing out into the fading light of the open desert, Smitty tested the rope. The string of livestock would help block the light of their fire. "Arrogant Easterners are one thing," he said uneasily. "But Indians are a horse of a different color altogether."

A voice behind Smitty spoke. "Mr. Wellington says you're to care for the horses."

Turning into the last rays of the blazing sun, Smitty squinted at Treadway. "He does, does he? All of 'em?"

"Yeah. I got to help set up camp, me and Hialeaha. When you're done with the horses, you're to pitch in, too."

Smitty shaded his eyes, checking the western sky. "Be dark soon. Best we get a move on."

Treadway grunted and then lumbered off to gather firewood. Smitty smiled and went to the extra water barrel. When no one was looking, he lifted the lid and removed a one-gallon canteen that floated empty on top of the water. Careful not to be seen, he filled the canteen. Observing the others, he laid it in the wagon box and covered it with a tarp.

LaFarge and Brooks stood to one side as Wellington and Davis climbed on top of the coach and tossed down a canvas wall tent. Hialeaha was approaching the supply wagon.

Smitty casually rested his forearm on the sideboard. "Evenin', Miss Hialeaha."

Hialeaha nodded. "Mr. Smitty."

Showing the gaps between his teeth, Smitty grinned. "Just Smitty, miss. Just call me Smitty. There ain't no mister 'bout it."

"Very well. I need the sheet-iron stove for cooking."

Careful not to expose the canteen, Smitty threw back a corner of the tarp. "Know just where it is."

Reaching over the sideboard, Smitty lifted the stove. "I'll carry it over for you."

"It is not heavy," said Hialeaha, taking the stove. "And Mr. Wellington likes his orders followed. I believe you must tend to the horses first."

Glancing at Wellington, Smitty said, "Got a hard nose, does he?"

Hialeaha looked to her left, then right. "Where is Mr. Fargo?"

"Gone. Lookin' for trouble, I reckon. Said he'd be back after dark."

"But supper will be over."

"There's plenty of airtights here. I never seen the like. Canned fish, meat, fruit. He can have his pick when he gets back. I don't s'pose a man like him cares if it's hot 'r cold.

"He won't be in camp nohow. Don't think he likes our company much. Or maybe he don't wanna sleep too close to Treadway without his guns on. Reed's got a score to settle with that old man. A couple of scores, I'd say."

Hialeaha faced Smitty. "Mr. Treadway would be advised to forget any foolish notions."

"Foolish?" questioned Smitty, studying the glint in the Indian's eyes. "Treadway may be slow in the head, but he's a curly wolf. If he ever gets hold of Fargo, he'll clean his plow quick enough. He liked to have killed that man in Lamy, and he was bigger'n younger than Fargo."

"Treadway will die," said Hialeaha flatly. Then, with Smitty watching, she spun on her heels and walked away.

Unhitching the teams, Smitty considered what the Cherokee had said. More importantly, he considered how she had said it. She spoke with certainty. Did she know something about Fargo no one else did? Did he carry a hidden knife in case he was caught without his pistols, a Derringer, perhaps? Was he, like Treadway, a known killer? If both were killers, one might eventually eliminate the other, simplifying matters considerably.

It was almost dark before the horses were watered and grained. Wellington insisted the polo horses be brushed. It made Smitty late for supper.

Hialeaha was busy at the stove when he arrived. Treadway sat on a small campstool with an empty plate in his lap.

The two couples lounged in wooden folding chairs at a dining table draped with a white linen. Elegant plates, glasses, and silverware were evenly spaced around platters of various meats and vegetables. On one side of the table, a campfire was blazing. Near it, the metal cookstove had been set up next to a smaller table and chair. On the other side of the table, a canvas wall tent faced the diners with its flaps tied open. Two cots with bedrolls and valises were inside. A glowing candle lantern hung from the support pole.

"Welcome, Smitty," said Wellington. "What do you think of our humble accommodations?"

Gazing at the half-eaten food and the dining table, Smitty was speechless.

Hialeaha handed him a plate. It held beef, fish, tomatoes, beans, and three biscuits.

"I'm in clover now," exclaimed Smitty, grasping his fork in his fist.

He started eating where he stood. He stabbed a piece of meat with his fork and began gnawing off a bite with his side teeth.

Hialeaha went to the small table and returned, handing Smitty a coffee cup filled with red wine.

Davis raised his glass. "I propose a toast. To the first day of our journey."

"Hear, hear," agreed Wellington. "Hear, hear," chimed LaFarge and Brooks. All took a liberal drink of the wine. Treadway and Smitty clumsily joined in the toast, gulping from their cups.

Hialeaha placed a bowl of peaches in front of each person for dessert. Wellington topped off his glass with the last of the wine. "Another bottle of the same, Hialeaha."

Coming to his feet, Wellington stumbled slightly. He waved his glass in a wide arc and looked out into the blackness surrounding him. Orange firelight reflected off his face. "To our intrepid pilot, our guide and protector, wherever you are."

Davis laughed. The women giggled.

Smitty, his mouth full of food, raised his cup and said, "Here's to him!"

Treadway sneered.

"Protecting us from what?" asked Brooks.

"Phantoms," jibed LaFarge. She raised her empty hand and made it into a claw. "And goblins that creep in the night."

"No," blurted Davis. "Windmills! He is looking for windmills."

The Easterners roared with laughter. Wellington plopped back into his chair. "Our own Don Quixote," he said, laughing, and then choked on his wine and started coughing.

Treadway and Smitty looked at each other and shrugged.

When the laughter subsided, Hialeaha tried to intervene. "Tomorrow will be a long day, Mahra. Perhaps you should retire. Remember you headaches."

"Nonsense. I feel delightful. The day was dreadfully hot, and the evening air is so cool. The night is simply delicious."

Hialeaha's head came up. She was the only one who had heard it. Somewhere far beyond the light of the fire and lantern, a hoof struck a stone. Such sounds traveled in the desert. So did voices.

Before sundown and miles from the camp, Fargo built a small smokeless fire. From the side of bacon he carried and some flour he made his supper and then rode back to the wagons. He found the .45-75 Winchester and scabbard by the front wagon wheel where Smitty had left it. After caring for his black, he tied the gelding to the back of the wagon and switched his saddle and the .45-75 to the bay.

With so much commotion coming from the dining table, Fargo's return had gone unnoticed. Now he was bedding down a hundred yards upwind from the camp on the side of a low hill. Their fire was far too big, and it was easy to deduce Wellington and his friends had been drinking too much.

Fargo positioned his pistols and hat next to his saddle, which would serve as his pillow. He rolled in his blanket and listened.

Treadway had asked a question and now was asking it again. "What do you mean, windmills? And who is this Damn Coyote you're laughing at?"

After another round of sidesplitting laughter, Davis answered. "Not damn coyote, Don Quixote. Like 'keeotay.' He was an old Spaniard who thought windmills were monstrous giants. He believed himself a valiant knight out to save fair damsels in distress. Much like our old Mr. Fargo, don't you see? Now he is somewhere out in the dark saving us from imaginary ruffians and wild aborigines."

"We have seen nothing but empty desert for miles," added Wellington, "and he is out scouring the wilderness searching for giants to slay. No doubt, he is trying to impress our two fair damsels."

"Dreaming of his past glory days," snipped LaFarge. "I, for one, want to be there when he is awakened from his vainglorious imaginations."

"I bet," offered Smitty, "Reed would be more'n happy to wake him up for you, Miss LaFarge. Wouldn't you, Reed?"

The camp grew silent waiting for Treadway to respond.

"I don't like trouble," answered Treadway. He recited the words slowly.

"Good for you, Reed," said Mahra, as if speaking to a child. "No one should want trouble. And I like Mr. Fargo."

Fargo gazed thoughtfully into the star-filled sky. Treadway was pretending to be something he wasn't, but why? And did LaFarge know he was acting, that he was both calculating and ruthless? If she didn't, then his ruse was of less importance. But if, in fact, she knew what he was, she would be an accomplice to whatever he was up to. Perhaps even a partner.

LaFarge scoffed. "I think Fargo is arrogant and insulting."

"Well," said Smitty, "I for one think he's sleepin' outside of camp on account he'll have to take them pistols off to get some shut-eye. I calculate he don't wanna be anywhere near big Reed Treadway without them irons strapped on."

"Perhaps we should replace him," suggested Davis.

"Not until I have satisfaction," said LaFarge. Her words were beginning to slur. "I want to hear him apologize to me, beg my forgiveness. No. I want to see him crawl to me on his hands and knees."

Fargo snorted. "That'll be the day," he muttered, and then glanced down the hill. The fire was dying down. Hialeaha was washing dishes in a basin. It had been a long day, and whatever they were drinking had gotten the best of them. They would turn in soon.

"Are you sure, Reed," teased LaFarge, "that you do not wish any trouble with Fargo?"

"No, Miss LaFarge," replied Treadway, ponderously swinging his head from side to side. "I don't like fighting."

LaFarge poked Wellington's shoulder with her finger. "Now you see, Miles. I told you Reed was harmless. He was just trying to protect you from that awful man."

Wellington stiffened. "I hardly needed protection!"

The camp grew suddenly quiet. Fargo heard the fire pop, a horse blew, but otherwise, there was silence. Her drinking had caused LaFarge to slip.

Smitty broke the silence. "I heard you boxed that hombre real good, Mr. Wellington. But you gotta watch them busted teeth. I had me a plenty of 'em from fightin'. If it turns colors, pinkish like, or gets dark, you're in for it. Nothin' like an ulcerated tooth to ruin a good time. No sir, I heard women say they'd sooner have a baby than a ulcerated tooth."

Davis came to his feet and stretched. "I am going to retire. This desert air has made me drowsy."

Wellington stood, wobbled, and then steadied himself. "We have a long day tomorrow. I suggest we all call it a day."

Fargo tugged on his blanket, pulling it up close to his neck. It was the first night he had slept under the stars in weeks. The voices below were fewer now and too muffled to understand. The stars enshrined the desert in a hazy, silver-gray light. A gentle breeze drifted across his face. His eyes grew heavy.

While Smitty finished eating, he watched Brooks and LaFarge pull down the shades in their coach and the men close the flaps of their tent. Treadway, like a loyal dog, made his bed beside the coach.

Taking his plate and cup to Hialeaha, Smitty put them in the dishwater. "Where you sleepin' tonight?"

Hialeaha continued washing. She motioned with her head. "The coach is a sleeper. There is room for three."

"That was some feast," said Smitty, eyeing a pile of cans just beyond the stove. "We eat that much?"

Taking her hands from the dishwater, Hialeaha pointed to a bucket next to the cans. Beside the bucket, a small shovel was stuck in the sand. "That is full of what was not eaten. All of it wasted. I will have to bury it before I go to sleep. It may draw scavengers."

"Never you mind," offered Smitty, picking up the shovel and bucket. "I'll do the honors."

"Thank you."

"Night, Miss Hialeaha."

"Goodnight."

Walking behind the string of horses, Smitty found a soft stretch of sand and started digging. "They've never been hungry a day in their lives," he whispered, grinning as he spoke. "They've never been thirsty, either. Never, never. They've never been anything but fat and sassy."

Smitty dug deep, deeper than necessary. He poured the garbage into the hole and then took the bucket back to the supply wagon. Careful to make no sound, he pulled back the tarp and filled the bucket with unopened cans. Moments later, he finished burying the garbage and with it a two-day supply of canned goods.

Hialeaha was already in the coach when he unrolled his blankets under the wagon bed. When he was certain no one would see him, he retrieved the hidden canteen of water and tied it under the wagon onto the bolster and axle assembly.

Smitty crawled into his bedroll and lay on his back. He sucked a piece of meat from between his teeth and spit it out, smiling. "God suffers fools to reap what they have sown."

Chapter 8

Before the stars faded in the east, Fargo was up and armed. Instead of his boots, he wore knee-high moccasins. Squatting on his heels in the gray light, he listened, tested the air, and watched his horse's ears. The bay could smell man or beast as well as any dog. If there was going to be trouble, it would come before sunrise, when there was just enough light to see down the barrel of a rifle.

Fargo stood slowly, surveying the shapes around him. When it was light enough to make out the ground, he grabbed the Winchester and started in a wide arc around the camp. At first he walked and then broke into an easy dogtrot, carefully winding his way through the brush. Learning from the Apaches, he breathed only through his nostrils, saving water and forcing his lungs to work. Like the Apaches, he preferred to scout and hunt on foot. And like them, he had developed a remarkable physical endurance.

By the time the horizon brightened to pale yellow, Fargo's moccasins were in his saddlebags and he was back in his boots. He stepped into his stirrups and rode in for breakfast. Smitty sat on the campstool grinding coffee. Hialeaha was busy at the cookstove. They were the only two up.

Fargo tied his bay next to the black. He walked toward the stove, passing by Smitty without speaking.

Smitty glanced up but kept cranking. "You oversleep?" he jested.

"He was up before either of us," said Hialeaha, offering Fargo a fork and plate with a serving of peaches on it.

Accepting the plate, Fargo's eyes met those of Hialeaha's. Without words, there was an exchange of mutual respect.

Hialeaha opened the lid on a coffee pot. "That is enough grinding. Pour it in."

Coming to his feet, Smitty eagerly poured the coffee into the steaming water. He leaned over the stove, inhaling deeply. "Them slapjacks smell mighty tasty."

"Get your plate," said Hialeaha. "I call them griddle cakes."

Treadway stirred in his bed. Hialeaha poured hot syrup over Smitty's slapjacks and then poured more batter onto her griddle.

Continually scanning the desert, Fargo ate his peaches. "For folks who were in such a hurry to get where they're going, they sure sleep late."

"Hungover, I 'spect," offered Smitty. "You missed quite a fandango last night. You ain't never seen such a spread'a food and likker. And way out here in the middle of nowhere."

"I saw it. And anybody in forty miles could have seen it. The fire was too big."

The flap of the tent opened. Wellington emerged, followed by Davis. Their eyes were bloodshot but full of disdain.

"I built the fire the way I wanted it," said Wellington. "We rode all day and saw not so much as a hoofprint. There was no danger."

"Mr. Fargo," interjected Hialeaha, "your griddle cake."

Fargo held out his plate until the syrup was added. "Your funeral."

Tossing off his blanket, Treadway came to his feet. "Well now," he said, momentarily losing his gentle-giant façade, "I thought I heard a 'damned coyote' out here."

Smitty huffed. Wellington and Davis snickered. None seemed to notice the subtle difference in Treadway.

Treadway took a step. Fargo smoothly transferred his plate to his left hand. His right hung free.

A devilish light flashed in Fargo's eyes. "When was the last time you were in a church, Treadway?"

"Enough!" shouted Hialeaha.

The coach door swung open. LaFarge stuck her head out, as did Brooks.

All eyes except Fargo's locked on Hialeaha.

She glared at them all. "If you want to eat, do it now!"

A long silence followed. No one had ever heard Hialeaha raise her voice. LaFarge had never seen Treadway so pale. And Smitty had never met the likes of Conway Fargo.

Keeping his eyes on Treadway, Fargo handed his plate to Hialeaha. "My apologies, ma'am. You all go ahead and eat. I'm riding on ahead." He paused and grabbed a tin cup. After filling it with coffee, he took a step toward the supply wagon. He stopped. Turning back, he spoke to no one in particular. "If you see Sancho Panza, tell him which way I went."

For several seconds, everyone watched Fargo ride off to the south. Brooks finally spoke. "Who is Sancho Panza? Is he a friend of Mr. Fargo?"

Davis raised an eyebrow. "It appears that our guide is not the country bumpkin we took him for. And he has excellent hearing."

"Why do you say that?" asked Brooks.

"Sancho Panza was the friend of Don Quixote."

"My word!" gasped Mahra. "He heard what we said about him?"

"So, he got an earful," said LaFarge. "What does it matter? We said nothing that was not true."

Wellington rubbed the side of his head, squinting his eyes. "What I do not understand is why he asked Reed when he had last been in church. That makes no sense. Does it to you, Reed?"

Treadway shrugged. In his usual tone and cadence, he replied, "No, Mr. Wellington."

"Anyone?"

LaFarge stared at Hialeaha, who was now flipping griddle cakes as if nothing had happened. "Hialeaha appears to get along with him. Maybe she knows."

"Hialeaha?" questioned Wellington.

Shifting the coffee pot to a cooler part of the stove, Hialeaha answered, "Perhaps he is a religious man, one that is concerned about Mr. Treadway's soul."

"I hardly think that," said Davis.

"Perhaps," returned Hialeaha, "he is like the diamondback snake… the snake that rattles before it strikes. Who can say what is in another man's mind so early in the morning?"

"But why would he want to hurt poor Reed?" asked Brooks.

Smitty studied the faces around him. Clearly, Wellington and Davis knew nothing about the pistol-whipping in Dodge. Hialeaha knew. She was keeping quiet, which meant she favored Fargo. By keeping quiet himself, he might end up on the good side of LaFarge and Treadway, a good place to be.

"Sun'll be up soon," said Smitty. "Best we get as far as we can while it's cool."

Wellington shook his head. "I'm not hungry."

"Nor am I," agreed Davis, as did LaFarge.

"I'll eat," grunted Treadway.

"I want some of those delicious peaches," smiled Brooks. "Just peaches, though."

"Then we will break camp in the meantime," said Wellington. "And Smitty, tie my horse to the coach. I'm riding inside."

"And mine as well," added Davis. "I am not up to another twenty miles in a saddle. My backside is raw, and my head is about to explode."

***

In the blinding glare of late afternoon, Fargo reined his horse toward a flat-roofed, two-room adobe. Except for a small garden next to it, the building sat in the middle of five acres of barren sand. On the east wall, tilted off center, hung a crude white cross. Off the west wall stood an empty corral built of stacked rocks and twisted juniper limbs. Inside the corral, chickens scratched and pecked through scattered piles of crusted manure. A *ramada* of gnarled mesquite sticks shaded an open front door that was guarded on each side by two snarling black statues.

Fifty feet in front of the adobe, a dozen sun-bleached animal skulls and a scattering of leg bones hung from a single dead mesquite. Nailed to the trunk, a rusted sign was lettered with faded white paint. It read, *"Poco Onate, Remedios y Yerbas."*

Fargo dismounted in front of a hitch rail and watering trough. He slapped the trail dust from his chest and shoulders. With no clouds in the sky, the temperature had passed ninety well before noon.

Letting his horse drink, he took off his hat and dunked his head in next to the sucking lips of the gelding. Standing with his eyes closed, he leaned his head back, letting the water run down his neck and then trickle under his sweat-stained shirt. When he opened his eyes, a Mexican was standing in the shade of the *ramada*. Little more than five feet tall, he wore soiled muslin clothes and leather sandals. In his hands, however, he gripped a ten-gauge double-barreled shotgun.

"If I didn't know better, Poco," remarked Fargo, "I'd think you've grown a couple of inches."

The Mexican lowered the shotgun. "*Señor* Fargo? Is that you?"

"Got a haircut since I last saw you. And a shave."

Poco laughed. "And some gray hairs too, *amigo*. *Venga*! Come in out of the sun. It has been too long since we see you at Antelope Springs!"

"How long's it been, Poco? Three, four years?"

Poco loosed his right hand from the scattergun and stepped into the glare. He rubbed his palm on the side of his pants and shook Fargo's hand. "Four. Maria is now nine. Wait until you see her. She is a *muy bonia señorita* like her mother was, God rest her soul. She will be so happy to see you. She never stops talking about you. I will go wake her."

"No. Let her sleep. I got people coming behind me."

Poco squinted to the north, studying the gentle grade. "Enemies?"

"Not enemies, not friends," answered Fargo, noticing a lock of feathers dangling from a string around Poco's neck.

"Got a new charm?" asked Fargo, indicating the necklace with a nod.

"The leg of a *nagual*," answered Poco, pulling out the taloned leg of an owl. "He came a week ago. I knew he was here to cast a spell, so I shot at him. I only took his leg. Now the spirits warn me to watch for a man to come with only one leg. This will be the evil *brujo* that came to visit me as an owl. The spirits say the one-legged man is *muy malo*, and his *bujeria* is strong."

Fargo merely nodded. Poco was a *curandero* and a *brujo,* a healer and a witch. To the Mexicans and Indians, there were good *brujos* and bad ones. Poco was a good witch. Their superstitions were hard to understand, but some of the healings Poco performed were inexplicable. In the vast deserts and dark mountains of the Southwest, Fargo kept his mouth shut and his mind open.

Poco turned and motioned with a wave of his hand. "*Venga, amigo. It is too hot in the sun.*"

Fargo glanced at the two hand-carved statues beside the doorway and then followed Poco inside. "Those that are coming are Easterners. I'm piloting them for a week or two. They'll pay for the water. They like to see different places and people. Could be they'll want to pay for a good Mexican meal."

Poco brought a clay mug and pitcher full of cool water. He handed the mug to Fargo and then gazed out his open front door again to the north. "I see a stage coach and a wagon. That is them?"

"Four men and three women," said Fargo, letting his eyes adjust to the dim light. He took a long drink of cool water.

Poco set the pitcher on the crude plank table. "Three *womens*! Out here?"

Fargo wiped his mouth with the back of his hand. "It's a long story. We're headed for Zuni."

Poco slid both hands down the front of his shirt and over the roundness of his belly where the cloth stretched tight. "*Gringos locos!*"

"They're *ricos*, Poco. *Muy rico.*"

"Their money will do them no good if they die in this desert," replied Poco.

"Out here it doesn't do them much good anyway. All but one of them are about as useful as tits on a boar hog."

"What are you doing with *ricos, Señor* Fargo? Did they lose someone?"

"No. I'm just taking them to Zuni and then back as far as Lamy. That's what they're paying me for. After that, they are on their own. I'll be done with them."

Fargo refilled his mug and then arched his back to work the stiffness out of his long ride. "Have any trouble around here lately?"

Poco kept his eyes on the wagons as they neared. "No. A few pass through, but no troubles. No *banditos*, no *Indios*. Maria, she always hides. You know. Until we know for sure."

Fargo nodded and took another drink. The air was cool in the thick-walled adobe. "How's she sleeping?"

"Good, but always the candle burns. She stays below still. The nightmares…they do not come so much anymore."

"I got to warn you, Poco, one of the women is an Indian. She doesn't look like one except for her moccasins. She's their cook."

Poco turned from the doorway. His brown eyes narrowing, he studied Fargo for several seconds. "You trust this Indian?"

"So far I do. And that's more than I can say for the rest of them."

"I will tell Maria you trust her. I think it will be enough. She is strong like her mother."

The coach rattled to a dusty stop in front of the adobe. A moment later the supply wagon pulled alongside. Smitty was first to step down. He beat the dust from his clothes as Treadway sluggishly climbed off the coach and opened the door.

"Welcome, *amigos*," greeted Poco, coming through the doorway but staying in the shade. "I am Poco. Welcome to Antelope Springs. *Mi casa es su casa.*"

"*Gracias*," grinned Smitty. "Is your water cold? Ours is 'bout to come to a boil."

"*Sí, Sí.* Come in, come in," said Poco, watching Wellington and Davis emerge from the ornate coach. "We have good water and *tamales and pappas fritas* this evening if you are hungry."

When LaFarge reached out for Wellington's hand, she caught a glimpse of the adobe. She scowled as she stepped down into the blistering sand. She wore no bonnet. A few strands of hair, uncharacteristically out of place, hung loose.

Brooks, her hair more unkempt than LaFarge's, came out smiling and was helped down by Davis. Hialeaha, appearing unaffected by the long ride, helped herself out of the coach.

Poco waved his arm encouragingly. "*Venga.* Come inside, *por favor.* It is cool inside. *Señor* Fargo is here already."

No one moved.

Brooks hooked her arm through Davis's, holding him close. Shading her pale forehead, she looked first at the black statues. She half turned toward the dead mesquite and then back again to Poco. "Why do you have those dreadful bones hanging from your tree?"

Poco smiled. "I am *curandero*."

Blinking against the sun's rays, Davis asked, "And what might that be?"

"I cure with plants, the diseases. God gives all plants a purpose for curing. I use the power in them to make others well. I am a *curandero*."

Wellington smiled sarcastically. "So you are a country doctor, and this is your office."

"*Sí.* Yes, yes, *amigo*. A *medico*." Poco continued to smile.

Mahra started to take a step but stopped suddenly. She took a closer look at the statues. Each resembled a nightmarish cross between man and beast.

"What are those?" she asked. "They are hideous!"

Poco studied Mahra Brooks for several seconds. His eyelids fluttered slightly. He followed her gaze to the statues. "They are to keep the evil spirits out. The bad spirits cannot pass by them. If the magic in the herbs does not work, I am also a *brujo*."

LaFarge shook her head. She was thirsty and sweaty but not ready to step inside a squalid mud shack. And Fargo was nowhere to be seen. "And just what is a *brujo*?"

"If you have a spell cast on you by a *bruja*, a witch, or if you have the *embrujada* of an evil spirit, I can remove it. I perform the *brujeria*." Poco glanced appraisingly at Mahra from the corner of his eye. "Sometimes a person does not know they have an evil spirit. They need it removed, *tambien*. Only a *brujo* can do these things."

Wellington's smile raised only one corner of his mouth. He indicated the cross on the outer wall. "And what about that?"

Poco glanced in the direction of the cross and traced another across his chest. "It is for the Holy Church. I am of the Galisteo parish."

"You are a witch doctor and a Catholic?" chided Wellington. "Anything else we should know?"

"No." answered Poco, simply. "Just these things, I think."

Wellington smirked at Davis and Brooks. "He's harmless. Let's go inside and get out of this heat."

"Wait," said LaFarge. She raised her voice. "Mr. Fargo."

A few seconds passed before a hatless Fargo appeared in the frame of the door. He took a drink of water from his mug. "It's safe. I've known Poco for years."

Without hesitation, LaFarge started forward. The others followed. Brooks stumbled, but hanging onto Davis's arm, she caught her balance.

Leading the way into the large room, Poco pointed to a rough-sawn table and two benches on either side. "*Por favor*, sit," he said, fetching an armful of mugs and another pitcher of water.

The group walked inside the adobe. When their eyes adjusted to the dim light, they saw Fargo leaning against the far wall. A *rastra* of red chili peppers hung to his left, a wooden crucifix to his right. He wore a faint smile.

Arranging the mugs in a rough circle, Poco filled each to the brim, splashing water onto the tabletop. "Drink," he said. "It is fresh from the well."

Davis was first to pick up a mug. He peered into the water and smelled it. He took a sip, then another. "It is wonderful," he announced. "Delicious and refreshingly cool."

The others stepped to the table and took mugs. Raising them to their dry lips, they started to drink. Wellington suddenly jerked his head to the side and yelped.

"What is it?" asked Davis.

Wellington winced in pain, rolling his lips over his teeth for several seconds. "My tooth! The damn water hurt my broken tooth."

Smitty took a drink. "It ain't the water. Nothin's wrong with it. It's the cold of it. Water's fine."

Satisfied at the explanation, all but Wellington eagerly turned their mugs up, drinking deeply. Wellington watched them, his eyes reflecting disbelief that they should drink without him. It was a look that quickly turned to envy.

Finishing his water first, Smitty held his mug out. "Hit 'er agin, *amigo*."

As Poco poured, Smitty eyed Wellington. "Better hope that tooth don't start paining you to hot next. If it does, it's Katy bar the door."

"What do you mean?"

"Hot means it's 'bout to ulcerate." Smitty lifted his lip and pointed to a dark space where there once had been a tooth. "You ain't never felt pain like a ulcerated tooth. I'll swear to that."

Poco set the pitcher down. "I will wake my daughter, Maria. She will cook for us a good supper. Come, *Señor* Fargo. She will be happy to open her eyes to you."

After watching Fargo and Poco disappear into the next room, LaFarge surveyed the adobe. Other than the *rastra* and a crucifix, the drab walls were bare. Each had a small window framed by hand-cut timbers. There was no glass, not even a screen. Instead, heavy wooden shutters, made to close from the inside, were bolted to the timbers. The floor was a collection of loose-fitting planks.

"You could not pay me to eat in here," said LaFarge.

"Nor I," agreed Wellington.

Davis looked uncomfortably at Hialeaha. "We do not wish to be rude to the Mexican. Would you explain to the gentleman about our eating arrangements?"

Hialeaha nodded. "Be sure to pay him well for his water."

"Pay for water?" scoffed Wellington. "I have never heard of paying for a drink of water."

"Twelve horses, seven people, and two water barrels to fill," said Hialeaha. "That is much more than a drink of water. And out here, water can be worth more than gold."

Davis cringed. His cousin was unaccustomed to being contradicted, especially by the hired help. And unless he missed his guess, Fargo would not allow Hialeaha to be openly castigated for a second time.

Attempting to intervene, Davis said, "She does have a point, Miles. It may be customary."

Wellington started to speak, but a muffled voice squealed excitedly. It came from the second room of the adobe. "*Señor* Fargo! *Señor* Fargo!"

Out of sight, a door slammed with a heavy thud. The young voice continued. "You are here! You are here!"

Then Fargo said, "*Como estsa, bonita? Como estas?*"

Poco returned to the main room, followed by Fargo. They stopped several feet from the others.

"This is my daughter, Maria," Poco said, turning back to Fargo.

Behind Fargo, a raven-haired girl leaned her head out. Her brown eyes were wide with uncertainty. She grasped Fargo's hand and took a half step but remained partially hidden.

"These are…" began Fargo, but hesitated. "These people are with me, Maria." Fargo pointed at Hialeaha. "*Ella es mi amiga. No tengas miedo.*"

"*India?*"

"*Sí. Pero no malo. Tu amiga, tambien.*"

Clearly surprised, Davis asked, "Do you speak Spanish, Mr. Fargo?"

"Mexicans were here first. Out here whites learn Spanish, and Mexicans learn English. Sometimes we mix them together."

"Like mongrels," moaned LaFarge. Lifting her nose, she turned her head aside. "Would it be too much to ask if we could bathe this evening?"

Poco cocked his head. "Bathe? Here?"

"*En la agua de los caballos,*" grinned Fargo.

Poco smiled, and his daughter giggled. "No. We have no tub for you."

"Then what are they laughing at?" demanded LaFarge.

"I told them you might want to use the horse trough," answered Fargo.

"We have no tub for you," said Poco, "but we have *tamales* and potatoes for supper. And plenty of good water for you to drink."

Hialeaha spoke quickly. "Thank you, Mr. Poco. It is very kind of you to offer to feed us, but we have our own food. We will need wood, though, for our cookstove."

Poco shrugged but smiled. "I have some mesquite in the back. Put your horses in the corral. You may sleep inside my *casa* tonight, my adobe. You will be safer in here, I think."

Treadway turned his back and walked outside, ducking his head slightly at the doorway.

"We have a tent," said Davis, "and the women have beds in the coach."

Hialeaha saw Poco's smile fading. "Mr. Poco, we want to thank you for your hospitality. Will you and Maria join us after supper for coffee and fruit? Tonight it will be cherries. Please join us and be our guest this evening."

Poco's smile returned. "*Muchas gracias, Señora.*"

"And Maria," continued Hialeaha as the others followed Treadway. "I have to cook for my people, but I have never had a *tamale*. Would you please bring one for me when you come?"

Maria smiled timidly and nodded. "*Sí.*"

Poco's eyes followed Hialeaha out the door until she was beyond hearing distance. "To have womens out here is bad, *amigo*, but to have three such beautiful ones...*es muy malo.*"

"I tried to get them to stay back east where they belonged. When they told me they were dead set on the trip, I signed on to help the one called Mahra. Not the mouthy one. Mahra's the frail one. I'm riding for her and as a favor to Hialeaha."

"The mouthy *mujer*," said Maria, taking Fargo's hand, "I do not like her."

Fargo peered out the door. "Neither do I, Maria. Neither do I."

Looking up, Maria tugged on Fargo's hand. "Will you stay here with us?"

Going to one knee, Fargo shook his head. "No, pumpkin. I can't. The young woman named Mahra needs my help."

"You mean," sighed Maria, "like *mamasita* and me needed you?"

"Something like that. But I'll be here for supper. Are you cooking for your papa already?"

A grin brightened Maria's face. "Yes. I cook for Papa and me. And for those that come here for the water."

"Well now, I'm powerful hungry. You think you can cook enough for me?"

"Yes! You will see."

Fargo stood. "Then you best get started."

"I will," chirped Maria, scampering off to the kitchen.

His brow wrinkling with unpleasant memories, Fargo said, "She seems happy, Poco. You've done a good job."

"No, not me. The day she was born, the Holy Father gave my little Maria the strength of her mother. Maria is a miracle. And you brought her back to me unharmed. You are *la mano de Dios*."

Before Fargo could object, Poco shoved out his hand. "I know you do not want to hear those words, *amigo*. Though the words are true, I will say no more today."

Frowning uncomfortably, Fargo changed the subject. "Don't let these folks get under your skin, Poco, especially that LaFarge woman. She's the worst of the lot."

"I think maybe she is a *bruja*."

Fargo chuckled. "Close, I'd say."

"How long will you stay tonight? I can roll out a feather mat for you on the roof. You can see the desert good up there."

"Thanks, Poco, but nothing has changed. I doubt it ever will."

"After the tamales, then?"

"Yeah. Can I count on breakfast with you two?"

"Always, *amigo*."

***

Poco placed two hot tamales on a cloth and folded it. When he approached the gringos' campfire, they were still sitting around their dinner table. Amber candlelight from a silver-encased lamp illuminated their faces. A single wine bottle sat empty.

Four paces from the table, Treadway and Smitty sat crossed legged on a blanket by the campfire. Just beyond them, Hialeaha stood working at a stove. As he approached the cookstove, Poco nodded to the two men. He handed Hialeaha the *tamales*. Before she could accept them, LaFarge cleared her throat.

"Excuse me, Mr. Poco. May we see what Mexican food looks like?"

Half nodding and half bowing to Hialeaha, Poco excused himself and crossed to the table. Holding the bundle in one hand, he proudly unfolded the cloth with the other. Steam curled up into the cool evening air.

"*Tamales*. Made by my *hija*, Maria."

"They are brown?" questioned Brooks.

"Yes, but what you see now is only the husks of corn. The *tamales* are wrapped in the husks before they are cooked."

Mahra winkled her nose. "Corn husks?"

Poco seemed puzzled. "*Sí*. What else would we use, *señorita?*"

LaFarge laughed. "Of course, Mahra, what else would they use?"

Poco took a half step backward. For the first time, he eyed the visitors with suspicion. He turned slightly, glancing back at Hialeaha.

"I am sure they will taste as good as they smell, Mr. Poco," Hialeaha said. "Let me see."

Poco stepped toward Hialeaha. Smitty stood to take a look as well. "I ain't had me one of them in a coon's age."

"Get your plate," said Hialeaha. "I'll share."

Smitty went back to the fire for his plate as Hialeaha served bowls of fruit to the table.

"Mr. Poco," said Wellington, waving a hand. "Please come and sit with us. We set a place for you. We are enjoying cherries tonight— canned, of course, but still quite good."

Poco handed the *tamales* to Smitty and started for the table. He looked at the white tablecloth and silverware before awkwardly sitting on the edge of an empty chair.

"Please, *Señor*, call me just Poco. To everyone, I am Poco."

"Very well," agreed Wellington. "Poco it is. Where is your daughter? I thought she was coming."

"No. She is not so good with strangers. She has gone to bed."

Davis looked around. "Then where is Mr. Fargo? He is not with you?"

Curious, Poco squinted at Davis and then at the others. "You have known *Señor* Fargo long?"

"Heavens no!" said LaFarge, taking a dainty spoonful of cherries. "A few days only."

"It is his way to sleep apart," said Poco. "He listens and watches always in the night. You know…for just in case."

"How long have you known Mr. Fargo?" asked Davis.

Wait," Mahra injected. "In case of what? Watches for what?"

His eyes sliding from Brooks to Davis, Poco ignored the question. "I have known him five years, almost."

Wellington chewed some cherries and washed them down with wine. "You say Fargo does this often? Sleeps away, as you call it?"

"Sí."

"Then he is always this unsociable?"

Poco looked down at his uneaten cherries. "My American is not so good. I do not know that word."

"Unsociable means not liking people very much." offered Davis. "So Mr. Fargo usually stays away from people?"

"Yes. That is it."

"The farther the better," quipped LaFarge, scooping another spoonful of cherries.

Poco glanced at LaFarge. For several seconds, he pondered what Davis had said. "Yes, he is that word you say, but more. Much more. My people call it *separado*. He is a *separado*."

"*Separado*," repeated Wellington. "So what exactly is that?"

Thinking hard, Poco looked up at the black sky as if searching the stars for an answer. "Is like when the wolf hunts alone. He is *el lobo separado*."

"Lone wolf," blurted Smitty, his mouth full of *tamale*. "He means Fargo hunts like a lone wolf, that's all."

LaFarge rolled her eyes. "And what, pray tell, does this 'lone wolf' hunt?"

This time, Poco looked long and hard at LaFarge. What he saw, he did not like. Shifting his attention from her, he studied each of the faces at the table before returning to LaFarge.

"Men," Poco said flatly. "He hunts men."

The campfire crackled sending sparks into the night. A squeak came from a cup Hialeaha was washing. Otherwise, the camp was suspended in silence.

It was Treadway who broke the spell. "What do you mean he hunts men?"

Poco began to eat his cherries. "Bad men only. Many are Indians, but Mexicans and gringos too. He hunts them all."

"What does he do with them when he finds them?" asked Brooks.

"Mostly," answered Poco, wiping his mouth with his sleeve, "he kills them."

Brooks gasped, covering her mouth with her fingertips. LaFarge only scowled. "How do you know this?"

Poco nonchalantly took another spoonful of cherries. He took his time chewing. When he finished he answered, choosing his words carefully.

"Five years ago we live in Tubac. There, the Apaches murder some people and take my wife and child. *Señor* Fargo was known to us and close by. We send for him, and he came. He led me and some men after the Apaches.

"He can see sign no other white man can see. We rode day and night until we find their *rancheria*. We prepare to attack at first light, but everyone knows the Apaches will kill my wife and child as soon as we fire our first shots.

"*Señor* Fargo crawls into the *rancheria* that night by himself. It took him all night. He move like the snail on his belly, by inches just like the Apache.

"When we can see, we go in shooting. In this way my Maria is saved by *Señor* Fargo."

"But what of your wife?" Wellington asked.

"Before *Señor* Fargo can stop her, a squaw kill my Rosetta. Then *Señor* Fargo kill her, before she kill my Maria."

LaFarge cringed. "He killed a woman?"

A half smile was hidden under Poco's drooping mustache. He nodded. "Yes, he killed her good, and many warriors that day too. We kill any Apache with a weapon, anyone close to a weapon. Man, woman, boy. No matter.

"A squaw, she can kill as good as any warrior. At torture, the squaws are better than many of the men."

"Now, see here!" scolded Davis. "These tales of Indians are frightening the women."

Wellington let loose a bored sigh. "That was five years ago, Poco. The Indians are all on reservations now. There is no need for anyone to be alarmed."

Poco somberly shook his head. "Reservations, *Señor?* Reservations only keep the white men *out.* They do not keep the Apache *in.*"

The shock that Fargo might be a man hunter and would even kill a woman was wearing off LaFarge. Her cynicism was returning, and with it her self-assurance. "If there was any danger from Indians, you would not be out here alone, would you, Poco? If all you have told us about the Apaches is true, you would not live out here with your daughter."

Poco sat up straight. "I live here for my own reasons, *Señora.* It is far from Tubac. As for my daughter, she sleeps in a room under the floor. There is a door with no handle. It has only a hidden spring. She is safe there. They will not find her again.

"But you, señor, go west. From here, every day you go closer to the Apache."

Smitty stood. He yawned and scratched his chest. "Say, Mr. Wellington, where is it, 'xactly, we're goin', anyhow?"

Wellington looked at Davis. Davis shrugged.

"I suppose we can tell you now," said Wellington. "Our destination is the Zuni reservation."

Smitty used his fingernail to pick a piece of gristle from his teeth and wiped it on his shirt. "Zuni, eh? I hear them's friendly Injuns. Fact is, they's enemies of the Apache. We'll be safe enough on Zuni land."

"Do you know anything of the Zuni, Poco?" asked Davis.

Poco shrugged indifferently. "Only that the padres went there many, many years ago, but it did no good. Their church they build is empty for a long time. They worship the dead, I think. And they have many witches…and spells."

"Ah," said Davis cheerily, "witches and spells. Not long ago, there were some in our country who believed in witches, too. Well then, if witches and goblins are all we have ahead of us, we need not worry. I trust we can readily handle a few aboriginal superstitions."

"Hear, hear," agreed Wellington, raising his glass and taking a gulp of wine. "That's the spirit."

Poco's eyes narrowed. "Sometimes it is not so easy as you think. Only a week ago I saw a *nagual*."

Wellington shook his head. "A what?"

"A *nagual*. This one was an owl, but sometimes they are a cat. They can be anything they want."

Davis winked at Wellington. "Go on, Poco."

Poco reached inside his shirt. Dangling the owl foot from his fingertips, he continued. "A witch can change into an animal and go looking around. This *nagual* came as an owl, so I shoot at him. But I have only the leg. He got away. He was here to cast a spell on me.

"After I scare him away, the spirits came to me. They told me to watch for the witch, that I would know him because he now walks with only one leg. So I am looking for a man with one leg, or a cat or some other animal with only three legs."

Poco stole a look at LaFarge from the corner of his eye. "So you see, it is not so easy to know when you are looking at a *bruja*. They can be right in front of you. Only this *brujo* will be walking on one leg if he is a man. So if you meet a man with one leg, beware. He is evil."

LaFarge stole a glance at Treadway. His eyes met hers. The man who had sold them the map and helmet had a peg leg. The two exchanged smiles before LaFarge spoke.

"Where we come from, Poco, there are many men who fought the rebels and now walk on one leg."

"May we speak of something else?" Brooks pleaded. "All these stories are giving me a headache."

"Certainly, dear," replied Davis, putting his arm around Mahra. "What would you like to talk about?"

"Well, how far is it to the river? I simply must bathe."

Poco dropped the owl foot under his shirt. "From here it is two hours to the Manzano Mountains. There are many canyons, but you will follow the Cañada del Chinchonte until it comes to the Cañada de Chilili. It is best to camp there. Sometimes there is water. The next day you will find the Rio Grande before night falls. There is plenty of water there."

"Wouldn't it have been better," asked Smitty, "to have gone from Lamy right on to Albuquerque?"

"Sometimes is better," answered Poco. "But many bandits are on that road. And it is not so much different in miles. You will be safer this way, I think.

"After you cross the river, there will be little water this year. There was no snow and little rain. A bad year for water."

"We brung an extry water barrel," assured Smitty. "We'll get through just fine."

Poco shrugged again. He put down his spoon and stood. "*Gracias* for the fruit. It is time I go to sleep. *Buenas noches.*"

With his back to the table, he went to Hialeaha and paused. Tapping the owl foot under his shirt with the tip of his finger, he said gravely, "*Vaya con Dios, Señora. Vaya con Dios.*"

Chapter 9

P oco watched the wagons roll west until they disappeared into the gray-green thickets of mesquite and juniper. Unlike the night before, the desert air did not cool. Before the rising sun cut through the haze on the eastern horizon, it was nearing eighty. Why the gringos had risen so late and left when the sun was already up was a mystery to the Mexican.

Walking past where the supply wagon had been, he noticed a patch of ground that had recently been disturbed. Curious, Poco dug the tip of his sandal into the sand. Going to his knees, he dug with both hands until he saw the tops of unopened cans. In all, there were a dozen of them. Using the front of his shirt as a basket, he carried his new supply of meat and fruit inside the adobe. "*Ricos locos*," he muttered.

***

By noon, the wagons were threading their way through the narrow passes of the Manzanos Mountains. Fargo led them up Chinchonte Canyon following a faint road with a dusty uphill grade. The junipers grew taller and thicker along the steep walls of the canyons. Yucca clung to the parched earth growing between clumps of scrub oak and low-growing pine, all withered by the heat. The horses, lathered with sweat, were beginning to stumble over rocks that peppered the road.

Fargo waited in the meager shade of a juniper for the wagons to catch up. From here on, the grade was gradually downhill, but the horses would need water before making it to the Rio Grande. He took off his hat, wiping the sweatband and then rubbing his forehead where the band pressed into his skin.

They were on the edge of Apache country now but were more likely to encounter bandits or highwaymen. Fargo, however, scanned the ragged mountainsides just as he would if they were in the heart of *Apacheria*. There was no such thing as being too careful.

Fargo replaced his hat and thoughtfully scratched the stubble on his jaw. Before Fargo had left Antelope Springs, Poco had taken his sacred healing stone and rubbed it down Fargo's spine and across his shoulders. He chanted as he made the sign of the cross on his back and then his chest.

Poco said the spirits had instructed him to do so, that the ritual was needed to ward off the one-legged *brujo*. Poco was adamant about performing the ceremony, and so was little Maria. It was Poco's way, a way shared by thousands like him from West Texas to California. Fargo respected their beliefs and accepted their customs. And he had seen enough, heard enough, and experienced enough to know that it wasn't all superstition.

Poco also thought Mahra was very ill, that a spirit made her so. He had offered his most powerful herbs, but Davis refused. He said their doctor in Chicago had already prescribed the proper remedy, and all she had was a few headaches. Davis scoffed at Poco's dire warnings.

The coach rounded a jagged outcropping, the horses trudging up the last hundred yards of the grade. Fargo thought of Hialeaha sitting next to LaFarge and Brooks. Did she speak during the day? If she did, what did she talk about? Was there enough Indian left in her to believe in witches and spells? Poco seemed to think she did.

As for Clarissa LaFarge, Poco was still debating whether or not she was a *bruja*. It seemed to the Mexican that Wellington might have had a spell cast on him. Why else, he said, was a rich man with such an unpleasant woman, a woman who could do nothing worthwhile? Surely he had many women to choose from, yet he had chosen this one.

Fargo pulled his hat brim low, shielding his eyes from the scorching sun. He nudged his mount out of the shade and into the path of the coach. Treadway pulled back on the lines as dust wafted into the heat.

"We'll noon here and water the horses. This is the summit. From now on, it's a gradual slope back down into the open desert."

Avoiding eye contact, Treadway set the brake. Fargo rode fifty feet past the coach and out of the settling dust. He waited for the supply wagon to catch up.

"Far-go," said a voice from behind him.

Fargo turned. He had heard no footsteps, but Hialeaha stood behind him shading her eyes and looking up at him. She no longer wore a long dress but had changed into a riding skirt. "Would it be all right if I ride with you for a while? The coach is stuffy, and Mr. Davis said I am welcome to use his mare."

A jolt pulsated through Fargo, but he replied impassively. "Suit yourself."

Fargo took a deep breath and quietly exhaled. Acutely aware of the pounding his chest, he gazed at the upturned face. Without thinking, he let his eyes drift down the front of her blouse to the small waistband of the riding skirt.

She was a fine-looking woman, even if she was Cherokee. He had realized that the moment he saw her. But after their conversation in Lamy, he tried to put her out of his thoughts. At times he wished he had never said anything to her. Now he was not so sure.

"You want me to saddle him up?"

Hialeaha took her hand down. "I will do it."

Smitty was bringing the wagon around the outcropping, coming on slowly. Hialeaha took two steps and came alongside Fargo. Her shoulder was inches from his leg.

"It's hotter on a horse," said Fargo, focusing his attention on the approaching supply wagon. "No shade."

"The air is dry," replied Hialeaha, her attention also on the wagon. "Chicago is worse. And I prefer your company over the others."

Fargo resisted the urge to look down at Hialeaha. "That's not saying much."

"I suppose not," answered Hialeaha. She paused. "When Mahra weds, my work will be done. She will have chosen her husband…and her friends. It will be time for me to leave."

"Have any plans?"

"Only for today," said Hialeaha. "And you? When this is done?"

"I quit making plans twenty years ago."

Hialeaha looked up at Fargo. The Indians said he was a man without a heart, that it was burned out of him years ago. Now only a scar remained where his heart used to be. That was why he was Quick Killer. He felt nothing. No joy, no happiness, no fear or regret. He knew only hate.

That was the legend, but this was the man. Poco's daughter Maria loved Far-go. And Conway Fargo clearly loved the little girl. And he had signed on with Wellington only to protect Mahra Brooks. If nothing else, he had compassion for helpless women and children.

He treated Poco with respect and spoke of the Mexicans as equals. And he risked his life to save a mother and child. A man filled only with hate could not do those things.

"Then, Far-go, neither of us has plans for the future. We have at least that in common."

"Water stop?" asked Smitty, calling out over the rattle of trace chains and snorting horses.

Fargo nodded, allowing Smitty to come alongside and set his brake.

"Make sure Treadway lets his team cool before he gives them water," said Fargo. "I don't know how much he's driven outside of Chicago."

Winding the lines around the brake handle, Smitty leaned his elbows on his knees. "You figurin' to stay clear of him all the way to Zuni?"

"If I can."

"To hear him talk, I'd say that's not likely."

"They are requesting peaches," said Hialeaha. "It is too hot for much else."

"I'll fetch 'em, miss," answered Smitty, climbing over the back of his seat. "I'll bring 'em to ya."

Fargo wheeled his horse and rode on by Wellington and Davis, who were off to the side of the road spreading a blanket in the shade of a twisted pine. LaFarge and Brooks stood by, cooling themselves with lace fans. Treadway sat on a boulder across from the blanket. He made no attempt to tend to his sweat-lathered team.

Smitty smiled, watching Hialeaha walk back to the coach. He was put in charge of the canned goods, a job he gladly accepted. No use, he told Hialeaha, having her climb up in the wagon every day when she had so much to do. He would take care of it for her.

Hooking a dirty fingernail under the larder's metal latch, Smitty flipped it up and swung the food crate open. Half the fruit was already gone. He took out four cans. When he reached for the fifth, he jerked his hand back and swore.

Tilting his head to the side, he studied the small scorpion that had tried to sting him. "Well, well what have we here?"

After a quick check of Treadway and the others, Smitty ducked down behind the crate and took out a pocketknife. Hurriedly cutting around the top of one of the cans, he bent the lid back and drank all the juice. Stealing another look over the crate, he tossed the peaches into a clump of scrub oak.

With the empty can, he maneuvered the scorpion into a corner. Avoiding its stinging tail and using his knife blade, he flicked the scorpion into the can and bent the lid back down.

Holding a bundle of seven cans in his arms, Smitty gave five to Hialeaha and then crossed the road and gave one to Treadway. The last he kept for himself, saying he would eat his under the shade of his wagon.

He casually strolled to the far side of the coach and stopped where no one could see him. Opening the lid of the can, he twirled it several times then spit on the enraged scorpion. With the can firmly in his palm, he reached inside the coach and flicked his wrist.

***

When Fargo rode back to the wagons, Treadway was holding a bucket under the nose of his nigh leader. Smitty was filling another bucket at the water barrel. Hialeaha had the mare tied to the rear of the supply wagon and was tightening the cinch.

Fargo dismounted near the shaded blanket. Both Wellington and Davis were seated leaning back on their palms. The women, lying on their backs, had their heads in the laps of the men.

"See any witches?" snipped LaFarge.

Loosening the cinch on his horse, Fargo looked directly at LaFarge. "Up the road, no."

LaFarge's face, already rosy from the heat, flushed bright red.

"You missed some good stories last night," said Wellington. "We were just discussing how Poco could spin some tall tales."

"He's been known to."

"Rather strange," offered Davis, "to hear of such superstitious beliefs in the modern age, don't you think?"

"Comes with the country. Most Mexicans don't have a drop of Spanish blood in them. For the most part, they don't act it, but they're descended from Indians. They mix their old Indian beliefs in with the new."

"So the Mexicans really believe a man can turn into an animal?" asked Mahra.

"Lots of them do. And so do Indians. They believe in the *nagual.* The Apaches and Navajo call them shapeshifters."

"Preposterous," berated Wellington.

"To us it is," said Fargo. "To them it is powerful medicine."

"Hialeaha is not like that," said Brooks. "She is perfectly civilized."

"How about you, Mr. Fargo?" asked LaFarge. "Are you civilized? Just how civilized can a *separado* be?"

Fargo paused, his gaze moving from one face to the other. "No matter where you are, civilization is paper thin. It's just a set of rules that most people discard the minute it suits them. That minute came and went for me a long time ago."

"How long until we reach the Rio Grande?" asked Mahra, oblivious to the cutting edge in Fargo's voice. "I cannot wait to be rid of this infernal dust."

Fargo glanced at Brooks, catching her in her just the right light. A few strands of hair dangled down her cheeks, shading her blue eyes and delicate nose. She was, at that moment, the face of innocence, and, at that moment, a wave of guilt washed over him. It had been nearly twenty years, but the memory had never faded.

"If we get on our way, Miss Brooks, we'll be there before sundown."

Brooks sat up, as did LaFarge. Fargo turned. Treadway was approaching from his rear. He stopped three paces back, his face unreadable.

"The watering's all done, Miss LaFarge."

They all came to their feet. Keeping distance between them, Fargo led his bay past Treadway to the supply wagon. A bucket of water was waiting by the rear wheel. The horse immediately buried its nose in it.

Fargo nodded to Hialeaha. Keeping an eye on her, he began unsaddling the bay.

Hialeaha checked her cinch a second time. The mare had relaxed, and she tugged hard on the latigo, taking up the slack. Fargo had seen plenty of squaws fork a saddle, but never a white woman. But then, he reminded himself, Hialeaha was Cherokee.

On his ride down the road and back, he wrestled with the question of whether it even mattered what she was. Weren't Mexicans like Poco just Indians whose ancestors had been converted by Spanish priests? If Hialeaha were Mexican, he would not have questioned the feelings taking root inside him.

"Did you adjust the stirrups?" asked Fargo.

"While you were talking with the others."

Fargo threw his saddle onto the black. He noticed the saddle on the mare held an empty rifle scabbard. "You know how to shoot a rifle?"

Finishing the latigo knot, Hialeaha looked over her saddle. "My father showed me how with his flintlock. Rear sight, front sight, then squeeze."

Without speaking, Fargo walked away. In a moment he returned with Wellington's lever action and slid it into the scabbard. "If we need it, I'll show you how to use it. Never go unarmed out here. Never."

Hialeaha nodded, then took the reins in her right hand and grabbed a handful of mane with her left. She put a foot in the stirrup and swung her leg up and over the back of the horse.

Fargo looked away but not in time to miss the flash of her knee and thigh. Tugging at the collar of his shirt, he went to the water barrel. He took a cup off a peg and filled it. Looking squarely into Hialeaha's eyes, he gulped the cup dry and then swiped his mouth with the back of his hand.

"Do I make you uncomfortable?"

Fargo mounted. "It's been a while," he said. "That's all."

Hialeaha's eyes flickered knowingly. "Well then, Far-go, we have two things in common."

Working his neck and hearing it pop, Fargo nudged his heels into the black, putting it into a smooth gallop.

Hialeaha waited for a moment before heeling her mare into a jarring trot. She had covered one hundred yards before she remembered to stand in the stirrups, to take the shock of the hooves with her knees. It had been decades since she had ridden, but the memories came back quickly. By the time she caught up with Fargo, she was staying in the saddle more than she was leaving it.

Fargo heard her coming and waved his hand. "Side by side. No need to eat my dust."

Hialeaha trotted forward, coming alongside the black. For several minutes they headed west in silence. As they rode, Hialeaha paid attention to the trail ahead but studied Fargo from the corner of her eye.

His head swung slowly from side to side. His eyes, never fixed, darted into every shadow, under every tangled clump of brush, and into every thicket of trees.

Those eyes were brown like hers. There were crow's feet at the corners, like the ones she was starting to get. Square jaws were covered with two days of stubble, and his mustache had hints of gray.

Like Fargo, Hialeaha began to scan the rock-strewn slopes of the canyon for anything that did not fit, for movement in the shadows or tracks in the sand. Another forgotten memory, a lesson from her father, had returned.

"Poco said," began Hialeaha, breaking the silence, "you are called Separado."

Fargo's saddle creaked as he shifted is weight. "Some call me that."

Hooves cut into the packed sand as Hialeaha chose her next words carefully.

"So, is it you do not like people?"

"Most of them I don't like. Some I do."

Fargo now looked skyward, triggering another forgotten lesson for Hialeaha. Her father had taught her that birds sometimes flared, revealing the hiding place of an enemy. This Separado would have impressed her father.

"You are darker than I, Far-go."

Hialeaha sensed it more than she saw it, but she knew Fargo smiled.

"I noticed that. It's partly the sun and partly my Portuguese grandfather. They tell me they were a dark bunch."

"You speak Spanish. I thought you might be part Mexican."

"Live here long enough, and you pick up the lingo."

"Were you born in this land?"

"No. But I was born to it. I came in sixty-two as a Confederate and ended up a 'galvanized' Yankee."

Hialeaha stared at Fargo. "A what?"

"I was in a Yankee prison camp in Yuma. They let me and some of the other boys out to fight Apaches. Called us 'galvanized' Yankees."

A long minute passed. A dry breeze worked its way up the canyon, too hot to be refreshing. Hialeaha reflected on the stories she had heard of Tats-a-das-ago, the killer of Indians. But here was that man, speaking freely with her, a Cherokee. Was Quick Killer as bad as they said? Was his hate for Indians any different than her father's hate for white men?

Again scanning the mountainsides, Hialeaha thought of the crow's feet tracing their way into her once-smooth skin. It was better to know quickly and not act like a fool. There had been so few men in her life, and now she was with a man like none she had ever known. Time was too short to harbor secrets.

"You are known by many names, Far-go."

Fargo reigned in suddenly. He peered deeply into Hialeaha's eyes. She felt her heart begin to pound. Did he know what she was about to say? Did he truly possess the medicine they said protected him? If he did have that power, there was no use trying to hide, no use lying.

"I like you, Far-go. It is said you are a killer of Indians, yet I believe you have an interest in me. Am I wrong?"

After several seconds, Fargo relaxed the grip on his reigns. The tension drained from his face. "I won't deny I have feelings for you. But there's a lot about me you don't know, things I don't want you or anybody else to know. And there are some things I'm trying to figure out about myself."

Hialeaha shook her head. "I told you I do not dwell on the past. Neither should you. It does no good."

"Maybe. Maybe not."

"Then what is it you are trying to figure out about yourself?"

Fargo took a deep breath. He was about to speak when a woman's scream pierced the air.

"Mahra!" gasped Hialeaha, wheeling her horse. "That's Mahra!"

Hialeaha's horse burst into a full run back down the road toward the wagons. Instead of following, Fargo instinctively spurred his black up the side of the canyon then skirted its edge. If they were under attack, it would be better to gain the high ground than ride into a barrel shoot.

Within seconds he saw the coach and wagon two hundred feet below him. Hearing no shots, he pulled up behind a scrub oak and searched for signs of trouble.

Wellington and Davis were kneeling several feet from the coach. Mahra, apparently writhing in pain, was between them screaming and holding her left hand. A few feet away, LaFarge was pulling up her dress and shaking it frantically. Treadway, bent at the waist, seemed to be looking her over in desperation.

Hialeaha jumped from her horse and ran to Mahra. Words were exchanged, and the screaming slowed. Smitty emerged from the coach holding up an ax. He said something, but Fargo could not make it out. Everyone's attention was focused on Mahra and LaFarge. Whatever the reason for the commotion, it was not due to an attack.

Fargo waited until the screams turned to moans before picking his way down the mountainside. By the time he reached the coach, he had forgotten what he was about to say to Hialeaha. The words, if there had been any to start with, had vanished from his thoughts.

LaFarge was straightening the folds of her dress when Fargo rode in. She glared up at him. "Where have you been? Are you deaf?"

Fargo ignored her. He looked at Smitty. "What happened?"

Holding up the ax, Smitty pointed to a greasy spot with a tail still attached. "Scorpion. Stung Miss Brooks on the arm."

"It's a little one," said Fargo. "They're worse than the big ones."

Davis hurried to the coach and returned with a bottle of Mother Bailey's. He held it to Brooks's quivering lips and gave her a dose. She grabbed his hand and made him give her another.

"It burns!" wailed Brooks. "It's like fire!"

Hialeaha examined Mahra's hand. Already red, it was beginning to swell, the once-delicate fingers starting to look like carrots.

"I need a fire and boiling water," said Hialeaha. Her voice was controlled but commanding. "Mr. Fargo, I need cactus. The beavertail cactus. Several pieces."

Spinning his horse, Fargo dashed up the road only to veer up the side of the mountain and out of sight. Wellington stood and glanced all around, his head jerking from side to side, but he did nothing.

"I'll get the water," offered Smitty. "Reed, you get the fire goin'."

Brooks began to cry. Hialeaha rubbed her forehead. She was beginning to sweat. "Get some blankets, Mr. Wellington. We'll make a pallet."

"Is she going to be all right?" asked Davis, still on his knees holding the bottle of Mother Bailey's.

"I don't know. Mr. Fargo will know. I will do what I can."

Treadway struck a match on a nearby stone. It spewed flame and sulfur into a pile of gathered twigs. He began shoving rocks around the flames and then more sticks.

After laying out the blankets, Wellington went to LaFarge. "Are you...did you find any of those beasts on you?"

Wide-eyed and pale, LaFarge swore softly. "No. I have never seen anything like it. It was like a spider with the tail of a snake!"

Eyeing Brooks lying on the makeshift bed, Wellington whispered, "Perhaps we should turn back, Clarissa."

"No!" snapped LaFarge, but quickly gathered her wits and her charm. "No. If Mahra needs care, would it not be closer to continue on to Albuquerque or even Santa Fe?"

"Yes," agreed Wellington, nodding his head and rubbing his sweaty palms on the front of his pants. "Yes, of course."

The distant sound of hooves pounding rapid fire echoed down the canyon. They grew louder by the second. Fargo came into view, leaning forward, his head just above the streaming mane of the racing gelding.

Sand flew as Fargo slid the horse to a stop and dismounted in one smooth maneuver. Speared on his Bowie knife was a row of beavertail cactus.

Without being asked, he went to the fire and began burning off the needles.

"These what you had in mind?" he asked.

"Yes." For a moment, Hialeaha took her eyes off Mahra. Smitty was coming with a pot of water. "When the spines are off, put them in the water. I'm going to make a poultice of jelly."

"Heard of it for scorpion stings," said Fargo. "Never seen it done."

Mahra's crying was getting worse.

"Mr. Davis," said Hialeaha, taking the bottle of Mother Bailey's from him, "talk to her until I return. Try to comfort her."

Davis nodded feebly. He scooted close to Brooks, speaking softly and stroking her hair.

Going quickly to the coach, Hialeaha stepped inside. A moment later, she returned with something in her hand. With the fire crackling and the water heating, Hialeaha sat down cross-legged next to Mahra and began to play a wooden flute.

The soothing notes were low and soft. Mahra immediately calmed. In seconds her crying faded into a whimper.

With the spines burned off, Fargo fingered the scorched pieces of cactus into the water. Glancing around, he saw total bewilderment stamped on everyone's faces. Except for Hialeaha, none of them had the slightest idea what needed to be done. They were city people, far from paved streets, theaters, and baseball games. Now they were on the frontier, watching Hialeaha's every move and glaring at her as if she were a total stranger.

"Cherokee flute," said Fargo, smiling at their ignorance. "And cactus juice will take away some of the burn. More than that bottle of poison she's been drinking."

Fargo stood, his eyes on LaFarge. "You're not in Chicago anymore. You're in Poco's world now."

As Hialeaha continued to play the flute, Mahra's whimpering ceased, but when her sight began to fade, she started to panic. Fargo assured her it would pass. His assurance was gentle, even tender. It shocked everyone.

Hialeaha applied the poultice, changing it every half hour. By nightfall, the burning was minimal, but it took another large dose of Mother Bailey's to put Brooks to sleep. They thoroughly inspected the coach and moved her back inside. It was unthinkable to leave her on the ground.

No tables were set up for supper, only chairs around the campfire. Coffee was put on, and, for the first time, they ate straight out of the cans, just fish and peaches. No one had much of an appetite.

They sat in a circle facing the amber flames. Behind them it was inky black, the kind of darkness that comes deep in the jaws of a canyon. They sipped their coffee, each keeping his or her own thoughts.

Finally, Davis spoke. "Hialeaha, how did you know about the cactus? There is none where you live."

"Relatives," answered Hialeaha. "Some were…relocated…to the west. They told me."

"And the flute?" asked Wellington.

"It was my father's. It is a courting flute…for love songs. He made it for my mother. I have played it for Mahra all her life, since the day she was born."

"Your playin' was awful purty," said Smitty. "Bet you love her like she was your own."

"I do."

LaFarge thoughtfully took a sip of coffee. Her eyes narrowed as she eased the cup down in her lap. "Then what do you think of Mr. Fargo?"

Warily, Hialeaha raised her eyes. "What do you mean?"

"When you heard Mahra this afternoon, you came running. Your friend took his sweet time getting here. If there had been real trouble, we could have all been dead by the time he arrived. And you did notice he rode into the hills rather than coming directly to our aid?"

"You know," said Smitty in a gruff whisper, "he can porb'ly hear you?"

LaFarge huffed. "And what if he can?"

Hialeaha sat up straight, her eyes roaming beyond the flames into the night. Yes, Fargo was near. He would hear all that was said.

"I was born before the Cherokee were conquered. I was a child when my father was a warrior. He was a brave man, but he would have done the same as Mr. Fargo. The white generals call it a tactic."

Wellington looked up. Even Treadway perked his ears.

"Why do you say that?" asked Wellington.

"If enemies had attacked us, they would have done so from above. Mr. Fargo would have come in behind them. When there is trouble, a cunning warrior does not ride directly toward it. That is how traps are laid and sprung…on the foolish."

"Your defense of our intrepid guide is most generous," said LaFarge.

"It might just be," suggested Smitty. "Fargo was lookin' out for his own skin. I say he could just as well been hightailin' it lickety-cut. That's one way to stay alive in a mix-up.

"And another thing I been askin' myself all day is, what was a man like him doin' in Chicago? So I finally says to myself, maybe he's a man that's lost his nerve, that took off back east where it was safe.

"So far, I ain't seen nothin' to prove otherwise."

His eyes shrinking into cunning slits, Smitty surveyed the faces gathered around the dancing flames. "Course, it's just my opinion."

"You have a point," mused Wellington. "What would a supposed *separado* be doing in a crowded city?"

"I had not thought of that," said Davis. "It does seem to be a contradiction."

Separado

"All we have seen of his bravado thus far," said LaFarge, "is his taking a shot at poor Reed. And even that brave deed occurred when Reed was unarmed and defenseless."

Smiling paternally, LaFarge leaned forward looking at Treadway. "What do you think, Reed? We never hear from you."

Treadway was resting his elbows on his knees, twirling a coffee cup between his thick fingers. "I wonder what he would be like if he didn't have a gun."

Hialeaha had not taken her attention off LaFarge. She had always wondered what Wellington saw in the woman, but after Treadway spoke, she was puzzled by something else.

Even in the soft light and shadows, Hialeaha saw an exchange of glances, knowing glances, between LaFarge and Treadway. In that instant, they shared a common thought. Whatever had passed between them was not good.

"Mahra does not belong out here," said Hialeaha. "She is not well."

Arching her eyebrows, LaFarge sat back in her chair. She gracefully waved a hand, palm up. "The four of us are but travelers. None of us *belong* here. However, I see you have adapted quite... naturally."

A smirk twisted Wellington's lips. Davis pensively shifted his weight, causing his chair to squeak.

LaFarge meant to be degrading, but Hialeaha suddenly realized the woman's jibe was actually an astute observation. "Yes, Miss LaFarge, I have. But you all should go back."

"My, my!" mocked LaFarge. "The hired help is chatty this evening."
This time Hialeaha bristled.

Davis spoke quickly. "We will reach the Rio Grande tomorrow. I for one am looking forward to a swim."

"Plenty of water for that," said Smitty. "There's plenty of cool shade in them cottonwoods along the bank." The teamster paused. "Or so I been told."

Not finished with Hialeaha, LaFarge turned to Wellington. "Dear, when we are wed, promise me you will hire servants who know their place."

Patting the top of LaFarge's hand, Wellington said, "Certainly, my love. I will make it a priority."

Smitty smiled and took a sip of coffee. He had hoped the scorpion would sting Wellington or LaFarge, but this was even better. The Cherokee was starting to stand up for herself. That would make her a bitter enemy of LaFarge. Squaws were born fighters. If this one got the chance, she would tear LaFarge to ribbons.

Chapter 10

The wagons made repeated stops to allow Mahra to vomit. Her arms and legs twitched so badly it took both Davis and Wellington to get her in and out of the coach. It was noon before they rolled out of the shadowy canyon back into the blistering desert. Before them lay a sloping plain of red sand, scattered as far as the eye could see with blue-green sage.

A half mile beyond the mouth of the canyon, Fargo wiped the sweat from his hatband and waited for the others to catch up.

"I don't see any river," growled Treadway, bringing the stage to a stop. "All I see is a road any blind man could follow!"

Wellington stuck his head out the window. Shading his eyes, he scanned the western horizon. "I see absolutely nothing. How can there be a river anywhere out there? I would at least see cottonwood trees. Even twenty miles away, I would see them!"

Fargo replaced his hat. "Who said there were cottonwoods?"

"Smitty."

Fargo dropped his reins over his saddle horn. He glanced back at Smitty. "They're there. Ten miles out."

"If they were that close," snapped Treadway, "we'd see trees."

Taking the cork from his canteen, Fargo thoughtfully took a drink. Smitty, a man who claimed to have never been to the Rio Grande, said they would see cottonwoods. And in the sweltering heat, Treadway was starting to speak more like a man than a half-wit.

"The river runs along low ground," said Fargo. "In the desert, rivers and sometimes even canyons can't be seen until you're right on them. The cottonwoods grow along the Rio Grande for miles. Its banks stretch a half mile across. But from here, you'd swear there was nothing but desert out there. Nothing but desert and that mountain range on the skyline."

"It is hard to believe," said Wellington. "A river like that...out there."

Fargo shrugged. "It's a river. Up north, it's clear water. Where we're headed, it's cloudy red."

"Just so it's wet," grumbled Wellington, ducking back inside the coach. "And the quicker we get there, the better."

Fargo wheeled his horse and started off in an easy trot. Over packed sand and down a gradual grade, it took him only two hours to cover the ten miles. It was only in the last mile that the trees came into view.

Fargo stopped at the edge of the cottonwoods, already feeling the cooler air of the river bottom. In front of him, the road cut down an embankment and then passed under thousands of trees. The thick canopy of leaves shaded miles of tangled willow brush, piles of driftwood, and clumps of green grass.

A twig snapped in the river bottom. Fargo's hand went to his Colt but stopped. Two Mexican boys trudged out of the brush, each with a load of sticks strapped to his back.

Fargo spoke with them briefly as they came up out of the trees.

They were from the village of Peralta. The older of the two told Fargo where there was a good place to camp and not far from it, a place deep enough to swim. But the river was lower than usual, he said, no more than to their knees. He also said that west of the river, there was almost no water. The rains had not come. Witchcraft was the reason, but they had not yet discovered the identity of the witch. They said even the Zuni River might be dry.

When the wagons caught up, Fargo led them down the bank and into the trees for two hundred yards. He then veered left, as the boys had advised. He drew up in a sandy clearing bordered on the west by the flowing red water of the Rio Grande.

Fargo leaned on his saddle horn, watching everyone step down. He studied every face, seeing in them the same wonder and disbelief he had felt the first time he saw the cottonwood forest and its desert river. He saw it on every face but Smitty's.

Supported by Davis, Mahra was able to walk, but she was still under the influence of scorpion venom and Mother Bailey's syrup.

Davis gazed up at the green leaves rustling in a gentle breeze. "It defies logic," he said exuberantly. "It must be ten degrees cooler in here."

Fargo shoved his hat off his forehead and pointed to the south. "There's a hole downriver deep enough to swim in."

Wellington slowly turned in a complete circle, taking in the contradiction of being in a desert one moment and a forest the next. "Unbelievable. Simply unbelievable."

The collar of LaFarge's dress was unbuttoned down past her throat. She dragged her fingers down her chin onto her dust-covered neck. "And we can finally bathe!"

Wobbling in Davis's arms, Brooks giggled. "Is this an oasis? Are we in Egypt again?"

"No, dear," answered Davis, taking a firmer grip around her waist. "You need to lie down and rest."

Arching his back and stretching his arms, Wellington said, "Wonderful! Invigorating! Who is up for a hunt? I saw a buck deer coming in. We could use some fresh meat for a change."

Davis shook his head. "I will stay with Mahra. Perhaps tomorrow."

"Well then," said Wellington. "Reed and Smitty can set up camp. The women can make their toilet before dark. We have two hours before sundown. I shall try to return with venison for our evening repast."

As Wellington went for his rifle, Fargo started to leave. LaFarge stepped in front of his horse.

"Before you go, Mr. Fargo, would you please locate the swimming pool you spoke of? I am certain we would all be more at ease, knowing more precisely its location."

Fargo nodded and then disappeared down river. Wellington came out of the coach with his Winchester and went to LaFarge. Sliding three .45-75 cartridges into the loading gate, he levered one into the chamber. He winked at LaFarge.

"That should get the job done," said Wellington.

With Mahra being looked after, Hialeaha started gathering driftwood from the base of a massive cottonwood. Smitty began unloading the supply wagon. LaFarge walked to the edge of the river, followed by Treadway.

"When you hear me scream," she whispered.

Treadway rolled his neck to loosen it. "I'm going to enjoy this."

LaFarge continued. "Smitty says he knows the way from here. If not, we can find a wretched Mexican who does.

"Miles thinks you're only going to teach him a lesson, put him in his place. So make it look accidental, like you didn't know your own strength."

Treadway smiled.

Hialeaha turned with an armload of firewood just in time to see Treadway grin and LaFarge step away from him. She thoughtfully shook her head. There was something between them. There always had been.

Hialeaha was going for more wood when Fargo rode back to camp. He went to LaFarge, showing his knife before sheathing it. "I marked the trail coming and going. It's about seventy yards." Gathering his reins, he said. "You can't miss it."

LaFarge held up her hand. "As you may recall, I cannot swim. And there might be Mexicans about. I want you to stand guard nearby, with your back turned, of course."

Fargo frowned. "Sounds more like a job for Treadway or Davis."

"Poor Reed never learned to swim. And Edward will not leave Mahra's side."

Staring in the direction Wellington had gone, Fargo saw no movement. "Suit yourself. Get your things. Follow the trail. I'll be there… with my back turned…of course."

Following the trail he had just marked, Fargo passed close to Hialeaha and paused. She watched LaFarge step inside the coach before speaking. When Hialeaha spoke, it was softly. "She is a snake. Careful you are not bitten."

"No chance," said Fargo, nudging the gelding back down the trail. "Not by the likes of her, anyway."

Coming to the pool, Fargo wrapped his reins around a sapling and took a seat behind a cottonwood, his back to the river. Five minutes later, twigs snapped, and then heels dug into sand.

"I assume you are present, Mr. Fargo."

"I'm here."

"Good. I feel much more at ease."

A few more branches snapped. It became quiet. Cloth rustled, and then leaves. Clothes were being hung on limbs. Fargo felt a wave of heat but kept his mind occupied. He wanted no part of that kind of woman.

Water rippled. Feet waded.

"It is warm. Is it always so dirty?"

"You mean the water?"

LaFarge chuckled pleasantly. "What else would I mean?"

"Yeah. It's always like that."

"And Mexicans drink this?"

"You get used to it."

"I hardly think so."

Fargo sighed. What did she think she would be drinking west of the Rio Grande? This was the water that would fill their barrels.

"I am sitting now, up to my neck. It is heavenly. I am sorry I doubted you, Mr. Fargo. It has been a difficult journey. I fear, on occasion, I have been...well...rude to you. It has been the hardship. I am not accustomed to it. Can you find it in your heart to forgive me?"

His eyes narrowing, Fargo turned his head. Had he heard correctly? He considered himself a good judge of character. His life often depended on it. But there were a few times his judgment had been wrong. Was Clarissa LaFarge apologizing?

"Please, Mr. Fargo. It would mean so much to me."

"Well, I..." the words caught in his throat. He could not refuse to accept her apology. At least, if she was serious, he could not. With LaFarge the actress, it was difficult to tell.

A scream shattered his thoughts, then a frantic cry.

"Help! Mr. Fargo, please!"

Instantly Fargo was on his feet. He palmed the walnut grips of his Colt. His thumb arced across the hammer. Looking left, then right, he saw nothing.

He heard a gurgle, splashing, then another scream, this one choking.

Crouched, he spun around the cottonwood, thumbing back the hammer. Instead of bandits, Indians, or even a snake, he saw no one—not even LaFarge.

Holstering his pistol, he unbuckled his gun belt, dropping it as he ran for the river. When he was chest deep in the water, he started to swim. LaFarge surfaced and then went under, leaving one frantic hand swinging above the water. Fargo's fingers locked around the wrist and jerked upward, bringing her head up. She gasped, clawing at him like a wild animal.

Fargo dodged, spun her around, and cradled her neck in the bend of his elbow. When he started swimming for the bank, she went limp. Feeling the sandy river bottom, Fargo gained his footing. With his back to the trees, he dragged LaFarge out of the water, her wet camisole and bloomers caking with sand.

Fargo leaned her back and knelt next to her, catching his breath. LaFarge coughed and took a few breaths. Her eyes opened. She smiled.

"How was I?" she asked.

Fargo blinked.

"Convincing as always," said a voice from behind them. It was Treadway.

Refusing to give them the satisfaction, Fargo suppressed his impulse to swear. He stood slowly, knowing he had been made a fool. And knowing what was coming next, his mind raced.

Treadway was a brawler and a wrestler. He had power and strength but likely was not conditioned to the heat or high altitude. His wind would be his weakness, and his overconfidence could be used against him. Fargo knew he would have to stay on his feet and out of Treadway's grip. He would take his best blows and be patient.

In his younger days, he had made a living fighting in the ring up and down the Mississippi. He fought big men then, too. He was older now, but the strategy was the same. Defend, then defend some more. When his opponent's punches began to weaken, when he started sucking wind…attack.

Turning slowly, Fargo saw not only Treadway but Wellington and Smitty. Wellington was grinning, casually holding his Winchester in one hand and a woman's robe in the other. Treadway held Fargo's gun belt. Both pistols were holstered and the knife sheathed.

Treadway held out the belt. "Looking for these, Fargo?"

LaFarge came to her feet. Wringing the water from her hair, she sauntered back to Wellington and put on the robe.

Wagging her finger at Fargo, she said, "I would say Reed is within ten feet of you now, Mr. Fargo."

Tossing the gun belt back toward Wellington, Treadway held his arms wide apart. "You going to kill me now, Fargo?"

Smitty nodded at Wellington. "That's what he said, Mr. Wellington. Said he'd kill Reed if he come within ten feet of him."

"My, my, Mr. Fargo," taunted Wellington, "you might regret saying that. And you might recall your general rudeness and insubordination while you are at it."

Fargo took a small step sideways, edging his way to higher ground. He took another step, but his boot rolled on a stone. He stumbled, and Treadway charged.

Off balance already, Fargo dropped and dove into Treadway's legs, tripping him.

Fargo was up first with his guard ready. Treadway rolled, catlike, and sprang back on his feet. His fists came up. He closed the distance between them, his boots grinding deep into the sand.

A roundhouse right came first, followed by a powerful left. Fargo blocked both but barely kept his balance. A right hook grazed his ribcage. He countered with a light jab into Treadway's nose and then retreated, circling to stay clear of the entangling brush.

Treadway swung another right. Fargo ducked, then blocked a clumsy hook and jab. Now it was clear that Fargo could move and block punches. A kick came next, Treadway trying to take out Fargo's left knee.

After the ring, Fargo had spent his share of years in Arizona bars. He was no stranger to no-holds-barred fighting. He raised his left leg. Bending it sharply at the knee, he absorbed the blow. Treadway's kick was no more than a nuisance.

A sudden flurry of fists pummeled Fargo as he covered his head. His forearms and the sides of his head were taking a beating, but his face and jaw were buried deep in his guard. To the unschooled, he appeared to be in serious trouble.

Somehow, he heard LaFarge. "Not so high and mighty now, are you, Fargo?"

Three minutes, he thought. If he could last three minutes, Treadway would be his. But if the brawler wised up and slowed his punches or backed off for a rest, all bets were off.

Fargo swung, deliberately missing, deliberately feeble. Again blocking the blows, he staggered backward but kept his balance. Still circling, his ears were burning and starting to ring. He could feel bruises on his cheekbones, but he was not hurt. And Treadway was breathing hard—sooner than expected.

In a surprising move, Treadway caught Fargo with an uppercut to the gut that folded him in two. A fist to the top of the head sent him to his knees.

"Finish him!" screamed LaFarge.

Scooping a handful of sand, Fargo blasted Treadway's face. The big man quickly cleared his eyes, but not fast enough. Fargo was back on his feet and with air in his lungs.

Again LaFarge screamed, but this time it was more of a command: "Finish him, Reed! Do it!"

Fargo straightened, now breathing easily. Treadway's chest was heaving. He looked into Fargo's eyes then lunged for his throat.

Swatting away the clutching arms, Fargo sidestepped, spun, and buried a fist into Treadway's ribs. The blond grunted and stumbled. He turned and caught a calloused row of knuckles in the point of his chin. He staggered backward, with Fargo closing in like a snake on a rat.

Fargo's blood was white hot. A fist thudded deep into Treadway's belly. Making a half fist, he drove his middle knuckles straight into Treadway's Adam's apple.

Treadway's hands grasped his throat. He tried to breathe but could only wheeze and cough. Fargo stepped closer. The open jaw was his target. Driving all his weight with his back leg, he landed a crushing right cross.

Eyes glazed over and rolled to the top of their sockets. Treadway collapsed and rolled onto his back.

Fargo's face was lobster red, his eyes cauldrons of fury. He took two steps toward the river and pulled a melon-sized rock from the riverbank. Raising it to his chest, he walked to the fallen man. Standing over Treadway's head, he raised the rock high.

"No, Conway!" screamed Hialeaha, almost out of breath.

Fargo jerked his head up, glaring at her. He let out a savage growl, turned slightly, and slammed the stone down on Treadway's right hand. Bones snapped.

His blood still boiling, Fargo went for Wellington.

Wellington took an involuntary step back, trying to control the fear that showed on his face.

Fargo stopped, picked up his gun belt, and buckled it on.

"Your employment is terminated," managed Wellington, glancing uneasily at his Winchester. "We no longer require your services."

"I should have known," said Hialeaha, catching her breath but standing clear of the two men.

"Me, too," grunted Fargo, as he checked each cylinder of his pistols. "I go where Mahra Brooks goes. And Hialeaha. The rest of you can be damned. Get in my way and I'll send you all straight to hell."

"How dare you speak to me…" bellowed Wellington, but a blur of movement put a pistol barrel ten inches from his chest.

Fargo jerked the Winchester out of Wellington's hand and turned to Smitty. Pointing with the pistol barrel, he said, "Treadway has a pistol in his pocket. Get it. Empty it and hand it over easy."

Smitty found the pistol, a short-barreled Smith and Wesson. He opened the top and dumped the cartridges. "I had nothin' to do with this." He snapped the pistol closed and held it out by the barrel, grips first. "I come along just to see the show, that's all."

Fargo shoved the pistol in his belt. "I'm taking both the Winchesters for payment. Whether you turn back or go ahead, don't get within rifle range of me during the day. If I come into camp, I want all your weapons in a pile where I can see them. That includes those two shotguns you have. I know what you brought, and they all better be there."

Wellington's nostrils blanched with indignation. "And if we do not do as you say?"

Fargo holstered his Colt. "Then you'll have hell to pay."

Gathering the reins of his horse, Fargo swung into the saddle. "My advice to you is to go back where you came from...as fast as you can."

"We will do no such thing," LaFarge sneered. Her hair now clung to her skull in a knotted mass. "You are nothing but a scoundrel."

Fargo spurred his gelding. "Count on it."

***

After splinting Treadway's shattered hand, Hialeaha observed the others as she prepared the evening meal. Brooks had gone to bed early. Wellington, Davis, and LaFarge were gathered around the dinner table studying something by lantern light. Treadway was off by himself, quiet and sullen. Only Smitty seemed unmoved by the turn of events.

Absent-mindedly, Hialeaha lifted the coffee grinder, slowly turning the handle. She looked at the coach, thinking of the many nights she had put Mahra to bed, tucked her in, and told her a story. She was a grown woman now, but in so many ways still a child. When she married, Mahra would be a wife, no longer needing an Indian nanny. But that inevitable day had not yet come. And she was in more danger than any of them realized. Like Fargo said, they all should go back to Chicago.

Hialeaha stopped grinding for a moment and then started again. Selfishness was an ugly trait, yet in the shadows of her soul, it was gnawing away at her best intentions. She loved Mahra more than her own life, a life she had all but given up. Now, however, she felt the coming of spring in her heart, like the blossoming of a long-forgotten rose. While there was still time, she wanted to be the woman of a good man.

Smitty came toward the cookstove smiling, his grin showing black gaps where teeth used to be. "That old man sure is hell on wheels, ain't he?"

Hialeaha set the grinder down and picked up a wooden spoon. She stirred a skillet of canned beef while adding a pinch of red pepper from Poco's *rastra*. "He is not old."

"Figure of speech," said Smitty, leaning over the stove and taking a sniff. "Just a figure of speech.

"Guess you're the only one of us he'll trust now…with Miss Brooks bein' the way she is and all."

Hialeaha stopped stirring. "What about Miss Brooks?"

"Thought you knew," said Smitty, feigning concern. "That Mother Bailey's is got hold of her. It's nothin' but laudanum, a hook with a mighty big barb. Hard to get off it once you're on."

"You have seen this before?"

"Enough times to know it when I see it. She's hooked."

Hialeaha went back to cooking. "I will speak to her."

Smitty scratched at his ribs. "You think Treadway was tryin' to kill Fargo?"

With no answer from Hialeaha, Smitty continued. "I'm thinking," he said, looking over his shoulder and seeing Treadway in the distant shadows, "that's just what he had in mind."

Hialeaha looked up but kept stirring. "Why do you think that?"

"On account of what happened between the two of 'em at that saloon back in Dodge. And because I think Treadway would'a killed that fella in Lamy if Fargo hadn't stopped him. I seen it in his eyes."

Smitty's eyes followed the spoon as it scraped the edges of the skillet. Steam rose, grease popped and sizzled. It was time to stir his own pot.

The Indian was developing a friendship with Fargo. The actress had made a fool of him and might have gotten him seriously injured, if not killed. Hialeaha could be of use now. If the situation arose, she would side against Clarissa LaFarge.

"Did you see how Miss LaFarge was fawnin' over that big Swede today? Mighty peculiar, him and her, I'd say."

Leaning toward Hialeaha, Smitty spoke in a near whisper. "You must'a noticed it your own self. A fool could see there's more between them two than meets the eye."

"I would not know anything about that," said Hialeaha.

Under his scraggly mustache, a smile thinned Smitty's lips. The Cherokee was a good woman but a bad liar.

"Think we'll turn back?" Smitty asked.

"We should. But we will not."

"Why's that?"

"Pride. No one tells Miles Wellington what to do. He will press on to save face. I do not think even Miss LaFarge could change his mind now."

Smitty raised an eyebrow. The Indian was right. Greed was a powerful motivator, but pride was even better. Davis and Brooks might turn back, but LaFarge and Wellington were sure to go on. And it was another hundred miles to Zuni, enough time to figure out how to handle Fargo.

"What do you calculate Fargo is gonna do now?"

Hialeaha thought for a moment. "He knows the people along the river. Likely, he will get supplies from one of the villages, enough for a few days, maybe longer. He will ride ahead or behind us, always out of pistol range. We may only see his tracks, and those we see will be left so we might follow."

"Makes sense. What I don't get, though, is why he went on today about Miss Brooks. Him talking about stickin' with you, I could understand. But he don't even talk to her."

"She is the only reason he agreed to come with us."

His eyes narrowing with anticipation, Smitty asked, "Why's that?"

"Something happened long ago. I do not know what it was, but it made him what he is today. All I know is that he wants no harm to come to Mahra."

"Well, none of us wants that."

"It is different with him," said Hialeaha, picking up the skillet. She started toward the dinner table. "Very, very different."

Watching Hialeaha serve the beef, Smitty stroked his mustache with satisfaction. "Well, well," he muttered. "Mr. Fargo has a soft spot."

Wellington placed a napkin in his lap and waved Smitty to the table. "Need somethin', Mr. Wellington?"

"Are there any law officers in this godforsaken country? Fargo stole Edward's rifle as well as mine."

Squinting one eye in concentration, Smitty chewed the inside of his lip for several seconds. "Could be some law in Albuquerque. But you'd be out'a their jurisdiction, if there was. Best bet to find a marshal of any kind would be Santa Fe."

"Where is Santa Fe?"

"Two days north."

Wellington swore softly. He forked in some fried beef and chili pepper. He glanced at Hialeaha but did not compliment her on the new seasoning.

"You seem to know this country well enough. Do you think you could get us to Zuni?"

As if pondering the question, Smitty inhaled deeply. Treadway was all but useless. Fargo was an outcast. Thanks to the drought, there was almost no water west of the Rio Grande, and though they didn't know it, they were rapidly running out of food. Best of all, he had their trust.

"Well I never been there before, but I listen good. So when Fargo come in to switch his horses off, we talked a bunch.

"He said there was a road across the river that goes west to a river called the Rio Puerco, about twelve to fifteen miles from here. From there the road crosses the river and heads northwest to a village called Mesita. It's on another river, the San Jose, as I recollect. From here, that place is 'bout thirty miles. We could make that in a good day.

"From Mesita, we head up river a ways then climb into pine trees. Fargo said there's a nice camp at a place called Agua Fria. Means cold water. Not far from there, he claims...well, I can't say as I hardly believe what he said."

"What?" LaFarge asked.

Smitty shook his head. "He claimed there was a cave up there with ice in it all year, never melted even though the cave's not deep at all. Says the ice is kinda blue."

"Ice?" questioned Davis. "Out here?"

LaFarge looked out into the darkness. "Cold water…ice? It sounds good, even if it is half true."

"And from there?" prompted Wellington.

"Well, from the cave, it's just a long day to a rock called El Moro. There's supposed to be big, clear pool at the bottom of the rock, seventy foot across and ten foot or so deep.

"The next day, you hit Zuni."

Wellington glanced at LaFarge, and then his eyes held on Davis. "Sounds simple enough."

"It sounds like the worst is over, Edward," said LaFarge. "And Mahra will be well rested by tomorrow. After bathing here, she will also be refreshed. The next river is only one day's ride. It seems likely we can bathe each day now."

Wellington suddenly sat erect. "What do you say, Cousin? We have never balked in the face of adventure. Remember why we came. Relish the pure challenge of it all.

"Come on, man. Through thick and thin, we have always stuck together."

Davis sat back in his chair, a smile slowly spreading across his sunburned cheeks. "Quite right," he said, then swatted his palm down on the tablecloth. "Indeed," he bellowed, ceremoniously raising his glass of red wine. "To the challenge."

Wellington and LaFarge joined the toast.

"Westward," said LaFarge.

"Westward," repeated Wellington.

Smitty watched them, mindful to hide his contempt. They had taken the bait. In time, he would be the one drinking their wine. In time, he would see them crawl.

"Guess that means we're goin' on?"

After dabbing the corners of his mouth with a spotless white napkin, Wellington answered, "Most assuredly. And I am doubling your pay...as of tomorrow."

"Much obliged," said Smitty. "Much obliged."

***

With everyone but Smitty bathed and the water barrels full of silty Rio Grande water, the wagons rolled across the shallow river at midmorning. A half hour later, they found the road to Mesita and rolled out of the shaded cottonwood grove up a desolate grade of sand and scattered sage. Within seconds, they were driving into a hot north wind that had been blowing just above the treetops.

Inside the coach, Hialeaha sat opposite Brooks. She studied the delicate features of her face and saw the color had returned. Mahra said the scorpion sting was still painful. She explained that was why she needed Mother Bailey's medicine more often than she did for her occasional headaches. But she also thought the sting had made her headaches worse.

With hooves plodding rhythmically and trace chains rattling, the coach rocked and swayed in the stifling heat. For miles, Wellington and Davis reminisced about Egypt and Africa. LaFarge fanned herself when she wasn't napping. Wearing a constant, lazy smile and with eyes half open, Mahra listened to the men's stories.

Hialeaha spent most of her time gazing out the window at the monotonous mosaic of sage and sand. Now, however, she leaned forward and focused on the increasing number of small mounds piled underneath limbs of the sage. Soon she could see the mounds were burrows made by what appeared to be squirrels. Everywhere she looked, they stood on their hind legs, watching the wagons pass. Near several mounds, and only inches from the squirrels, small owls also stood watching.

Hialeaha's brow wrinkled. As far as she knew, owls and squirrels were natural enemies. However, here they apparently lived side by side. It was an impossible harmony yet one not to be denied.

Thoughtfully, Hialeaha leaned back. If the owl and squirrel could stand side by side, why not the white man and Indian? Could not someday, even a man like Tats-a-das-ago choose to be with a Cherokee woman?

Hialeaha was starting to smile when something beyond the burrows caught her attention and broke into her thoughts.

A dark cloud was forming on the northern horizon. It was not a rain cloud. She had never seen anything like it.

"Mr. Wellington," she said, pointing out the window, "look at that."

Wellington stopped talking and leaned forward. "At what?" he asked. Following Hialeaha's finger, he swore. "Sandstorm!"

The coach stopped abruptly. LaFarge looked north. "Is it coming this way?"

Treadway jerked the door open with his good hand. Smitty stood next to him. "Smitty says we got trouble."

"We have to stop," Smitty said, holding the brim of his hat down against an increasing wind. "A sandstorm's coming fast. We best get ready to sit it out."

"How?" asked Wellington.

"We'll turn the wagons and face 'em downwind with the horses hitched. That'll help keep some of the sand out of your coach. Get them shades tied down, and get somethin' to put over your face to breathe through. And cover your eyes."

LaFarge scooted over, making room next to her. "Reed, you will come inside. We have no room for you, Smitty."

Smitty shrugged. "I need to tend to the stock, anyhow. I'll make a tent out of blankets under my wagon."

Hialeaha took one last look out her window before pulling down the canvas shade. "Did you see any sign of Mr. Fargo?"

Blinking against the whipping wind, Smitty raised his voice. "Saw him behind us a while back, but nothin' lately."

Treadway slammed the door shut. He climbed to his seat on top and turned the coach. A moment later the door opened again, and Treadway stepped inside, taking a seat next to LaFarge.

Hialeaha stole a glance at Wellington. If he was at all disturbed, he hid it well.

In minutes, the wall of sand hit them. The teams jerked. Smitty's swearing was muffled by the rising wind and sand pelting against the coach's varnished wooden hull. The horses settled, took a few more steps, and then stopped. Then the full force of the storm hit, roaring, twisting, howling. With the wind came choking clouds of dust, blasting sand, and hours upon hours of grit.

***

Light was fading when knuckles banged on the coach door. Wellington opened his eyes to slits, then closed them. He brushed a layer of dust from his eyelashes with his fingertips and opened his eyes again. Pulling a silk neckerchief from his nose and mouth, he opened the door a crack.

Smitty peered inside. Only his bloodshot eyes looked human. "Worst of it's over, folks. You can get out and stretch if you've a mind to. Maybe clean up 'fore dark."

The others began lifting their heads and uncovering their faces. Mahra's teeth suddenly glistened behind a mask of dust. She began to laugh. "You should see yourselves!"

In a cloud of dust, Wellington shook his head and surveyed the interior of the coach. Everyone and everything was covered in a cream-colored powder. Rolling his neck, he forced a smile. "Mahra, you *are* a cheery one."

Wellington threw the door open and stepped out. Sand streamed from his clothes as if through an hour glass. He began to laugh.

Davis exited next. He slapped Wellington on the shoulder, sending up another cloud of fine dust. As he laughed and held out his arms, sheets of sand poured off his sleeves.

LaFarge was next to exit, but she only managed a smile. Neither Treadway nor Hialeaha showed any emotion.

Everyone began pounding and shaking the desert from their clothes and hair. As they did so, Hialeaha scanned the windswept desert. There was no sign of Fargo. In fact, there was no sign of anything else.

"The road," she said.

Only Treadway heard her. He looked up, then over both shoulders. "It's gone," he blurted. "The road is gone!"

The others suddenly took notice. In unison they searched the skyline for the setting sun, now a faint silhouette floating above a dingy orange horizon.

"We know west," declared Davis. He turned to Smitty, his voice quivering. "We just go west. Right, Smitty?"

Smitty starred at the sun. West was a vague direction in a vast desert with little water.

"I wasn't countin' on this. All I knowed was to follow the road."

Wellington resumed dusting the front of his shirt. "The next river can be only two or three miles west of here. If we do not find it in that distance, we shall simply return to the Rio Grande. We have nothing to worry about."

"Of course," agreed Davis, his panic subsiding.

"In the morning," continued Wellington, "the air will be clear. We can decide then what to do. Now we should merely change into clean clothes."

Swatting his pants with his hat, Smitty said, "I'll water the stock. They'll need extry after all this. And tomorrow they'll be pulling over blown sand, not hard packed. It'll be lots harder on 'em, no matter which way we take out."

Glancing at the setting sun, Hialeaha said, "I will get a fire started."

She recalled Fargo saying flames could be seen for fifty miles in the desert. If he had been lost in the storm, he would need water. He might see the fire. If he did, he likely would not come near camp until late. The fire would have to last well into the night.

Seeing a distant juniper stump, Hialeaha started for it. After dragging it into camp, she went back to gather more branches. When she returned, the tent was up, and the table was covered with a linen cloth. A lantern burned inside the tent and another on the table.

The women had changed their clothes and even used the Rio Grande water to wash their face and hands. They sat at the table sipping white wine and swearing to each other they might bathe in river water, but would never succumb to drinking it.

Davis emerged from the tent wearing a starched white shirt and striped pants. "I would drink the water…if it were cut with a fine whiskey."

LaFarge winced. "Perhaps, Edward, but only then."

"I will drink it!" Wellington announced, tossing back the tent flap. He approached the table holding a shot glass. He swirled its contents close to the lantern, revealing the murky red tint of the Rio Grande.

"You would not!" protested LaFarge.

"Bottoms up," scoffed Wellington. He tossed his head back and downed the water. He winced, as if having swallowed a shot of whiskey, and then smiled.

Brooks's mouth dropped open. "My gracious."

Davis rolled his eyes. "Miles, you beat everything. Always the daredevil."

Mahra wrinkled her nose. "How is it?"

"It is a bit gritty. However, my good friends, after eating sand all afternoon, it tastes like springwater."

"Disgusting," groaned LaFarge. "Miles, you are behaving like a savage."

Hialeaha stopped loading kindling into the stove. Her dislike of LaFarge turned into a simmering hatred on the banks on the Rio Grande. The woman was pure evil. She needed to have her hair jerked out and her face ground into the dirt.

Standing erect, Hialeaha took a deep breath. She turned her back on the table, searching the sky. The evening star glowed brightly. A faint breeze moved over the desert, brushing the hair back from her face.

If LaFarge thought the water from the Rio Grande was unfit to drink, she was in for a surprise. The canteens that held the last of the good water would be empty by morning. Did the others think the water in the Rio Puerco would be different from the Rio Grande? If the water was the same, would they then turn back?

Smitty came out of the darkness. His skin and hair were still caked with dust. "Them horses drank up a whole barrel. Good thing they got a bellyful of grass yesterday."

"Did Mr. Fargo give you any details about the Rio Puerco?" asked Hialeaha.

Sticking his finger in his ear, Smitty dug out some sand and flicked it away. "Like I told Wellington, he just told me the names of the rivers and about how far they was."

"So, without the road, we are lost?"

"No. We just don't know 'xactly where we are or the 'xact way to the river. But we ain't lost."

"Still, we are alone."

"That we be," agreed Smitty. "Unless Fargo's still around. Could be that duster sent him packin'. I'd of gone to Albuquerque to one of them nice cantinas, if I was him."

Hialeaha felt certain Fargo was nearby but kept her thoughts to herself. The less anyone knew about him the better, and Smitty had a penchant for talking too much.

After sending Smitty for cans of beef, Hialeaha prepared it as usual but spooned an extra portion into a tin pail. Covering it with a lid, she set it aside and then served the food. When supper was finished, Hialeaha sat on a blanket next to the campfire. To save water, she scrubbed the plates and skillets with sand. After she deemed each one clean enough, she buffed it with a towel. Working slowly, she pretended to clean long after everyone was asleep.

Finally, hearing Smitty begin to snore, Hialeaha crept to his wagon. Silently, she filled a bucket from the full water barrel. Taking the pail and bucket, she tested the breeze.

To avoid being detected by the horses, Fargo would approach downwind. Going that direction, Hialeaha walked fifty yards out and set the food and water in a clear patch of sand. She waited five minutes before returning to the fire.

By sliding the juniper trunk into the flames inch by inch, she kept the fire burning for hours. Just before sunrise, she returned to the spot where she had left the bucket and pail. Both were empty. Around them, she saw no boot tracks, only smooth depressions left by moccasins.

She quietly replaced the bucket and went back to the campfire. She lay down next to it and closed her eyes. In what seemed like seconds, a voice cut the air.

"You fall asleep out here?"

It was Treadway, and the sun was rising.

"I must have been tired," said Hialeaha. She stood, blinking sleep from her eyes. "I'll start breakfast."

Treadway grunted and walked out past the wagons.

Wanting a clean skillet, Hialeaha went to the supply wagon. Smitty was still asleep under the rear axle. She looked over the sideboards into the bed and reached for the tarp.

"What do you think you're doing?" barked Smitty, scrambling from under the wagon and onto his feet.

Hialeaha jerked back. "Just looking for a clean skillet," she said, eyeing him curiously.

Wiping a hand over his dirty face, Smitty focused his gaze on Hialeaha.

"Oh. You kinda snuck up on me. I'll fetch you a skillet and bring it to you."

"I am here now," returned Hialeaha. Smitty was defiant, almost hostile. It was a side of him she had not seen.

Again Smitty wiped a hand over his face, but this time more vigorously. When he took it down, he wore his familiar smile.

"Sure," he said, stepping on a wagon spoke and lifting the tarp. Grabbing an iron skillet, he held it out. "Just takes me a bit to wake up."

"I can see that."

As Hialeaha prepared griddle cakes, she heard muted voices, first from the tent, then the coach. She could understand nothing. A few moments later, Wellington and Davis emerged to stand in the amber rays of the rising sun.

Both men stretched, apparently well rested.

"Across the Rio Puerco and to Mesita by noon," yawned Wellington. "Then up the Rio San Jose. No sandstorm can bury a river."

Turning a griddle cake, Hialeaha realized they were going farther west. She felt her heart jump, and then, feeling a twinge of guilt, she frowned.

She shook her head. They should turn back, of course. It was the only sensible thing to do.

Gazing at the steam rising from the stove top, she sighed. Perhaps, however, they would go as far as Mesita before ending the journey. And there, for the last time, she could see Conway Fargo. She at least deserved the chance to bid him a proper farewell.

Treadway trudged into camp, his steps gouging deep into the smooth sand. He thumbed over his shoulder as he made his way past the stove to the dining table. "I saw horse tracks. They rode off sometime after the wind died down."

"Which way?" asked Wellington.

Treadway turned and pointed.

"South?" questioned Davis. "But if it was Fargo, that makes no sense."

Wellington thoughtfully rubbed his knuckles across his clean-shaven face. "It does if he wants to see what we will do next, to wait and see which direction we will travel. He knows we will not follow him south, and I doubt he would lead us west."

Smitty came from the wagon to the stove. He sniffed the griddle cakes and looked out into the desert. "No water to the south. He musta watered at the Puerco last night, or he'd be headed back to the Rio Grande."

Hialeaha was suddenly worried. If there was water at the Rio Puerco, an easy ride for a man on horseback, why was the water in the bucket gone? What kind of river was the Rio Puerco?

"What is your best guess, Smitty?" asked Wellington. "How far is it to that river?"

"Two, maybe three miles. Four at the most."

"I agree. Even if we stray from the trail a few degrees, we should be there in two hours, at most. No one can miss an entire river."

Smitty took another whiff of the griddle cakes. He smacked his lips. "Sounds 'bout right to me."

***

Four hours after breaking camp, they came to a stop at the edge of an abrupt twenty-foot drop. Across one hundred feet of dry river bottom, another wall of red sand formed a barrier as far as the eye could see.

Everyone stepped out of the coach. They stood on the banks of the Rio Puerco, the smothering noonday heat engulfing them.

Shading her eyes from the glare, Mahra said, "This cannot be it. There is no water."

Smitty shrugged. "I'm thinkin' maybe this ain't it. Whatever it is, we got to get across to the other side anyhow."

Wellington surveyed the sandy riverbed. In its center, a few green willowlike shrubs held on to life among brown tufts of dead grass. "I'll ride north, and Edward, you south. The wagons will wait here until we locate a way across."

On the opposite bank, a quarter mile to the north, Hialeaha saw movement. "We need to go north," she said, staring at some distant object.

Wellington turned, following Hialeaha's eyes. "And just what makes you so certain?"

Hialeaha said nothing. Instead, she pointed.

All eyes narrowed, searching for what Hialeaha could see easily. Davis walked next to her. Leaning his head, he sighted down her arm and finger as he would a rifle. "I see nothing, Hialeaha. What are you looking at?"

Slowly lowering her arm, Hialeaha said, "Far-go."

"Where?" demanded Wellington, still unable to see what was obvious to Hialeaha.

Puzzled, Hialeaha looked at Wellington. Before she could answer his question, the muffled blast of a rifle echoed down the ravine.

Brooks squealed in frustration, "Why can I not see him?"

Smitty chuckled, glancing at Hialeaha. "None of us do, Miss Brooks. White eyes don't see what Injun eyes do."

LaFarge frowned at Hialeaha. A hint of jealousy flashed in her eyes. "Apparently not."

Savoring the expression on Wellington's face, Smitty asked, "So, do we head north?"

Wellington took long strides back to the coach and jerked the door open. "That is a stupid question!"

***

An hour passed before a cut in the banks came into view. In a matter of minutes, the coach and wagon rolled down the east bank and up the west side of the dry riverbed.

Fargo was nowhere to be seen, but his double set of tracks led them steadily northwest. Near sundown, they came to a mesa that glowed brilliant red-orange in the last rays of the sun. At its base, in the darkening shadows, was a small group of stone buildings. Smoke rose from their flat rooftops, and the glimmer of firelight escaped through small, irregularly shaped windows. The air began to cool.

A few hundred yards from the village, wagon ruts appeared out of the drifted sand. Treadway halted the coach and then leaned down and back toward the passengers.

"Looks like Fargo's tracks go off into the desert, but I can see the road now."

Wellington stuck his head out. "Then go into that village. This must be Mesita. We need to locate the river as soon as possible. We need water first and foremost."

Smitty called out to Treadway. "When we get to that pueblo yonder, take any trail that goes downhill. All these places are built on high ground above a river. You can likely just give the horses their head. They'll smell the water and go right for it."

Treadway nodded and snapped his lines.

They rolled slowly toward the squat adobes, all haphazardly scattered and built atop mounds of rock and sand. To their right, they passed a dead burro, its gray belly bloated to the point of bursting and its head crawling with a carpet of flies.

Mahra buried her face in her hands. Her words were garbled by her fingers. "I do not like seeing dead animals!"

The carcass was downwind, but the heavy stench flowed into the coach.

"Barbarians," uttered Davis, unable to take his eyes off the burro, "simply barbarians."

As they neared the first building, a small child with a wild thatch of black hair poked his head above a rock. He darted for the house, naked from head to toe.

An old man wearing a faded calico shirt and soiled cotton pants stepped out. He held out his hand. Treadway ignored him, guiding his team around another adobe and then down a steep grade. With the wagons creaking and trace chains jingling, they maneuvered past two more houses and several more onlookers. All of the men were dressed like the old man. The women wore similar shirts above plain skirts that reached past the knees.

A narrow, green riverbed came into view. Treadway relaxed the lines and allowed the horses to find their way to water. They followed the road a few more yards until it turned into a worn path. A minute later, the coach came to a halt at a circle of rocks no more than six feet across.

It was dusk when Treadway climbed down and opened the coach door. Smitty pulled up with the supply wagon as the last passenger stepped out of the coach and began to stretch. A warm breeze drifted across the riverbed. Insects began chirping softly from somewhere in the grass.

Wellington looked at the lead horses. Their heads were down and they were sucking water, but he saw no river. "Where is the river?" he asked Treadway.

Treadway was hot from riding in the sun. His fair skin was beet red. "There's water in those rocks. That's all I know."

Smitty walked up to the group. "Gettin' dark. We campin' here?"

"We need to find the river first," said LaFarge.

Craning his neck, Smitty looked over the riverbed. The far bank was no more than thirty paces from them. "May be it's up that'a way," he said, pointing farther west.

"Why don't we ask him?" said Mahra.

The old man they passed when they had first entered the village was walking toward them.

"Excellent idea," agreed Wellington. Taking a few steps toward the man, he asked, "Would you be kind enough to direct us to the river?"

Continuing to walk, the old man said something unintelligible. He came within two steps of Wellington and stopped. His gray hair was shoulder length and tied with a bandana off to the right side of his head.

"The river?" repeated Wellington.

The old man rattled off several choppy, guttural words. He looked and sounded angry.

"Agua," said Smitty. "Agua."

The old man nodded his head but resumed what now seemed like a rant. Several residents of the pueblo were gathering on the trail to watch from a distance.

"I don't know what he's jabberin' about," said Smitty. "But I do know Spanish when I hear it. And that ain't it."

Davis rolled his eyes. "That is *just* splendid!"

Hialeaha stepped away from the group. The old man's eyes locked on her as she raised a cupped hand to her mouth.

The old man stretched out a flat hand, flipping up and then down before rubbing it on his stomach.

Wellington looked at Smitty, a question in his eyes.

Smitty huffed in disbelief. "She's usin' sign language. 'magine that. Way out here."

"But that is a lost art," said Davis. "That is what they taught us at Harvard. They knew of no Indians, anywhere, who still used it."

Smiling, Smitty cut his eyes toward Davis. "Then I reckon not ever' thing they taught you at Harvard was on the money."

For several minutes, the old man and Hialeaha made signs with their hands, arms, and heads. They paused, and she turned to Wellington.

"The river is all but dry. Even the Zuni River is dry this year. There is some water at Agua Fria, and it is true there are ice caves nearby. The next water after that is at the rock with the writing on it.

"As for this water, the water the horses are drinking, this water is his. He wants no money, but he is willing to trade for food, cloth, pots. He wanted a gun, but I told him no."

For a moment, there was silence as the news took hold.

Glaring at the old man, Wellington ran his tongue over his broken tooth. "His water? He says this is *his* water?"

"He is their chief," said Hialeaha.

"The last I checked, this worthless piece of land is still in the territory of the United States. No one owns this water! I bought that bill of goods once, but, by damn, I will not play the fool twice!

"Tell him this water belongs to us just as much as to him, and we will take what we require."

Hialeaha started to disagree, but Miles Wellington was not accustomed to being corrected, especially by a servant. It was better he learn on his own.

Turning back to the old man, Hialeaha made several more gestures. The man's expression was unreadable. When the signing ceased, the old man turned and walked back up the trail. In seconds, the villagers were gone.

"So what did you tell him?" demanded Wellington.

"That you were a chief, that you had guns and would take the water."

Wellington scowled. "Why tell him I am a chief?"

"It is what they understand."

"I do not understand," said Davis. "The professors at Harvard extensively researched sign language. They could find no Indians who used it. They concluded it was a lost art."

Hialeaha stood more erect. "I was taught. Many of the old ones know sign, but they will not admit it to whites. And the young Indians do not care to learn. This old man knew it. In his day, it was known from sea to sea and from Mexico to Canada."

LaFarge heard the pride in Hialeaha's response. She smiled at the Indian with lips devoid of humor. "Well, are we not fortunate to have one of the 'old ones' among us? Thank you so much, Hialeaha."

On impulse, Hialeaha smiled in return, mimicking LaFarge as best she could. "Anytime, Miss LaFarge."

Pointing toward the adobes, Smitty said, "You best wear your pistols from now on."

"For what reason?" scoffed LaFarge. "Those pathetic worms would not dare harm us."

"Maybe, maybe not. But you best not show 'em no weakness. Them is Injuns. You don't never want to show no weakness to no Injuns, even ones the likes'a these here."

"To hell with them!" said Wellington, rubbing a fingertip along his mustache.

LaFarge glanced at Wellington and raised an eyebrow.

"Sorry for the swearing, my dear. This tooth has been acting up since the Rio Puerco."

Smitty ran his own finger along his scraggly mustache. "Feel a lump rising 'bout here and painful?"

"No. But when I press there, it is somewhat sore but merely a nuisance."

Tilting his head toward Hialeaha, Smitty asked, "You got a poultice for a ulcerated tooth?"

"Cloves sometimes help, but I have none," answered Hialeaha.

"I need no poultice. During my athletic training at Harvard, I learned to endure far greater discomfort than this."

Scratching his chin, Smitty said, "Well, that trainin' just might come in handy if'n the pain comes on you." He glanced at the grassy river bottom. "We can turn the stock out tonight and let 'em eat their fill. With things being so dry, you never know what's ahead."

"Nothing we cannot overcome, I assure you," said Wellington. "But if this is our only source of water, get those horses out of it until we draw our own."

"Should we wear our pistols, then?" asked Davis.

"Why not?" answered Wellington. "I suppose it is time."

***

The sound of shattering glass pierced the darkness, jolting Hialeaha to full consciousness. Her eyes opened, but she did not move. Outside the coach, she could hear sand grinding underfoot. No Indian would be so clumsy.

Tossing off the light cover, she slowly peered out the coach window. A dim glow from the campfire illuminated Wellington's face as he sat cross-legged in the sand. He was struggling to uncork a bottle of brandy.

Pulling on her robe, Hialeaha eased out of the coach. She quietly approached Wellington. Speaking softly, she asked, "Are you ill?"

Wellington looked up, trying to focus his eyes. "My head," he bellowed, slurring his words, "is about to 'splode."

"Your tooth?"

"Of course it is my tooth!"

"May I take a look?"

"You're no dentist!"

"May I see anyway?"

Waving his arm in a wide circle, Wellington announced, "Sure! The whole damn world can look for all I care."

Hialeaha took a lantern from the dinner table, lit it, and turned up the wick. Davis was coming out of the tent, and Smitty was stirring. She held the lantern close to Wellington's face.

The side of Wellington's nose was swollen as well as his lower eyelid.

Without asking permission, Hialeaha pulled Wellington's lip up.

Trying to talk with his mouth held open and his head back, Wellington asked, "Can ooo gid ee ouwt?"

"No," answered Hialeaha, releasing the lip. "But I may be able to take the pain away."

Uncorking the brandy, Wellington took a long swig. "Do it, then."

Davis squatted next to his cousin. "You look ghastly, Miles."

Wellington grabbed Davis's arm. "I do not care how I look at the moment, damn you. This is agony."

"Got 'im, did it?" said Smitty, coming into the lantern light. He yawned and then bent over for a better look. "Figured it would."

"Let him drink," said Hialeaha, and then she corrected herself. "No. Make him drink."

Watching Hialeaha go to the rear of the coach, Smitty asked, "Gonna yank it out, are you?"

"Do what I asked, Smitty, and build up the fire."

Throwing up the leather boot cover, Hialeaha retrieved a carpetbag. She removed two sticks. One was straight. The other was as long as her forearm and slightly curved. The curved stick had a leather thong tied to one end. She worked on the straight stick for a moment and attached a fine metal tip to one end.

When she returned, Brooks, LaFarge, and Treadway were standing near Wellington. In unison, they looked up.

"What are you doing?" asked LaFarge. Her tone was a mix of accusation and uncertainty.

"The poison must come out. You all will have to hold him."

"Hold him for what?" demanded LaFarge.

"I am going to make a hole in his tooth and let the poison out. Then the pain will go away."

"So now you are a dentist," said LaFarge sarcastically.

Wellington snarled, "Let her do it unless you have a better idea."

LaFarge flinched. Mahra put her hands to her ears, turned her back, and began to hum.

"What do we do?" asked Davis.

"Lay him down, head near the fire. Miss LaFarge, you will need to hold the lantern close. I need all the light I can get.

"Smitty, get on one side, and you, Mr. Davis, on the other, to hold him down. Reed, you will be at his head, with your good hand on his forehead and your knees clasping his head like a vice."

"Where'll you be?" asked Smitty.

"Sitting unladylike on his chest."

The men rolled Wellington onto his back and took their positions. As Brooks hummed louder, Hialeaha directed Treadway to tilt Wellington's head back until his tooth pointed up toward the stars and into the lantern light.

Wellington began to sing. "Fair Harvard! We join in thy jubilee throng, and with blessings surrender the o'er."

"The Harvard fight song," explained Davis.

Everyone watched Hialeaha wrap the leather thong around the stick with the metal point and then tie it to the other end of the curved stick.

"I get it," said Smitty, above the humming and singing. "I seen Injuns start fires the same way. You use that bow thing to turn that pointed stick."

Hialeaha hiked up her robe and straddled Wellington's chest. She carefully placed the tip of the makeshift drill on the flat edge of the broken tooth. Then she moved the bow slowly to the left and right, causing the point on her drill to turn back and forth. Hialeaha stopped to make sure it had made a small indentation in the tooth. Wellington continued to growl out his version of the Harvard fight song.

"Now hold him tighter," she said. She replaced her drill in the indentation.

Without warning, Hialeaha sawed the bow back and forth as fast as she could.

Wellington stiffened and screamed.

In seconds the point sank into the tooth a quarter inch. Hialeaha stopped and quickly removed the drill.

When she did, a milky drop of pus mixed with blood oozed out of the tooth and down the roof of Wellington's mouth. He immediately stopped screaming. His body went limp.

"You can release him now," said Hialeaha as she got to her feet.

The men backed a few inches away. Wellington's head relaxed. He took a deep breath and continued to sing. "Be the herald of light, and the bearer of love, till the stock of the Puritans die."

"I ain't never seen nothin' like it," said Smitty.

"Remarkable," agreed Davis, gazing up at Hialeaha. "Such pain, and gone so quickly."

Hialeaha shrugged. "All poison must drain. Teeth are no different."

For a moment LaFarge soured, but then, kneeling next to Wellington, she ran her fingers gently through his hair. "You were so brave, dear. I am so proud of you."

Nodding in rare agreement, Hialeaha said, "Yes. He did well."

Mahra turned around. Still holding her hands over her ears, she spoke loudly. "Is it over?"

Davis nodded. She slowly lowered her hands and smiled at everyone. "Is he better?"

Beyond the firelight, a horse nickered.

Davis smiled at Brooks. "Everything is fine, Mahra, just fine."

***

Hialeaha was packing away the last of the breakfast dishes. She shaded her eyes against the morning sun. One of the horses was missing; the coach's nigh leader had disappeared. Everyone assumed it had wandered off during the night. Smitty and Treadway had been searching downriver for over an hour. Now they were returning empty handed.

Wellington's swelling was gone. Other than having a hangover, he was in good spirits. With the others inside the coach waiting, he leaned against its shady side waiting.

Treadway shook his head in disgust. "That horse is dead."

Wellington came away from the coach. "Dead?"

"Eaten."

"By what? Wolves? Cougars?"

"Injuns," offered Smitty. "And by the way they cleaned them bones, I'd say they was hungry ones."

Wellington was speechless.

Davis stuck his head out the coach window. "I can hardly believe that. Who would eat a horse?"

Smitty felt the sun stinging the back of his neck. He scratched at it, squinting with one eye. "A hungry man'll eat most anything. And a thirsty one'll drink most anything."

"Most men, perhaps," scoffed Davis, "but not men of breeding."

Hialeaha opened the coach door, deliberately avoiding Wellington's eyes. She could feel them bearing down on her. If he asked, she would have to tell him it was the chief who had taken the horse. It was payment for the water. But surely he knew as much by now. They all knew it.

"Are we going to let them get away with this?" asked Treadway. "Isn't that showing we're weak?"

Wellington glanced at Treadway. "A very astute observation, Reed," he said, and then added thoughtfully, "I am impressed."

Treadway sheepishly dropped his eyes and shrugged.

"For now," said Wellington, "we will allow them to think that we have assumed it was wild beasts that killed our horse. We will have to come back this way. That will be the time to deal with these savages."

"The supply wagon's gettin' lighter as we go," said Smitty. "We can switch a horse from it to the coach."

"Very well," agreed Wellington. "The sooner we are out of here, the better."

In minutes, the horses were hitched. With two barrels of fresh water, the wagons rolled up the incline of the riverbed and veered westward through the pueblo. The villagers stopped what they were doing and stoically watched them pass.

At the edge of the village, the old chief stood on top of a flat roof. As the wagons rolled beneath him, he stretched out a bony hand. Gesturing wildly, he chanted in a voice pitched high by age.

Brooks scowled at Hialeaha. "What did he say?"

"It was nothing of importance."

"A curse, no doubt," LaFarge sighed.

"Was it?" asked Mahra. "Was it a curse?"

"It is nothing to worry about."

"So it was a curse?" asked Davis.

All eyes settled on Hialeaha. She considered their questions for a moment. She decided to answer even if it did make Mahra uneasy. They should know what the old Indian said even if they believed it was only superstition.

"He called for the spirits of the dead and their guardians to punish us."

"Is that all?" said LaFarge. "I was afraid he was transforming all of us into toads."

"Spirits do not concern me," said Wellington. "Their guardians, however, might be flesh and blood. We will continue to wear our pistols. Smitty and Reed will carry the shotguns."

LaFarge stared at Hialeaha for several seconds. "I cannot help but wonder what Mr. Fargo was doing while our horse was being stolen and butchered."

Hialeaha ignored the stare and gazed out the window. "He was watching."

"Watching? He was watching them steal our horse?"

"No," answered Hialeaha. "To Mr. Fargo, the horse was not being stolen."

Chapter 11

Since midafternoon, the wagons had been climbing steadily to the southwest. The sage and juniper were giving way to stunted Ponderosa pine and fir. The sand held tufts of sun-bleached grass amid jagged beds of lava rock.

Treadway reined in, stopping in the shade of a pine to give the horses another breather. They were lathered in foamy sweat and tiring quickly.

Smitty set his brake and stepped down. Going forward, he tipped his hat to the women in the coach before speaking to Treadway.

"We best give the horses some water. We keep this up, and we ain't gonna make it much farther."

"Agua Fria can't be too far," said Treadway.

"Still, we best be restin' 'em."

"How much water do we have left?" Treadway asked.

"Most of a barrel. We can spare half."

Treadway leaned back. "You heard him, Mr. Wellington. What do you want to do?"

Wellington rubbed his bloodshot eyes and opened the door. "Very well," he said. Starting to step down from the coach, he froze.

Fargo was riding toward them from a thicket of fir trees. He held a rifle across his saddle.

Following Wellington's eyes, Smitty and Treadway turned.

"You're going to kill those horses if you keep this up," said Fargo. "And you've got a long way to go."

Wellington eased himself out of the coach. Fargo took in the pistol on his hip and the glint of a shotgun barrel sticking up near Treadway's boots.

"I was just tellin' 'em the same thing," said Smitty. "We was gonna give the horses some water, after coolin' 'em down a bit."

Fargo's eyes shifted beneath the shade of his hat brim. He compared the hatred written on Treadway's face with the look of indifference on Smitty's. "Make sure you cool them good. You're at seven thousand feet. They'll founder easy."

"Seven thousand," repeated Smitty. "No wonder they're blowin' so hard."

Looking past Smitty, Fargo caught sight of Hileaha. Their eyes met and held for a few seconds. Glancing back at Smitty, Fargo said, "There's only enough water at Agua Fria for you to drink. The horses will have to make it to next water with what you have in the barrels. That would be El Moro, late tomorrow."

"How far are we from Agua Fria?" asked Smitty.

"Five, maybe six miles up the grade."

Wellington loosened his shoulders. "I might just have a look at Agua Fria myself."

"Saddle up, then. This ground doesn't hold tracks too well, anyway. I'll point it out so you don't miss it."

As Wellington saddled his polo pony, Fargo kept an eye on Treadway. If he made a move for the shotgun, he would have to be shot and shot dead. With scarcely twenty yards between them, Fargo was well within range of a double load of buckshot.

Wellington and Davis wore pistols, but they were too civilized to pose an immediate threat. LaFarge was capable of anything, but Smitty was still the wild card. He had shown up unexpectedly in Chicago, then eagerly hired on as a teamster. He claimed to have never been in the Southwest, but that was likely a lie. Though he tried to conceal it, he knew too much about the land and the customs.

A man who lied could never be trusted. Smitty appeared to go about unarmed, but a pistol was easily hidden. Whether he was just another shiftless no-account or something more, he would have to be watched the same as Treadway. One thing was certain: neither man was what he pretended to be.

Wellington pulled on a pair of polished riding boots, slid gracefully onto his English-style saddle, and trotted forward. He wore his pith helmet and green-colored eyeglasses.

With his eyes on Treadway, Fargo backed his horse several steps. Turning the bay parallel to the coach, he walked his horses through the dry grass and out of shotgun range before veering back onto the road.

Wellington galloped up alongside and then slowed to a walk. "I hardly think that was necessary. Reed is a simpleton, not a murderer."

"If I were you," said Fargo, "I'd keep an eye on him."

Twenty years in the Southwest had taught Fargo to size a man up quickly. He possessed almost a sixth sense about people, and he relied on his instincts. The Mexicans thought he could see into people's souls. They said it was because the saints protected him. The Indians claimed it was part of his medicine. When asked about it, Fargo would simply say: "The eyes are the light of the soul," he would tell them. "Just look at the eyes."

Fargo glanced at Wellington. He thought of how many times he had tried to warn people of impending danger, only to be ignored. It would do no good to tell Wellington about Treadway.

Things that were as sure as the sunrise to Fargo were often incomprehensible to the uninitiated. When he was younger, he had often wasted his breath trying to explain the obvious. Now, he said things only once.

Men like Miles Wellington only learned the hard way, if they ever learned at all. He had yet to face the dark side of life, to experience terror, agony, and grief. He knew nothing of how those demons would scar a man forever.

The two rode in silence for over an hour. At first Wellington rode stiffly, his eyes looking ahead, trying not to acknowledge the man next to him. But as they continued toward Agua Fria, he began to observe Fargo out of the corner of his eye. Tiring of that, he allowed his head to turn from side to side. Casually, his attention dropped to the grips of Fargo's pistols. They were heavily worn from use.

"Should we not be there by now?"

"Just about," said Fargo, veering off the trail and clattering up an embankment of loose rock. He reined in next to a twisted piñon pine. "Two hundred yards up the trail, there's a fork. To the right, across a meadow, is Agua Fria. I'm going to scout it out before we go in."

"But you were just there, were you not?"

"It's been a few hours."

"We have not seen a soul since leaving Mesita. You are overly cautious, Mr. Fargo."

"Damn right," said Fargo, spurring his bay and leading his black farther into the pines and out of sight.

Shaking his head, Wellington nudged the pony into a trot. In seconds, he saw the fork in the trail and then the meadow. A slash of green grass pointed to the spring. He followed it to hat-sized pool of clear water.

Without hesitation, he dismounted. Removing his pith helmet, he went to one knee. Cupping his hand, he gulped the water. It was cool, and it stayed cool as it trickled down his throat.

He reached for another handful of water.

"The water," said a voice behind him, "it is good, no?"

Wellington spun on his knee and saw not one but three men ten paces from him. They stood several feet apart, their brown faces shaded under broad-brimmed sombreros. Below black mustaches, they wore broad smiles. All three had pistols slung low on their hips.

Forty yards away, three horses were tied behind a deadfall. Wellington had ridden past them without taking notice. Now he looked in every direction, but Fargo was nowhere in sight.

"You ride in fast, *amigo*. You must be ver' thirsty."

The speaker stood between the other two. He was little more than five feet tall and slight in build. He wore striped pants tucked into knee-high boots. His steel spurs held four-inch spiked rowels.

"Yes. Yes, I was," answered Wellington. Thinking quickly, he added, "My friend is also thirsty. He should be along shortly."

Still smiling, the three Mexicans looked around. "Maybe we wait for your friend," said the little Mexican. "Maybe we don't."

Wiping his wet hand on his pants, Wellington stood slowly. He had never even fired the pistol buckled around his waist.

"You have a fine horse, *amigo*. I like your horse."

The Mexican to Wellington's left spoke in Spanish, then the one to his right.

"My name is Miles Wellington. I am from Chicago."

"Chi-ca-go?"

"Yes. Chicago."

"Well, *Señor* Chicago, we will take your horse and your *pistol*...And we will take your nice boots. You can keep your hat. We do not like your *sombrero*."

Wellington paled but managed to show no surprise. The others were at least an hour behind. He had never been robbed. In fact, he had never even been confronted by a thief. His knees began to tremble and then his hands.

The little Mexican pointed at Wellington and laughed. "*Tengas meido, amiga?*"

The other Mexicans laughed.

"I do not speak Spanish," said Wellington. Now even his voice quivered. "My friend, however, does. Perhaps you should wait—"

"No. I think we will not wait. And I think maybe you give us the *pistola* first."

Fargo had tied his horses in a narrow draw that led to the spring. Taking his sawed-off shotgun from his bedroll, he dropped in two loads of buckshot and crept toward the spring. Along the way, he gathered sticks the length of his arm. The draw would end near where the Mexicans had tied their horses. Their backs would be to him. From there, he would have to close twenty paces before the scattergun could do its work.

Where the draw spilled into the meadow, Fargo paused only long enough to conceal the shotgun under his armload of sticks. Holding it with his right hand, he rotated the stock sideways to prevent the mule-eared hammers from catching on a twig.

With both arms appearing to hold a load of firewood, Fargo deliberately stepped on a dry stick.

Hearing the snap, the Mexicans turned to see Fargo walking toward them with his head down. "Got the firewood, Mr. Wellington," he called out, and then he looked up. Smiling at all three men, he said, "*Hola, amigos.*"

"*Hola,*" returned the small Mexican. "*Buenos tardes.*"

"You speak any American?" asked Fargo, walking closer.

The Mexican smiled. "*Pocito.*"

"Shot a fat doe this morning," said Fargo, closing the distance. "You're welcome to some after I get the cook fire going."

Fargo stopped. Ten paces separated him from the closest Mexican, twenty from the third. If he got the chance, that one would have to be a pistol shot.

Without the slightest movement, Fargo squeezed a trigger. The first blast folded the closest man, and the second barrel knocked the little Mexican back on his heels. Dropping the wood and shotgun, Fargo reached for his right-hand Colt and then his left. The last Mexican standing was drawing as fast as he could.

A blast came from Fargo's left. He kept his attention on the Mexican, seeing his pistol belch flame and smoke. Fargo fired, then fired again. The Mexican staggered but fired back. Fargo let loose with both pistols, and the man went to his knees, then down on his face.

Smoke hung thick in the air. The quiet was deafening.

Fargo went to the first Mexican. He was clearly dead. The little man was still breathing. Fargo stepped back and put a slug into his heart. The third man had died before his face hit the grass.

Easing the hammers down on his Colts, Fargo looked at Wellington, who was still pointing his pistol at the third Mexican. He seemed frozen, his face white and pasty.

"You hit, Wellington?" asked Fargo.

Wellington blinked. He blinked again. With the whites of his eyes showing, he turned to Fargo. "Did I kill him?"

Fargo cocked his head. Holstering one pistol, he ran the shots back in his mind. Wellington had fired at least once.

"Maybe, a little," said Fargo.

Wellington's shoulders slumped, and his face turned a shade of green. "They said they only wanted my horse."

"*And* your pistol...*and* your boots. They were just playing cat and mouse with you. They'd have killed you."

Slowly lowering his pistol, Wellington spoke in a daze. "It was all so slow...Everything slowed down...I could only see a narrow space in front of me...Everything else went black."

"It happens sometimes. Early on, anyway."

"I was shaking uncontrollably."

Fargo shrugged. "You drew and fired while lead was flying. You could have run. You did fine."

Wellington's eyes began to focus. He stared at the dead Mexicans. "I have never seen men die. One moment...breathing...talking. Then they are dead...so quickly."

Ejecting his empty brass, Fargo said, "What's true for them is true for anybody. You could have been shot, too. Then you'd be lying there along with them. But if you would have died today, you'd have died well."

"What difference would it have made? I would be dead."

"Everybody dies. It doesn't matter so much what you die of, it's *how* you die that counts."

Wellington awkwardly holstered his Colt. "What do we do now?"

Fargo pulled a cartridge from his belt loop and slid it into the cylinder of his pistol. "You ride back to the others. Guide them back here and make camp for the night. Tomorrow morning, leave early, before the ravens or buzzards show up. Forget the ice cave and get on your way. The farther you are from here, the safer you'll be."

"What about them?" Wellington asked.

"I'll drag them up that draw I came down. If the others see the blood trail, tell them I shot a yearling elk and drug it to my camp.

"I'll set their horses free. No need to take chances on them being recognized by friends or relatives.

"The pistols, I'll keep for now."

Wellington swallowed hard. He hesitated and then asked, "Was it like this for you...the first time?"

In less than a heartbeat, the nightmare Fargo had seen for twenty years flashed through his mind. Apaches standing over the woman he loved, the flash of his Bowie knife, the flames from his pistol.

"No," said Fargo. "It was different for me. And you can thank God for that."

Fargo finished loading his first pistol and started on the second. He glanced at Wellington. Something was on his mind.

"What is it?" asked Fargo.

Wellington cleared his throat. "Are you going to tell the others what happened?"

It was not the question that surprised Fargo, but the tone. There was humility in it, and shame. Miles Wellington the pompous fool, at least for the moment, was gone.

Fargo flipped open the loading gate of his second Colt and started reloading. He thought of what he had been like when he first came to the Southwest. He never had money like Wellington, but he had been just as big a fool, if not a bigger one. Men sometimes changed. Maybe even this one would.

"They won't hear it from me."

Wellington's color began to return as Fargo finished reloading.

"One more thing," said Fargo. "You should reach El Moro late tomorrow. At the base of the wall where all the writing is, you'll find a deep pool of clear water. You'll all want to bathe in it. Don't. It's the only water fit to drink for forty miles. Use buckets if you want to wash up."

***

Miles Wellington found the wagons off the trail, two miles from Agua Fria. They were on level ground but had lost the last remnants of the road in a stand of dead grass and piñon pine. It had been less than an hour since the shooting, barely enough time for Wellington to pull himself together.

For the first time in his life, he had tasted fear—not just any fear, but the fear of death. He had trembled in the face of it. The best he could do was shoot at a man who wasn't even aiming at him. It was an act of desperation and panic.

The sun was dipping beneath the western treetops when Wellington rode up to Treadway. He pointed over his shoulder and off to his left.

"It is about one mile that direction," he said evenly, then rode past the coach and stopped beside Smitty.

"Fargo was right. There is only water enough for us, and he advises we try to make it to El Moro by sundown tomorrow."

Shading his eyes against the setting sun, Smitty skeptically dropped his chin and drew his head back. "You takin' Fargo's advice now, Mr. Wellington?"

Wellington's stomach was curdled. He fought off the urge to vomit. He had never tasted crow, but it was a small price to pay for his life. "If his advice is sound, there is no reason to ignore it."

Smitty was unconvinced, and it showed on his grizzled face.

"I may have," said Wellington, straining to get his words out, "mis-judge the man...somewhat."

Wellington wheeled his horse and rode past the coach, waving for Treadway to follow.

"Peculiar," muttered Smitty, snapping the leather reins. "Mighty peculiar indeed."

Tugging his hat brim down low, Smitty considered the sudden change in Wellington. If he warmed up to Fargo, it could complicate matters. Treadway, though, still had one good hand, enough to pull a trigger or thrust a blade. If the truth were known, LaFarge was likely as capable. Davis and Brooks remained bystanders, but Hialeaha was with Fargo. It was anyone's guess what the Indian could do.

***

Since the water barrels would have to be filled one cup at a time, they backed the supply wagon up to the trickling spring of Agua Fria. Blaming mosquitos, Wellington refused to make camp in a level meadow near the spring. Instead, he chose another in the opposite direction.

By the time Hialeaha assembled the cookstove, it was twilight. Seeing the gray outline of a deadfall across the small meadow, she started for it. Halfway there, she spotted a pile of sticks near the mouth of a sandy wash. Watching for snakes, she worked her way toward the firewood. Halfway there, her moccasin slipped on something wet, and she stumbled. Gaining her balance, she noticed a blackish streak and trail of bent grass.

Reaching down, she ran a finger over the grass. It felt syrupy. She rubbed her finger and thumb together and then pulled them apart. The slime was sticky. It was blood.

Hialeaha had long forgotten much of what her father had taught her, but some things she remembered. Slowly making her way to the sticks, she looked for signs. She saw drag marks and crushed blades of grass that led up the wash. Not one but several horses had gone that way.

Gathering the bundle of sticks, Hialeaha backtracked the horses to the deadfall. Counting the patches of flattened grass, she knew three horses had stood tied there. She broke off some branches and stole a look at the campsite.

Wellington appeared to be watching her. She snapped off another dead limb and started back.

Crossing in front of the supply wagon, Hialeaha paused. Wellington was lighting a lantern by the dining table and paying her no attention. While Smitty and Treadway erected the tent, she scanned the tracks at her feet. Smitty had backed his team up to the spring, so their tracks would appear to be leaving. But she could see one set of fresh horse tracks that had come to the spring.

Fargo had been to the spring first and then come back with Wellington. That would account for the three horses tied by the deadfall. But Fargo traveled with a led horse. If he came to the spring a second time, there should be two more sets of fresh tracks.

Keeping an eye on Wellington, Hialeaha followed the incoming tracks for several feet. Satisfied that only one horse had been ridden to the spring, she started back to camp.

She tried to think of an explanation for what she had seen but kept coming to the same conclusion. There had been four horses at the spring, not three. Four horses and a blood trail. One too many horses and something dragged away either dead or dying.

If there had been more light and more time, she might know more. Hialeaha considered the possibility that later in the evening, perhaps, Wellington would offer an explanation. Then she felt a jolt of fear. What if he said nothing at all? What if the blood belonged to Fargo?

Dropping the sticks beside the stove, Hialeaha opened the door and began stacking the kindling inside. She glanced at Wellington. He sat at the table cleaning his pistol. Their eyes met and held for several seconds. Hialeaha looked away, but she knew it was too late.

She lit the stove and watched the small flame lick the dry twigs. She heard footsteps behind her.

Wellington set a handful of cans down on the stove. "I thought we would have pork tonight."

Hialeaha added larger twigs to the fire but said nothing.

Wellington lowered his voice to a near whisper. "I was hoping to have fresh venison, but I think Mr. Fargo is not in the mood to share this evening."

"Why do you say that?" asked Hialeaha.

"When we rode up to the spring, I crippled a deer with a pistol shot. It was close to the water. I did not want Mahra to see the blood. That is why I chose this campsite.

"Fargo went to track it down. And you know how the man is about coming into camp at night."

"So, did you hire him again?"

"Certainly not," said Wellington. "I will consult with him if I must, but Clarissa wishes never to see him again. And there is the trouble between Fargo and poor Treadway."

Hialeaha gathered the cans and set them aside. Fargo had led them to the only water within miles and told them where to find the next water hole. Still, Wellington showed no signs of gratitude. And he was lying about what had happened earlier at the spring. There was a fourth horse and no deer that hobbled off. Whatever had bled had been dragged away.

"Do you think we will see him again?" asked Hialeaha.

"I suppose so. But I will not permit him in camp. As I said, I alone will deal with him."

Lifting the latch of the stove door, Hialeaha added more wood. As Wellington walked back to the others, her brow furrowed in thought.

Wellington spoke as if Fargo would return. If he had wounded or killed Fargo, he would not have hesitated to proclaim it. If Fargo had been injured or killed by someone else, Wellington would not keep it from them. Fargo was out there somewhere, likely alive and well.

One thing was certain. Wellington did not want Fargo anywhere near the others. And his reason had something to do with the fourth horse and bloody trail. Hialeaha was halfway through cooking supper when it came to her.

Conway Fargo was not the type to ride directly to the only water in the region. Its location would be known to anyone familiar with the country, good or bad.

Fargo would circle first and, even then, would approach cautiously. Wellington would find that foolish and ride straight in. Men were already there. They were going to kill him, and Fargo intervened.

That much made sense to Hialeaha, but it also created more questions. The fact that Wellington had been cleaning his pistol meant that it had been fired. He was arrogant and pompous. She had seen him mutilate a man in the boxing ring and take great pleasure in it. If he had been in a gunfight, he would be strutting about like a peacock, proclaiming his manhood. There would be no end to his bragging. What was he hiding?

She was setting the food on the dining table when another thought came to her. Miles Wellington had never been intimidated by anything or anyone until he met Fargo. In men like Wellington, that would induce jealousy, jealously that would grow into hatred.

Wellington had lost a fistfight in the streets of Lamy, and Fargo had won his fight on the banks of the Rio Grande. Wellington had bragged about his new rifles, and Fargo had taken them. And now, what if

Fargo had saved Wellington from an ambush, saved him from his own ignorant foolishness? Would he be able to concede that Conway Fargo was the better man?

Hialeaha smiled with satisfaction as she set a bowl of canned corn in the center of the table. Her father would have been proud of her for remembering the lessons he taught her. And because of him, she knew Tats-a-das-ago was alive.

Chapter 12

From Agua Fria, the trail led west. They rolled up easy grades now covered with only a few pine and then descended slopes of thickening juniper and sage. They were still over a mile high, and the sun penetrated the air, scorching what it did not wither.

The supply wagon left the meager spring with one barrel half full and the other empty. With the promise of water at El Moro, that barrel had been emptied at noon to water the horses. The two canteens held all that remained of the springwater. By midafternoon, they too were dry.

Treadway's lips were cracked and bleeding when the coach crested a rise that led onto an open plain covered in dry grama grass and patches of beavertail cactus. Some distance ahead, he saw sagebrush, a stand of trees, and what had to be the towering bluff of El Morro. He stood and turned back to Smitty.

"I see it," he yelled. Pointing at the bluff, he added, "That has to be it."

Smitty stood, shielding his eyes with his hand. "Gotta be."

In minutes, game trails sketched their way through the grass on both sides of the road. Like spokes of a wheel, they angled toward the bluff. Buzzing flies began zipping through the air. Grasshoppers jumped ahead of the horses' hooves.

The bluff grew larger, its two-hundred-foot wall jutting like a fortress into a cloudless sky. Except for an occasional gash, the sandstone was smooth, streaked with grays, whites, and tans of various shades.

Nearing the bluff, the wagons rolled into its shadow, facing an uphill climb. The sand deepened, and the wagons halted. The fatigued horses were unhitched. Smitty allowed them to roam free, saying they would find the water on their own.

Wellington and Davis grabbed a canteen while Hialeaha handed out tin cups. In unison they started for the base of the bluff. Wellington took the lead, the others falling in behind.

Single file, they started up the last rise, snaking their way around yucca spines and wading through patches of sage and primrose. Desert blue jays chattered from the tops of junipers. A warm wind rose from the south, cooling their sweating backs and arms.

Twenty paces from the base of the bluff, Wellington stopped suddenly. Davis came alongside, and then the others joined them. Shoulder to shoulder, they gazed in amazement at the carvings covering the sandstone wall. Scratched and chiseled at eye level, stick figures of men and animals were intermingled with scores of names and dates. The inscriptions stretched in both directions as far as they could see.

They started forward. Spreading slightly apart, each selected a section of the wall to inspect.

"There must be hundreds of them," said Davis. "Look at them!"

"This one says 1858," said LaFarge.

"My gracious," exclaimed Mahra, "1701!"

"I wonder what *paso por aqui* means," asked Wellington.

Davis and Wellington looked at each other and smiled.

"Conquistadors." Davis grinned. "Conquistadors!"

"We are getting close now!" said Wellington.

Smitty placed his palm over a chiseled handprint. "I ain't never seen the like. Here's some deer...and some stick men. Injuns no doubt carved these."

For several minutes their hands and fingers traced the rough grooves left by travelers long gone. Thirst was forgotten. Finally, with the light dwindling, Wellington called them together.

Fanning a fly from his face, Wellington said, "We can study these more closely tomorrow. But we need to find the pool before dark.

"I will go north along the bluff with Clarissa and Reed. Edward, you take Mahra, Hialeaha, and Smitty and go south. Call out when you find it. It cannot be far."

As usual, Mahra held onto Davis, slowing him. Hialeaha took the lead. Smitty trailed behind.

In less than five minutes, Hialeaha rounded a slight bend in the bluff and saw the mirrorlike surface of water. It was an elliptical pool nearly surrounded by walls of solid, smooth rock. The basin extended sixty feet into the heart of El Morro, leaving a thirty-foot opening across the front. Overhead, a dome of polished sandstone formed a partial roof. Above it, a dark-gray funnel marked where, for centuries, rainwater and melting snow had cascaded hundreds of feet into the rock tank below.

Hialeaha went to the edge of the pool. The light was poor, but she could see it was far deeper than a man was tall.

Davis and Brooks came up behind her.

"It is the most perfect place I have ever seen," exclaimed Mahra.

"It reminds me of ancient Rome," said Davis. "But this was not made with hands."

Davis took a few steps away from the pool, cupped his hands, and yelled to signal the others. His voice echoed back from the sandstone walls.

Hialeaha scooped up a cup of water and drank it down. "It is cool. And it is sweet."

Using Mahra's cup, Davis was next to drink. He agreed with Hialeaha. He was filling the cup for Brooks when Smitty ambled in.

"It is excellent water, Smitty," said Davis, refilling his own cup. "And we can drink all we want."

"Looks tasty enough," said Smitty, going down on a knee and dipping his cup. He drank a mouthful. "Yep. It's good water, sure 'nuff."

Hialeaha glanced at Smitty. She drank an entire cup without stopping. So did Davis and Brooks. Smitty merely took a taste.

She refilled her cup, tilted it up, and emptied it once again. Smitty, on the other hand, was sipping instead of gulping.

By the time the others made it to the pool, Hialeaha had lost count of how much water Davis and Brooks had drunk, but Smitty had finished only two cups.

At seven thousand feet, the air was dry, and the day was hot. Hialeaha knew no white man from Chicago would drink so little. Smitty had to be stealing water when no one was looking.

Treadway showed first and shouldered his way to the water's edge. He filled his cup and poured it over his head. Then he gulped down several cups in quick succession. Wellington and LaFarge appeared. Unlike Brooks, LaFarge went to the pool and knelt alongside Wellington. Both scooped up the water and drank feverishly.

A few moments later, Wellington wiped his lips. He focused on the pool. "It looks deep out there. There is enough water here for a small town."

"I cannot wait to bathe in it," said Brooks. "Is it not delicious?"

Still on his knees, Wellington shook his head. "No bathing or swimming."

LaFarge stopped drinking. "No bathing? And why not?"

Pointing at the walls around the pool with his cup, Wellington answered, "There is no water coming in or going out of here. Its source is the rain. This is drinking water. We do not want to foul it by bathing in it."

"Then," said LaFarge, "we will fill our water barrels before we bathe."

Wellington again shook his head but said nothing.

"Others drink here," explained Hialeaha.

LaFarge came to her feet. "And why should we care?"

"You, I am certain, do not care," returned Hialeaha. "But Mr. Far-go does."

Hialeaha paused, turning to face Wellington. "Does he not, Mr. Wellington?"

"How should I know that?" snapped Wellington. "We are one day from Zuni. This is their water. And I repeat: we do not want to foul it."

"Then we will use no soap," countered LaFarge. There was an edge to her voice. "How will they know what we did here?"

Hialeaha answered before Wellington could think of a response. "You will leave evidence you cannot see. There will be signs of your passing here. The Indians will read those signs as easily as you read a newspaper."

His eyes smoldering, Wellington raised his voice. It was the first time Hialeaha had ever seen him so agitated. "We have come too far to antagonize the Zunis now. Everyone, we must keep in mind why we are here. We can easily make our toilet with buckets of water poured over us. We may have all the water we want…as long as it is used outside the pool."

"Very well," said LaFarge, suddenly pleasant. She smiled as if nothing had happened. "Mahra and I will go first."

Brooks folded her arms and sulked. "It is such a perfect pool, Edward."

"I know, but Miles is right, dear. Perhaps on our return trip, things will be different."

***

Fargo retied his knee-high moccasins. Saving one last swallow of water, he corked his canteen and looped it over his saddle horn. The glow from the distant campfire had finally disappeared. He guessed it to be two hours past midnight when he led his bay and black to the pool.

His thirsty horses buried their muzzles in the water. Crouching under a rising half moon, Fargo submerged his canteen. As he listened to the bubbles pop, his eyes scanned the night, searching every vague silhouette and black shadow for danger. A gentle breeze brushed his cheek, hissing through branches of sage and primrose.

Raising the dripping canteen to his lips, Fargo drank long and deep. He submerged the canteen again. When it was full, he replaced the cork and palmed it tight.

For a moment the insects stopped their singing, then started again. Fargo stepped away from his horses. Listening, he slowly turned his head left and right. He heard nothing but sounds of the night.

He took another small step and bumped something with his toe, something that did not belong.

Fargo glanced down and saw an empty wooden bucket. A white cloth was draped over the rim. He nudged the bucket with his foot. In the moonlight, he saw a bar of soap in the bottom. Bending low, he touched the cloth, a towel. It was dry and had been neatly folded.

He looked back at his horses, as good as any two watch dogs. The black and bay stood relaxed.

Fargo thought of when he had had his last bath. The closest thing to it was his pulling LaFarge from the Rio Grande. He also thought of Hialeaha. He was going to find her in Zuni. They needed to talk. About what, exactly, he was unsure.

The thought crossed his mind that Hialeaha had left the bucket for him, but he quickly dismissed it. It had probably been left behind by mistake. But, just the same, the bucket and the opportunity were there.

Sitting on a pumpkin-size stone, Fargo pulled off his moccasins. He laid his gun belt on top of them and then stripped off his pants and shirt. His white skin and an even whiter scar on his chest glowed in the moonlight.

Years before in Tucson, the Yankees had been in a frenzy to brand him as a Confederate spy. They demanded the blacksmith hurry his work. Fashioning the iron as fast as he could, the blacksmith got it backward. Instead of an S, the scar Fargo wore was a ragged Z. An army sergeant, trying to kill instead of maim, had burned the red-hot iron deep into the muscle.

Fargo filled the bucket and dumped the water over his head and body. He lathered himself, dumped another bucket, and then one more.

He quickly dried himself and then placed his guns on his shirt and put on his pants and moccasins. As he buttoned up his pants, a twig snapped somewhere in the shadows.

Fargo grabbed the gun belt with his left hand and jerked a pistol with his right.

A voice whispered from the darkness. "It is Hialeaha."

Stunned, Fargo held the pistol at the ready. Then he began to breathe.

For several seconds, there was silence.

"Are you alone?"

"Yes."

Fargo eased the Colt back into its holster.

Hialeaha stepped into the open. Her raven-black hair glistened in the moonlight. She wore a white blouse open at the neck, only partially buttoned. A gust of wind pulled the collar open, exposing the subtle curvature of her breasts.

She hesitated. "May I come closer?"

Fargo nodded.

Stroking her hair, Hialeaha started slowly toward Fargo. "My hair is still wet. I want it to dry before I go to sleep."

She stopped an arm's length from Fargo and looked up at him. Her cheekbones were highlighted by the moon, and he could see the gentle rise and fall of her chest as her eyes searched his. He saw her attention drop to the scar.

She raised a hand, then stopped. "May I?"

"If you want."

Hialeaha stepped within inches. Slowly, she raised her hand and gently ran her fingers over the scar.

"They say the heart of Tats-a-das-ago was burned away. They say he has no feelings because he no longer has a heart."

Fargo let the gun belt slide from his grip. He brushed a strand of hair behind Hialeaha's ear.

"I used to believe that story too."

Hialeaha slid her other hand up and rested it on Fargo's chest. "And what do you believe now?"

Fargo put his hands around Hialeaha's waist and pulled her close. "This," he said and gently kissed her.

Feeling the heat of his skin, Hialeaha put her arms around him. Her grip tightened, and then her fingertips rolled into the muscles of his back.

"And this," he whispered and kissed her again.

Chapter 13

West of El Morro, the road meandered down a slight grade for the first ten miles, and the teams made good time. By late afternoon, the wagons were rolling past Dowa Haloni, a mesa crowned with green piñon pine and streaked with alternating layers of red and cream-colored sandstone.

When they reached the Zuni River, it was dry. Where water had once flowed, there was only a winding bed of sand bordered by barren, crusted banks. It ran through a plain of knee-high sage dotted with occasional stands of juniper. On a small rise, a cluster of drab buildings rose above the wasteland.

Treadway turned his head. "There it is! There's Zuni!"

Wellington stuck his head out one side of the coach and Davis the other.

"Splendid," said Wellington, waving the dust from his face and squinting against the dazzling glare of the sand. "Splendid indeed."

"It is precious little to look at," Davis said, coughing. "At least, not from here."

"Nonsense," said Wellington. "Just a few miles from this humble pueblo lies Cibola, my friends. Estevan awaits."

"Riders coming," said Treadway, pointing to a rising dust cloud.

"Greeters, no doubt," said Wellington. "The Zuni are known for their hospitality. Drive on. We are in good hands now."

Treadway crossed the riverbed and dove back up on the road. A half mile from the pueblo, he leaned back on the reins as three riders drew up in front of him.

Two of the riders were Zuni. The third, though dressed the same, was unquestionably white. He appeared to be in his early twenties.

The white man had a twisted bandana tied around his shoulder-length hair. Earrings hung from his lobes and a shell necklace from his neck. A mustache grew under an aquiline nose and two beady eyes. He wore blue wool pants lined with elk teeth and moccasins.

The coach unloaded.

"*Keshshi*," said the white man. "I am *Tenatsali*. Welcome to *Halona wa*. The *Ashiwi* welcome you to their *Hiwanna*."

"We were under the impression this was Zuni," said Davis.

"Ah, yes," said Tenatsali, eyeing the three women. "I must apologize. As you can readily observe, I have, to some degree, thrown off the cloak of the white race.

"My name is Cushing, Frank Hamilton Cushing, formerly with the Smithsonian Institute. Presently I am the resident ethnologist at Zuni Pueblo."

Wellington took an immediate dislike to the man and was unimpressed by his supposed credentials. Such impudence could not go unchallenged. "We are anthropologists from Harvard, Mr. Cushing."

Cushing dismounted. He approached swaggering with self-assured importance.

Wellington started the formal introductions. He took delight in the fact that Cushing was no more than five feet, three inches tall and small boned.

Saving LaFarge for last, Wellington introduced her as "Miss Clarissa LaFarge—*the* Clarissa LaFarge."

Cushing blinked. "I am sorry. I do not understand."

"The stage actress," explained Wellington.

"Ah, I see," said Cushing. "I fear my pursuits are so demanding I have no time for the theater."

LaFarge covered her contempt with a smile. She looked him over carefully. "I did not realize that pretending to be an Indian would place such great demands on one's time."

Uncertain of LaFarge's meaning, Cushing continued. "You say you are from Harvard. I was at Cornell for a time." He paused and sighed.

"I grew bored with it, however, and joined up with Powel. I assume that you are familiar with him.'"

"Yes," answered Wellington, but not to be outdone, he smiled. "We are associates of Professor Lewis Henry Morgan and Adolph Bandelier. Perhaps you have heard of them?"

Cushing stiffened. With a single eyebrow arching skyward, he raised his head as if trying to increase his height. "Not long ago, I had the pleasure of meeting the professor. I have no knowledge of Adolph Bandelier.

"May I ask, what is the purpose of your visit to Zuni?"

Sizing up Cushing to be a pompous ill-bred, Wellington took a chance. "We have no interest in Zuni or its culture. We are here to study the architecture of the Navajo."

Cushing seemed relieved. "Ah yes, the pesky Navajo. The Zuni are at odds with them at the moment. You do understand that the Navajo and Apache are traditional enemies of the Zuni?"

"Do the Indians fight *each other*?" asked Mahra.

Cushing smiled. "Always, Miss Brooks. And now I fight the Navajo alongside my brothers, the Ashiwi...or Zuni, as you refer to them."

"You?" questioned LaFarge, flashing her most innocent smile. "How daring you must be!"

Something caught Cushing's eye before he could respond to the flattery. He pointed. "Is he with you?"

Everyone turned to see Fargo riding across the sandy riverbed.

"No," said Wellington. "He was in my employ as far as the Rio Grande. But not since then."

"His name is Far-go," said Hialeaha. She raised her voice slightly. "Tats-a-das-ago."

Everyone standing, including Cushing, drew a blank. The Zunis on horseback, however, instantly sat up straight.

"His name means nothing to me," admitted Cushing.

The two Zunis rode to meet Fargo. They spoke for a moment, and then all three galloped toward the pueblo.

Watching the Zunis ride away without him, Cushing's face flushed red.

"Seems your friends might know 'im," said Smitty.

"Perhaps they do."

"Do them Injuns speak any Mexican?" asked Smitty.

"Most do. I myself do not."

"Well, Fargo speaks Mexican good. They musta been palaverin' together 'fore they rode off."

"We intend on stopping for the night," said Davis. "Is there any particular area we should occupy?"

"I will take you to the old mission," said Cushing, still flushed. "The land in front of it is flat and has a stone fence. It will hold your horses. Water is scarce this year. There is no grass, but the Zuni have corn enough for feed."

"We are most grateful," said Wellington. "May we invite you to dine with us this evening? We are well supplied with canned goods from Chicago. Hialeaha can prepare fish, meat, oysters, and even lobster. Side dishes may consist of beans, corn, strawberries, cherries, or peaches. The list goes on."

Cushing glanced at Hialeaha. "Canned lobster?"

Hialeaha nodded.

"Then I must bring some of the Zuni baked bread. They prepare it in stone ovens that resemble beehives. It is most delicious."

"Wonderful," said LaFarge. "So far from civilization, it will be a joy to converse with another gentleman—and one so knowledgeable as well."

Bowing at the waist, Cushing said, "It will be my pleasure, Miss LaFarge." He turned on his heels and went to his horse. Mounting it, he added needlessly, "Follow me."

It was not until the coach lunged forward that LaFarge snickered. Hearing her, Wellington and Edwards almost choked trying to quiet their laughter.

Brooks was confused. "What is it?"

Davis doubled over, tears running down his face. "I fight...I fight with my brothers against the Navajo!"

Wellington shook his head. He pitched his voice in a high falsetto. "How daring you must be, Mr. Cushing!"

242

Brooks began to laugh, although she was still confused.

Hialeaha merely listened as they ridiculed Cushing for several minutes. When the coach reached the edge of the pueblo, what they saw sobered them instantly.

An array of stone fences covered the ground leading up to the pueblo. As they approached, a half dozen scrawny dogs raced out, barking and nipping at the horses and wagon wheels.

The pueblo was a conglomeration of red adobe, stone walls, and log-supported flat roofs. Room after room had been constructed next to and on top of one another. Sun-bleached pole ladders jutted up through small openings in the roofs, their pointed ends extending ten feet in the air.

"Not exactly Egypt," said Davis.

Wellington scoffed. "It looks like the work of drunken masons. There is not a straight line anywhere."

Brooks leaned forward for a better look. "I see two bells on that large building. That must be a church."

Like a disturbed anthill, men, women, and children began to appear. They swarmed up through the roofs and, in seconds, lined the walls shoulder to shoulder. The entire pueblo was alive with movement.

"They do not look all that friendly to me," said Davis.

"Just curious," assured Wellington. "Notice they have no weapons."

Bouncing and swaying, the coach turned right through a narrow opening past walls of crumbling adobe and exposed flat stones. Burros, laden with firewood, were hurriedly pulled out of their path. Women with pots balanced on their heads quickly stepped aside. Chickens and dogs scattered in every direction.

With thousands of black eyes watching them, the wagons halted next to the only freestanding building, clearly the Spanish mission. In front of it stood a three-foot stone fence that marked off a half-acre plot for the church.

As the coach unloaded, Cushing rode back, this time staying mounted. "Feel free to camp here. If you encounter any Indians near the mission wearing green sashes, please understand they are harmless. They are but a curious remnant of the Catholic sacristan. They call themselves the Sakisti and, as I understand it, are caretakers of the mission."

Wellington nodded. "Shall we say sundown for supper?"

"Might I bring two guests? I should think you would want to entertain the governor of Zuni and his father."

"By all means, bring them. We shall be preparing more than enough."

"Excellent," said Cushing, and then he wheeled his horse and galloped out of sight.

Davis grinned. "Zuni has a governor?"

"We shall see," said Wellington. "But we have to make some plans before this evening."

"Such as?"

Wellington looked at the Indians lining the rooftops and walls. "Such as how best to extract the location of Hawikuh without arousing suspicion."

***

Camp was set up inside the stone wall in front of the church. The table was set with places for seven. Wellington and Davis put on their best hunting attire, and Brooks and LaFarge wore their finest traveling outfits. Hialeaha wore her nicest dress. Treadway and Smitty were told to keep their distance, that the evening encounter was critical to the success of their venture.

The last tinge of blue was fading from the evening sky when Cushing walked through the opening in the fence into the illuminated churchyard. He wore a bright-blue wool shirt, black pants lined with elk teeth, and a belt with silver discs attached. A turquoise necklace hung around his neck. He held a bundle covered with clean white muslin.

Wellington went to him, extending his hand. "Good evening, Mr. Cushing. Welcome."

Cushing shifted the bundle and shook hands. "I brought the bread. It is still warm from the oven."

Inhaling deeply, Wellington took the bread. "It smells delicious."

Davis emerged from the tent with Brooks and LaFarge. Cushing stopped in midstride. "I have not seen such beauty in all my days."

"You flatter us," said Mahra, smiling broadly. "But thank you just the same."

"Where are your other guests?" asked LaFarge. "Are they not coming?"

"Yes. However, I am afraid punctuality is not in their nature."

After ten minutes of exchanged compliments and small talk, a lone Indian stepped into the lamplight. He wore a headband and simple muslin clothing. Several strands of shells adorned his neck, and around his waist, he wore a red sash. He held a cane with a silver top.

Cushing went to him. "May I present Patrico Pino, governor of Zuni. If you will, notice his cane. It was a gift from President Lincoln to the Zuni. It is their symbol of governorship."

Another Indian appeared. A web of deep wrinkles creased his face. His eyes were deep and sunken. Next to him, wearing moccasins, stood Conway Fargo.

Approaching the old man, Cushing said, "And this is Pedro Pino, former governor of Zuni and father of Patrico. He is close to one hundred years old."

Glancing curiously up at Fargo, Cushing asked, "And who might you be, sir?"

Fargo searched the darkness for Treadway but did not see him. "A friend of the Zuni."

Pedro and Fargo said something to each other in Spanish.

Wellington looked to Cushing, a question in his eyes.

Cushing shrugged. "As I said, I do not speak Spanish. I am just beginning to learn Zuni."

"Supper is ready," offered Hialeaha, looking for the first time into Fargo's eyes.

"Mr. Cushing, here are places for you and your two guests," said Wellington, indicating where they were to sit. "Ladies, if you will be seated."

Fargo glanced at Hialeaha and nodded toward the campfire. Without a word, she went to the coach.

Cushing held the chair for LaFarge and then went to the governor and his father. He spoke to them and made hand gestures toward the table, but they did not move.

Hialeaha returned with a blanket and spread it by the campfire. To Cushing's surprise, the Indians went to the fire and sat down cross-legged on the blanket.

Without explanation, Fargo adjusted his pistols and joined them.

"Well," said Cushing, "I assume they are more comfortable over there. I suppose it is their custom."

Hialeaha kept busy serving lobster to the table and corned beef to those on the blanket. Cushing monopolized the conversation with long-winded explanations of what he had discovered about the Zuni while Fargo spoke Spanish in low tones with the Indians.

Stopping by the fire, Hialeaha stole a look at Fargo. Their eyes met for a moment. The old Zuni asked a question, and Fargo answered.

"What did he say?" asked Hialeaha.

"He wanted to know if you were my woman."

Hialeaha smiled. "The years have not weakened his eyes."

Smitty came in from the darkness as Hialeaha went back to the table to collect dishes. He knelt down by the fire, eyeing the Zuni.

"They don't look like much."

"No, they don't," agreed Fargo. "But they can stand toe to toe with the Navajo and the Apache."

A grunt expressed Smitty's doubt.

Pedro Pino studied Smitty for a long while. He spoke in Spanish to Fargo, and then the two Zuni rose soundlessly disappeared into the night.

"What was that all about?" asked Smitty. "They don't speak American, do they?"

"No."

"Then what was it that old man said?"

Fargo wiped his plate with a piece of Zuni bread. "He thinks you might be a witch. He said I should torture you to make you confess."

Smitty swore. "He's loco."

Fargo chewed on the bread. He had known Pedro Pino for years. The Zuni were highly superstitious, but Pedro knew how to read men. He did not like what he saw in Smitty. The patriarch of the tribe had no other way to express it but to call him a witch.

"Maybe he is loco," said Fargo, coming to his feet. "But no more than that greenhorn Cushing."

Taking a look around, Fargo worked his gun belt into position. Then, like the Zuni, he silently slid into the darkness.

"They are gone," whispered Davis. "All three have left."

"Without so much as a word," complained LaFarge.

"Again," said Cushing, "theirs is a different culture. Our customs and our concept of good manners are foreign to them, just as their customs and beliefs are foreign to us."

Wellington glanced over his shoulder at the campfire. Smitty sat by himself with his back to the table. Cushing had been lecturing throughout supper on the Zuni way of living. It was time to steer him in a different direction.

"Mr. Cushing, in our preparations to make this journey, Professor Morgan mentioned to us that Coronado was first to make contact with the Zuni. Was that encounter anywhere near here?"

"Oh, certainly it was," answered Cushing. "I have little interest in the site, but I have been there once. It is twelve miles or so southwest of here, down the Zuni River. It is just east of the river on a hill and easy to see. Coming in from the south, as he did, Coronado could not have missed it.

"All the pueblos seem to be built on hilltops. I assume for defensive purposes. At any rate, about 1680, the Zuni revolted against Spanish rule. They killed the priests and burned the mission at Hawikuh. After that, they inexplicably abandoned the entire site and never returned.

"I should correct myself. The Zuni do not believe it is completely abandoned. They say it is, to this day, inhabited by the nonliving."

"Ghosts?" asked Mahra.

"At least their version of them, I believe."

"Yes," said Davis, refilling Cushing's wine glass. "Professor Morgan mentioned something of that belief. He also told us a bit about a black Moroccan that I found quite mysterious."

Cushing took a sip of wine. "The Zuni have a legend of a fearsome black warrior who was thought to be a god. Some say he was good; others are convinced he was evil. They even have a doll that has a black body and red lips, called a *katsina* or *kachina*. The language is difficult to translate.

"According to legend, they killed the black warrior at Hawikuh and dismembered him to prove he was mortal. His body is said to be buried in a sacred location nearby."

"Oh, how horrid," exclaimed LaFarge. "Let us change the subject to something more pleasant, shall we? I have heard enough about these dreadful ruins. Do you not agree, Miles?"

Wellington winked at LaFarge. "Yes, we have heard all we need to know of them."

"You are quite right," chimed Davis. "Mr. Cushing, could you tell us what you know of the Navajo? After all, it is they we have come so far to research."

Obviously pleased to continue speaking, Cushing said, "Of course. You realize you will be taking some risk when you leave here. You will be virtually alone on Beale's Road. It is seldom used since the railroad chose to go by way of Gallup. The trade that once was conducted here has moved north and with it, the teamsters."

"Thank you for your concern," said Wellington. "We have come this far without incident. Please continue."

Chapter 14

Wellington did not break camp until after sunrise. He wanted to make certain their departure was witnessed. By the time they rolled out of Zuni, heat waves distorted every horizon.

When the pueblo was well out of sight, the wagons turned off Beale's Road. Heading southwest, the trudging hooves and steel rims dug deep into the sand, cutting a rough path across the sage.

Assured by Smitty that both water barrels were full, everyone in the coach drank freely from their canteens. Smitty and Treadway took turns with their own. Mahra nursed a heat-induced headache with frequent sips of Mother Bailey's while Hialeaha dozed. For over an hour, LaFarge, Davis, and Wellington discussed the meaning of three oval markings they had discovered on the buffalo-skin map.

Shortly after noon, Treadway caught sight of the dry riverbed. In minutes, they rolled down the shallow bank of the Zuni River to follow its smooth southerly route. Bordering the river to the east was a range of juniper-covered hills.

Near sundown, the hills began to slope into another plain, this one covered in dry grass. It spread eastward for two miles. Downriver, the grass extended as far as the eye could see before funneling into a small mountain pass.

Perplexed, Wellington ordered Treadway to stop. Everyone got out to stretch and then gathered by the water barrels. Smitty refilled the canteens while Wellington and Davis tried to determine where they were.

"We should have seen it by now," complained LaFarge. "Cushing said it was easy to see."

"Agreed," said Davis, accepting a canteen from Smitty and handing it to Mahra. "He said it was just east of the river on a hill."

Wellington wiped a hand over his face and took his turn on a canteen. Thoughtfully looking at the grassy plain, he waved his hand. "This is the first plain to the east we have seen, and there is no city. It must be farther down."

As they discussed their predicament, the sun began to set, its lower rim dipping below a distant mountain peak. In the thin, heated air, the desert was gradually bathed in a peculiar and strikingly vivid yellow light.

Suddenly Treadway's arm jutted out, his finger extended. "There! There it is!"

All eyes followed his.

Less than a mile away, walls appeared, walls painted gold by the setting sun.

For several seconds, no one spoke.

"They do look golden," exclaimed Brooks.

"The legend appears," proclaimed Davis. "Cibola rises out of nowhere before our very eyes."

"I'll be damned," said Smitty. "A feller might mistake it for gold, at that."

The color faded as fast as it had appeared, leaving only the gray outline of rectangular walls set against the dusky sky. A moment later, the walls blended perfectly into the red sand of the hillside.

Wellington climbed up next to Treadway. Before Davis could close the door, the coach began to turn around. Rocking up and over the eastern riverbank, the wagons struck out over the grass. In seconds, they started bouncing violently.

Looking down, Treadway slowed the horses to a walk.

"What is it?" asked Wellington.

"Holes. Lots of them."

"Prairie dogs," shouted Smitty. "They done dug up the whole place. Watch out the horses don't step in one of them holes and break a leg."

They slowed the horses, and it was twilight when the coach and wagon stopped at the base of Hawikuh. The low hill in front of them was covered at its crest with walls of flat sandstones stacked two feet thick. In some places, the walls had fallen into piles of rubble; in others, they stood seven feet tall.

Wellington pointed excitedly. "There is a space between the walls, Reed. It appears to be a passage through the center. I want to see how far it goes. Can we make it?"

"Let's find out," said Treadway and slapped the leather lines.

The horses started up the grade. After fifty yards they entered the ruins, passing crumbling stone walls on both sides of the narrow passage. A turn to the right and then a quick one to the left, and the coach stopped on top of a flat open ridge.

Wellington hopped down just as Smitty pulled up. Davis was first out of the coach.

"I thought it would be bigger," said Wellington. "It covers no more than an acre."

Davis shrugged and grinned. "No matter, my dear cousin. For our purposes, the smaller the better."

"This is a dandy campsite," said Smitty. He nodded, looking out over the walls. "Except for that little ridge behind us yonder, you can see all 'round for miles. I can see why they built up here."

Davis took Brooks by the shoulders. Turning her toward the south, he said, "Mahra, do you see that pass out beyond the grass? Coronado marched through that very pass to this city three hundred years ago. We now are standing in the exact place where he stood. And little has changed in all that time."

Smiling with indifference, Mahra shrugged. "How exciting. I am happy for you, Edward."

***

Fargo sat on his heels in the predawn light looking northwest from Ojo Caliente. There was water at the spring, drinkable but hot with the taste of sulfur. It could keep a white man alive for a day or two.

The campfire at Hawikuh had burned brightly for most of the night. Anyone within sixty miles could have seen it from all points south.

Now their horses were drifting toward Ojo Caliente, two miles from Hawikuh. No one was with them.

When Fargo first discovered the wagons had left the road, he was baffled. With no sign of trouble, he at least knew no one had forced them off. They headed directly for the Zuni River and then abruptly turned south. When he crossed their tracks in the riverbed, it became clear to him they were headed for the ruins.

The deserted pueblo of Hawikuh was sacred to the Zuni and located directly in the path taken by Apache and Navajo raiders. Whatever Wellington was after was at the ruins. He had gone out of his way to keep his destination a secret, but if he continued making big fires, he would be inviting company.

Mounting his black, Fargo checked his pistols and both Winchesters. He had a feeling in his gut, one that he had long since learned to trust. He called it a hunch. The Indians said it was his part of his power, the medicine that kept him alive.

Leading the bay, Fargo worked his way along a juniper-covered ridge that formed the southern border of the grassy plain of Hawikuh. Warily, he worked his way toward the riverbed and the small valley it formed. From the south, it was the natural gateway to Zuni.

***

Before the sun crested the eastern mountains, Wellington had found the remains of the old mission, but it was Davis who discovered the flat rock with three hand-sized depressions, likely the result of grinding piñon nuts. The marks were under a branch of juniper. The tree grew out of a crack in the rock, a wagon-sized piece of sandstone at the base of the hill. They had rolled over it the evening before.

Using the three depressions as a starting point and the buffalo cape as their map, they paced off to the east and then paced evenly off to the north. Both Wellington and Davis made their own calculations. They arrived at points within ten feet of each other. The point was also within an arm's length of a peculiar pile of stones. By midmorning, they agreed the place to dig was under the pile of stones, a spot almost in the shadow of the mission's south wall.

From the boot of the coach, they tossed down a tarp and unloaded picks, shovels, and various hand tools. With a pick in one hand and a shovel in the other, Wellington and Davis hurried along the fragmented walls of the ruins and down a steep incline of eighty feet to the stone pile.

Dropping the tools, both men slid their hands into new leather gloves and eagerly started tossing the stones aside. When the ground was clear, Wellington wiped the sweat from his face and picked up a shovel.

"Where is Smitty? We need that tarp."

"He went to cut some poles," said Davis, catching his breath. He looked up, studying the ruins for a moment, and then the remains of the mission. "Cushing said they killed the priests and burned the mission."

"The priests could have died right where we are standing...or where we are digging."

Placing his boot on the blade of the shovel, Wellington shoved it into the sand. "They are dead and gone," said Wellington, tossing the sand aside. "They are dead and gone."

They had dug a ten-foot square two feet deep by the time Smitty returned with Treadway to stake the tarp over the dig. Chairs were then brought down for LaFarge and Brooks. Wellington and Davis took off their pistols and hung them on the poles.

Davis stopped digging for a moment. "Reed, please bring us the other canteen, will you?"

"And bring one of the shotguns, also," added Wellington. "You can stand guard."

"Find anything yet?" asked Smitty, coming just inside the shade. "You two are working mighty hard."

"You need not be concerned," said Davis.

"You mind tellin' me what it is you're lookin' for, anyhow?"

"We do," LaFarge huffed. "If we need your assistance, we will call for you."

"Sure thing, miss," said Smitty, and he started back up slope to the ruins. At the first wall where there was enough shade, he sat down in plain view of everyone under the tarp. Leaning back, he felt the heat of the stones against his back and sighed with satisfaction.

How many years had it been now? Five? Or was it six? Sometimes it was hard for him to remember. The heat and the desert—and the beating he had taken—did that to him.

Reaching into his pants pocket, Smitty eased out a pistol and laid it in his lap. The glossy blue steel of the four-and-three-quarter-inch barrel reflected the blazing sun. Brand new and never fired, the Colt had cost him his last twelve dollars.

Smitty rotated the cylinder, enjoying the metallic clicking sound it made. Six cartridges, one for each of them. One left over if Fargo didn't show up. The hole they were digging would be big enough either way.

Savoring every moment, Smitty watched them dig deeper. When Treadway joined them under the tarp, the hole was waist deep. All had not gone exactly as planned, but then, what did? It was time to end it. But not before they knew why.

Standing triumphantly, Smitty slid the pistol back into his pocket. The only one missing was Hialeaha. She was the best of the lot but a loose end that would have to be dealt with.

With each step Smitty took, his boots dislodged small rocks, sending them rattling down the hill toward the tarp. He slipped and caught his balance. Grinning, he glanced from the dig to the mission walls. It was the closest he had been to a church since leaving Chicago and the closest Clarissa LaFarge had been in her entire life.

Smitty was still smiling when he stepped under the edge of the tarp into the shade. Wellington and Davis were in the pit sweating through their white shirts. Treadway stood next to LaFarge holding his double-barreled shotgun in the bend of his arm.

Seeing Smitty, Wellington stopped digging and wiped his forehead with the back of his sleeve. He pointed to a canteen on top of a pile of sand. "Smitty, can you get some more water for us? Hialeaha is supposed to come with some, but I cannot wait any longer."

"Sure," said Smitty, walking behind Treadway and picking up the empty canteen.

Mahra rose from her chair and adjusted her feathered broad-brimmed sunbonnet. Holding a small purse, she said, "I am going into the mission. Maybe I will find something to interest me there."

Davis paused. "Be careful, Mahra. Those old rock walls may be the harbinger of all sorts of beasts."

"Not to worry," smiled Brooks.

Smitty watched her leave, wondering for a moment whether it would be better to just leave her alone and let the desert take her.

The pistol belts of Wellington and Davis hung on the juniper poles, now out of easy reach. Smitty took a step back, positioning himself behind Treadway. He reached into his pocket for the pistol, but Treadway took two steps to his right, half turning in Smitty's direction.

"Here comes Hialeaha with that water," said Treadway.

Suddenly, a scream came from within the mission walls. Davis scrambled out of the pit, followed by Wellington. Empty-handed, both ran into the mission.

Brooks stood in a shaded corner holding her purse against her chest. A broken bottle of Mother Bailey's glittered at her feet. She pointed to a small mound of sand in the middle of the mission walls. "It moved!"

"What did?" blurted Davis.

"A creature came out of the ground," whimpered Brooks. "It was coming at me."

Hialeaha rounded the wall. Gasping for air, she hurried to Mahra. "Are you all right?"

Brooks nodded.

Unconcerned, Treadway and LaFarge casually stepped over one of the crumbled walls and into the mission to where the others had gathered. Smitty joined them, stopping a few feet to the rear.

Davis followed Mahra's eyes to a small mound of sand on the dirt floor. "Was it a snake?"

"No. It had a big head," answered Brooks. "And ears."

Davis went to the mound and scraped the toe of his boot across it. "Was it here, the thing you saw?"

"Yes. It was awful."

Davis sighed. His smile was humorless. "It was only a prairie dog, Mahra."

Noticing something white in the disturbed sand, Davis reached down. "They are harmless."

He picked up what at first appeared to be the tip of an arrowhead. "Look at this," he said, handing the sliver of bone to Wellington.

"A fingertip?" questioned Wellington. "Or possibly a toe."

Davis knelt by the burrow and ran his fingers through the loose sand. His fingers sifted out a small, jagged triangle.

Davis blew off the dust and then rubbed the object on his shirt-front. "It is a piece of glass." He paused. "Green glass."

"You mean pottery," corrected Wellington.

Wide-eyed, Davis looked at Wellington. "No, it is *green glass!*"

Wellington and Davis stared at each other.

"What difference does it make?" asked LaFarge. "I have seen bits of broken pottery all over the hill."

"The Zuni never had glass," said Wellington.

"But Estevan did," added Davis. "Remember, Professor Morgan said he traveled with two green plates for eating his food."

"Vaguely," said LaFarge.

"He was a big man," said Davis, excitedly. "What if he was taller than you, Miles? What if he was much taller and accustomed to walking long distances?"

"Then his stride would be far greater than ours," answered Wellington. "We could be off our mark by several feet, enough to put us here."

"But the mission wasn't even here when Estevan came," blurted Smitty. His reference to Estevan went unnoticed.

"True," replied Davis. "Cushing said that Estevan was buried in a sacred place near Hawikuh. The friars, wanting to dispel Zuni superstitions, might well have built their mission on the same ground. They have been known to do such things."

Smitty chuckled. "So, you want to dig some more, in the middle of a church?"

"You bet we do," said Treadway.

Smitty sighed, his eyes narrowing with curiosity. "Why not?"

"If this is Estevan, we will need a container," said Wellington. "Hialeaha, I assume you have a sewing kit."

"Yes."

"Please bring it here. And bring a blanket. We will need a sack made for our artifacts."

"And get the canteens under the tarp," said Davis. "We will need lots of water."

***

Hialeaha returned to the mission and paused in what had once been the doorway. Holding a satchel containing her sewing kit, a blanket, and a half-filled canteen, she thought for a moment before going inside.

Smitty had said the water barrels were full when they left Zuni. Now they were empty. She checked under the tarp in the supply wagon, and the food was gone as well.

Hialeaha looked into the room where Wellington and Davis were digging.

LaFarge and Brooks sat in the chairs that had been moved inside the walls. Two pistol belts were piled in a far corner. Treadway leaned against a wall, his shotgun propped next to him. Smitty stood away from everyone, seemingly unarmed.

The water might have leaked out of one barrel during the night, but not two. Smitty either had not filled them, as he had said, or someone had intentionally drained them. That someone would be LaFarge, Treadway, or Smitty.

Whoever it was had a plan, and whatever that plan was, it endangered Mahra.

Hialeaha handed the canteen to Wellington, but he set it aside and continued digging on his knees. Instead of a shovel, he was using a spoon and paintbrush. Davis sat next to him piecing together broken shards of glass.

Trying to think of what to do, Hialeaha picked up her satchel and eased herself against a wall. With her eyes glancing from person to person, she began to sew the blanket into a large sack.

In the floor of the mission, a rib cage gradually appeared, then an arm and leg. Wellington continued to scoop the sand away from the skeleton.

Davis swore suddenly. "These are plates, Miles. There is no doubt. These are green plates."

"Impossible!" said Smitty, clearly agitated. "That can't be!"

Treadway left his shotgun leaning against the wall and stepped in for a closer look. "They're plates, all right."

Wellington sat up, also swearing. "There is no skull. And the right arm and leg are missing."

"Dismembered!" said Davis. "They wanted to prove he was mortal."

Wellington sat back on his calves. "Ladies and gentlemen," he said, extending his hand, "may I introduce you to Estevan, the Moroccan slave!"

Smitty stomped over, his face red. He glared at the plates that Davis had pieced together and the partial skeleton lying in the shallow grave.

"Damn you all!" snarled Smitty. He stepped back, drew his pistol, and cocked it. "Damn you all to hell!"

Circling quickly, Smitty grabbed the shotgun from the wall and shoved the pistol in his belt. He walked around the shocked onlookers, stepping between them and the two pistols in the corner.

"What is the meaning of this?" demanded Wellington.

Smitty howled then shook like a dog. "What is the meaning of this?" he roared. "What...What indeed!"

"It is the heat," said Davis. "He has gone mad."

"Mad, am I?" said Smitty, cocking both hammers of the shotgun. "Better mad than a fool."

"Who are you?" asked Hialeaha.

"Ah. The Indian is brightest of you all. Who am I? she asks. She is the first to ask, the first to suspect. And that is indeed the question you all should ask. Not, what am I doing. No. The question should be… who *am* I?"

"Far-go was first to suspect," corrected Hialeaha.

"Well, then, it's too bad he is not here for the finale," said Smitty. "Clarissa, you have a flair for the dramatic. You will appreciate that I first offer a clue before disclosing my identity."

Smitty indicated the skeleton with the barrel of the shotgun. "It ends the way it started."

LaFarge sneered. "You are insane."

An exaggerated frown wrinkled Smitty's lips. "Would you like another clue?"

"You are a common thief," said Wellington. "You intend to rob us. That is all we need know."

"Rob you? Do you think I intend to *rob* you?"

"Take what you will and leave," said Davis.

"All in good time, all in good time. But first, another clue."

Smitty thoughtfully wagged his head side to side. "You were warned to watch for a witch with one leg. Your journey started with such and ends with such."

"You are a witch?" asked Mahra.

"Out with it!" demanded Davis.

"Any guesses…Reed?" asked Smitty. "Perhaps you should consult with your partner in crime. The one you financed by looting mansions after the Great Chicago Fire. Ask the one you sent to Yale and then to acting school…all in order to marry a rich gentleman. You know, Reed, your longtime mistress."

"You are completely mad," said LaFarge.

"Come, come, my dear," said Smitty. "Is that any way to speak to a beggar with a patch over his eye, a poor wretch selling artifacts in the streets of Chicago…a one-legged man?"

Wellington turned toward LaFarge, his eyes filling with confusion. "Clarissa? What is he saying?"

"Oh, there is more, Miles. Don't you want to know the rest? Surely you do. Of course you do."

Wellington was speechless.

Smitty took his hand from the forestock of the shotgun and raised his upper lip. "See the few teeth I have left, Miles?"

Wellington swore. "Who the hell are you and what do you want?"

"My, my, a Harvard graduate, and still you have no answers."

Hialeaha gasped.

Smitty glanced at her. "Aha. I can see the Indian has solved the mystery. Tell them who I am, Hialeaha."

"You are Bryce Stewart," said Hialeaha.

Smitty bowed slightly. "In the flesh."

Wellington squinted, studying Stewart's face, but said nothing.

"A broken nose and jaw, eyes cut and mutilated, teeth knocked out in front of hundreds of people. Is it so hard to recognize your work, Miles?

"And you Clarissa: if I still had all the money my father lost, would you marry me now?"

Stewart smirked. "I think not. Even if you did, you would have Treadway murder me and take my inheritance."

Wellington slumped, unable to speak.

"You see," said Stewart, "after the beating you gave me, I had nothing. I wandered through the streets of Chicago for weeks. I had to beg for food. I eventually discovered Chicago's darker side, the criminal side, and the criminal element accepted me.

"It was then that fate smiled on me. Reed Treadway's reputation was brought to my attention. He had an accomplice by the name of Mattie O'Brien.

Stewart extended his arm from Wellington to LaFarge. "Miles Wellington, may I present...Miss Mattie O'Brien."

"What now?" asked Davis, wrapping an arm tightly around Mahra.

"Mine was a clever plan, was it not? The conquistador helmet, the coin, the map, and the rocks I piled up for you to find were all brilliant deceptions. And I am proud of the Arabic I included. I think that was quite ingenious."

"You did all that?" asked Davis.

"Of course I did. After my days in the Chicago slums, I traveled up and down the east coast. Penniless, I decided to work my way west.

I made it as far as Zuni. Recalling the lectures of Professor Morgan, I wandered downriver searching for Cibola. I found this place and began digging, hoping to find artifacts to sell.

"One day an Indian appeared out of nowhere and tried to kill me. His arrow missed, but my bullet did not. He was wearing a conquistador helmet, and on his necklace was a Spanish coin.

"While holding that bloody helmet, the entire plan came to me in a matter of seconds."

"All of your misfortunes happened years ago, Bryce," said Davis. "And Mahra had nothing to do with any of them. Neither did Hialeaha. At least let them go."

"It's too late for that, much too late. As my worthless father often said, 'God suffers fools to reap what they have sown.'"

***

On the ridge, Fargo caught sight of the raiding party two hundred yards below. A dozen mounted Apaches waited in the riverbed. Motionless, they stared at a white speck two miles away. Two saddles were empty. In moments, a pair of scouts emerged from the grass. They pointed and then swung onto their horses.

Riding out of their concealment, the Apaches started boldly forward. Knowing they had nothing to fear, the raiding party walked their horses onto the plain of grass. If they broke into a run, Fargo knew he would have no chance to warn the camp. If he was to get in front of them, he had to go now.

Spurring his black and leading his bay, Fargo charged down the ridge, dodging junipers and bounding over deadfalls and rocks. In seconds he was on the grass at a full run, angling for the ruins. Glancing to his left, he saw the Apaches already trying to cut him off.

He had covered a fast quarter mile when the bay tripped, jerking the lead rope from Fargo's grasp. He leaned low to cut the wind and spurred the black. He was gaining distance. There would be a few seconds to get ready.

Hialeaha heard the rumbling first. She forced her eyes off the black holes at the end of Stewart's shotgun and looked over a low part of the mission wall.

"It may be too late for us all," she said.

Hearing the dull thundering, Stewart took two steps, trying to see what was coming.

"That has to be Fargo," said Hialeaha.

Stewart swore bitterly. He raised the shotgun, pointing it at Wellington. His finger danced on the trigger as he went to the wall for a better look. A large cloud of dust rose behind a single rider.

Ignoring Stewart, Hialeaha raced outside the mission, waving her arms in the air. Dirt was flying from the black's hooves. In seconds, Fargo slid to stop in front of the mission, wheeled, and fired five shots from his Winchester.

"Get to high ground," he yelled, and fired two more rounds at the scattering Apaches.

"Go...now!" Hialeaha screamed as she ran back into the mission.

No one inside the mission moved.

She pushed her way past Stewart and grabbed her satchel. Again she screamed, "Now!"

Running past a stunned Stewart, Hialeaha and the others ran out of the mission. They scrambled up the steep hill toward the ruins as lead slapped into the rocks around them. Fargo holstered the empty Winchester and drew the second. He rode halfway up the hill, turned, and fired at the puffs of smoke.

Stewart then came running out of the mission, firing both barrels of the shotgun at the Apaches. As he ran past Fargo, he pulled a pistol but did not stop to shoot. When he jumped over a stone wall, Fargo bolted up and into Hawikuh.

The shooting stopped as soon as Fargo rode into the ruins and dismounted. Following the sound of voices, he found everyone, including Stewart, gathering at the top of Hawikuh. There, the partially intact walls formed a modest fortress that had one large room and another one, much smaller.

Leading his horse inside the walls, Fargo went to the small room and dropped his reins. He took a box of shells and the three Mexican pistols from his saddlebags. Crouching low, he darted into the second room and dropped a pistol in LaFarge's lap. He tossed the other two to Wellington and Davis. Pivoting on one knee, he saw Treadway holding a pistol on him.

Fargo glared at Treadway, who clutched the two pistol belts taken from the mission. Fargo pointed to the fallen stones at Treadway's feet. "All of you, start stacking those rocks on the wall. Make shooting portals. Make them as small as you can and still be able to fire left and right!"

Turning his back on Treadway, Fargo faced Smitty. "Give your shot-gun to Hialeaha and use your pistol. Each of us needs to take a position along the wall."

Leaving Brooks, Hialeaha crawled to Smitty. Without asking, she jerked the shotgun from his hands.

Stooping low, she scurried to Treadway's corner and held out her hand.

Filling her palm, he said, "I only have four shells."

Hialeaha and Smitty took the southern wall facing the bulk of the ruins and the grassy plain. Fargo took the center of the wall facing the wagons while Wellington positioned himself in the corner to Fargo's left and Treadway to his right. Davis took the side wall facing the riverbed.

Keeping an eye out for Apaches, they carefully built up their walls, leaving gaps to shoot through. There was no sound, no sign of Apaches anywhere.

An hour passed. Fargo slid down the wall. Leaning his back against the stones, he looked around the room.

Clutching her purse, Mahra huddled next to Davis. Wellington stood alone, with LaFarge sitting beside Treadway. Smitty was talking to himself as he built his wall. Hialeaha glanced over her shoulder. She started to speak but turned back to her portal.

"What are they waiting for?" asked Davis.

"Apaches are never in a hurry," said Fargo. "Does anybody have any water?"

Hialeaha answered. "It's down in the mission. All we had left was half a canteen. Bryce drained the water barrels."

"What about you?" asked LaFarge.

"There's a small canteen on my horse."

Fargo took a quick look over the wall. The supply wagon and coach were thirty paces from the ruins, thirty paces across open ground. Behind the wagons to the north, a ridge covered in juniper and sage was sure to hold Apaches.

Sinking back behind the wall, Fargo shook his head. "Who the hell is *Bryce?*"

"Smitty," answered Brooks. Her sunbonnet was ripped and her face streaked with dust and sweat. "His real name is Bryce Stewart. He is a very bad man."

Fargo waited for Wellington to speak, but he kept his back turned to everyone. He was strangely silent.

That Smitty was not who he had claimed to be was no surprise to Fargo. Having an alias was nothing unusual, but LaFarge sitting next to Treadway, away from Wellington, made no sense. Neither did wasting water.

When no one offered an explanation, Fargo asked, "Smitty, did you drain the water barrels?"

Smitty stopped building his wall. Craning his neck, he stared at Fargo. "I wanted to see them die of thirst, but you kept interfering."

Fargo's mind began to race. He recalled what Mr. Pinkerton had told him about LaFarge. Then he remembered what Hialeaha had said about Treadway and his interest in women. One look at LaFarge and how she leaned into Treadway told him Hialeaha's suspicions were correct. Wellington had been duped, and now he knew it.

But what did that have to do with Smitty draining the water?

Hialeaha kept watching the ruins as she spoke. "Do you remember me telling you of the boxing match, about the man that was beaten by Mr. Wellington, the one that lost his fortune and his lover?"

Glancing from Smitty to Wellington and then to Treadway, Fargo swore. "Don't tell me this is him."

"It is," confirmed Davis. "And he was holding us all at gunpoint when you rode up. You interrupted whatever he had planned."

Smitty growled. "I was going to kill all of you and bury you in the hole you dug. That was my plan."

Davis jerked back from the wall, pointing his pistol at Smitty. "You would have murdered us?"

"Hold it!" ordered Fargo. "Right now, we fight together, or we all die."

"Maybe you'll die first," muttered Treadway.

"Maybe, but I'm guessing they'll take two or three days to kill you, big man. You'll be begging and crying like a baby long before they finish you off."

"You brought them," said LaFarge. "How do we know they're not just after you? They might let the rest of us go."

LaFarge paused, and her eyes flickered thoughtfully. "Or they might let us women go. I doubt they would hurt Mahra or me."

"If you can convince them you're crazy, they might not bother you," said Fargo. "You're welcome to walk out there and test your talent if you want. But your best bet is to stay put. If we can hold them off, they may give up and leave."

"We could all die of thirst before that," said LaFarge.

"There's water," said Smitty, "a big canteen full of it."

Davis sat up. "Where?"

"Tied under the rear axle of the supply wagon. I was keeping it for myself. It was part of my plan all along."

"It is no longer there," said Hialeaha. "When I saw the water barrels were empty, I searched the wagon and discovered it. I hid it inside the coach."

"It won't do much good out there," snapped LaFarge, and then she glared at Smitty. "I wish Miles would have killed you in that ring."

Smitty huffed and turned his back. "Why don't you walk out there and get that water, Clarissa? I'm sure they wouldn't harm a woman like you."

Falling silent, everyone turned their attention back to the Apaches. Peering again through their portals, they anxiously waited for an attack. As the minutes passed, the walls of the ruins reflected the sun's heat, turning it into an oven. Mahra let go of her purse and jerked off her bonnet. Digging her fingers into her hair, she began to moan—not from thirst, but for lack of Mother Bailey's.

A meager shadow slowly formed along the rear wall. Brooks hugged it, trying to avoid the searing rays of the sun. Following the shadow over the next hour, she squirmed inch by inch along the wall, moving farther and farther from Davis and Hialeaha. She finally stopped near the end of the wall, where it had collapsed into a jumbled pile of rocks.

With everyone at their posts, LaFarge crawled over to Brooks. She whispered something in her ear before crawling back to her wall.

Brooks lay where she was, her delicate, sand-crusted fingers beginning to tremble. She stared at LaFarge. LaFarge smiled back at her and nodded encouragingly.

A twig snapped in the juniper thicket. Every gun came up. Feet and knees dug into the sand.

Wellington's rifle erupted. He levered another round and fired a second time.

For several seconds, there was silence.

"I think I saw one," said Wellington.

"Make sure of it before you shoot," said Fargo. "Don't look for an Apache. Look for a piece of one. That's all you'll see. We have to save…"

A voice pierced the air. "Mahra?" It was Davis. He ran to where he had last seen her. He panicked and screamed, "Mahra, where are you?"

"There she is," shouted Wellington. "She's after that damned medicine."

Mahra was stumbling rapidly toward the coach.

Without hesitation, Davis sprang over the wall and ran for Brooks.

"Edward," Wellington yelled. "Come back!"

Fargo took aim. There was no target, but he knew there soon would be.

Just as Brooks opened the coach door, a tuft of sage moved under it. Two hands shot out and grabbed Mahra's ankles, jerking her off her feet.

Davis screamed as he ran. A shot rang out from the junipers, knocking a leg out from under him.

Screeching, Brooks was being dragged underneath the coach. Her flailing arms and body shielded the Apache from a clear shot. Davis crawled frantically toward her. When he was ten feet from the coach, a lariat flew over his neck. With his hands struggling to loosen the rope, he was rapidly being pulled into the brush.

Fargo fired two quick shots into the trees with no effect. He took careful aim. On his third shot, he put a bullet in Davis's head.

Wellington spun, leveling his Winchester at Fargo. "You shot him, you fool. You killed Edward!"

Hialeaha sprang between the two men. Her hand outstretched, she faced Wellington. "He had no choice. They would have tortured him to death."

"You do not know that!"

"I *do* know," said Fargo, "just as sure as I know those Mexicans at Agua Fria would have killed you."

As Wellington heard Mahra's screams, the rage drained from his face. He sank to his knees, clinging to the rifle and hanging his head.

Hialeaha sat and buried her head in her arms.

Mahra's screams at first were agonizing. Gradually, they faded into dead silence.

Fargo passed around what was left in his canteen. Now, their only chance was for him to break out and ride for Zuni. To stay put was to die.

"Why haven't they come at us from the ruins?" asked Smitty. "It would seem an easy task to work their way in close and finish us."

"I've been wondering the same thing," said Fargo. "My guess is they're afraid of the living dead, the dead they believe still walk these ruins."

"Lucky us," snipped Treadway.

"Fargo!" whispered Wellington. "By the tree."

Easing his head above the wall, Fargo saw Mahra being shoved in front of a juniper trunk. Ropes encircled her partially clothed body, but she was alive.

"Are you going to shoot her too?" asked Treadway.

Hialeaha crawled next to Fargo. Taking a quick look, she sank down next to him. "I have to save her."

"That's what they want," said Fargo. "Then they would have both of you."

"According to you," said LaFarge, "they don't bother crazy people. Maybe if Hialeaha acts crazy, it will work better for her than it did for Mahra. Or then again, maybe you don't know what you're talking about."

Hialeaha went to where Brooks had been sitting. She found her purse and sunbonnet. She tore the feathers from the bonnet and removed the lip pomade from the purse. "I have an idea," she said to Fargo. "I will need your sleeping blanket and your horse blanket."

For several seconds, Fargo looked into the eyes of Hialeaha. "What do you have in mind?"

"Kokopeli," answered Hialeaha, loosening her hair.

Adjusting the brim of his hat against the sun, Fargo nodded thoughtfully. "It might work."

Hialeaha was braiding her hair when Fargo returned with the blankets.

"The sleeping blanket should cover my body front and back."

Unsheathing his Bowie knife, Fargo cut a hole in the center of the blanket. "The Mexicans call this a *serapi*."

"The horse blanket must stay rolled on my shoulders. We have to tie it somehow."

Fargo went back to his saddle and removed the leather straps that held his blanket. In minutes, Hialeaha had four braids on each side of her head and had woven the feathers from the sunbonnet into them. From Mahra's purse, she took the red lip pomade and began painting her face from her nose to her forehead.

When she was finished with her face, she tore the bottom half of her dress off, leaving her knees exposed above her moccasins. She shredded what she had torn from her dress and tied bits of cloth on the ends of her braids.

She stood and bent slightly at the waist as Fargo tied the rolled horse blanket between her shoulders and then draped the serapi over her head. He tied the serapi around her waist and secured his Bowie knife behind it.

Stooping once more beside her satchel, Hialeaha withdrew her flute. She smiled at Fargo. "Wish me luck."

Fargo tilted her chin up. "Good luck," he said and kissed her.

Hialeaha crept out the back of the ruins and worked her way deeper into the interior of the crumbling walls. A few moments later, the light notes of the Cherokee flute floated in the air.

The Apaches no doubt had the hill surrounded, but Hialeaha chose to exit the ruin from the south. Playing the flute and hunching over like Kokopeli, she wound her way around the outside of Hawikuh. She paused occasionally, peering left and right, sometimes spinning in tight circles while raising and lowering the flute. In minutes, she rounded the western edge of the ruin. Upon seeing Mahra, she changed the tune and tempo of the flute.

Dancing as she approached, Hialeaha gesticulated as if courting a prospective mate. For several minutes, she played the flute and danced in front of Brooks. When Mahra finally raised her head, Hialeaha cut the ropes that held her.

Tying one end of the rope around Mahra's waist, Kokopeli again played the flute. But this time, however, he carefully led his woman along side the ruins and then back inside the city of the living dead.

Fargo left the wall and ducked deeper into Hawikuh. After a few strides, he went to one knee and listened.

Rocks clattered. Searching every corner and shadow, he moved toward the muffled sound.

Bent at the waist and holding one arm around Brooks, Hialeaha worked her way through the ruins. The horse blanket and rope were tucked under her other arm. Most of the red pomade had already been rubbed off.

Fargo moved toward them, all the while sweeping the walls with the barrel of his Winchester. Mahra saw him and started to speak, but Hialeaha clasped a hand over her mouth.

Shaking his head no, Fargo placed a finger to his lips and then waved them on. After they reached Fargo, Hialeaha removed the serapi and draped it across Mahra's shoulders. When they rejoined the others, Hialeaha led Brooks to a corner and eased her down in a patch of shade.

"How long until they figure out what happened?" asked Treadway. "They can't be that stupid."

Fargo glared at Treadway, fighting down the urge to put a bullet in him. "They're not stupid. Just superstitious."

"So," LaFarge scoffed, "we're back where we started, only minus one gun."

Wellington's face twisted with disbelief. "We're minus one *gun?* That is Edward out there!"

LaFarge was unmoved. "Not anymore it's not."

"My God!" cringed Wellington. "How could I have been such a fool?"

Treadway put his hand on LaFarge's shoulder. He smiled derisively. "You rich people are all the same. What's one less of you?"

Fargo took the horse blanket and untied it. "We've only got one chance now. I can try to make it to Zuni and get help. If I break through, my gelding can outrun anything in the territory. If we're lucky, I can be back before sundown."

"You mean, *if* you come back," said LaFarge.

"Saving your own skin," agreed Treadway. "That's what you're trying to do."

"We don't have time to waste," said Fargo. "Let's put it to a vote."

Wellington sighed. "I say yes."

"Yes," said Hialeaha.

"Well, I say no," returned LaFarge.

"Me too," said Treadway. He pointed at Brooks. "She's gone loco, so it's up to you, Smitty...or whoever you are. What's it going to be?"

His eyes darting from Fargo to Treadway, Smitty fingered the trigger of his Colt. His dry tongue licked drier lips. "I say go."

Fargo started for the gelding. When his back was turned, Treadway's pistol came up.

Hialeaha's shotgun roared, blasting a hole in Treadway's side and spinning him half around.

Fargo drew and fired at Treadway. Smitty's pistol exploded to his left.

Wellington's rifle belched flame and smoke as Fargo put another round into Treadway.

Smitty fell back against the wall with a .45-75 slug through his chest. Treadway landed with a thud, face down in the sand.

Smoke swirled inside the four walls. Fargo looked down at Smitty, who was taking his last breath. Fargo glanced at Hialeaha, and then Brooks and Wellington. "Are you hit?"

Wellington blinked several times before his eyes focused. "He missed me."

Fargo went to the wall. No Apaches were in sight, but it would not be long before they deduced what had happened.

LaFarge crawled to Treadway. She paused for a moment but made no sound.

"Take his gun," said Fargo. "Get ready to shoot."

LaFarge looked up at Fargo. "And die with the rest of you?" She started unbuttoning her blouse. "Those are men out there. You are all the same, red or white."

Tossing off her blouse, LaFarge slid her dress off. Standing in her chemise and drawers, she raised her head as if taking the stage. "You are such fools," she said and walked out of the ruins into the open.

Holding her arms extended, she turned slowly in a circle. Starting toward the coach, she rested her hands on her hips. She gracefully passed by the wagons and vanished into the junipers.

Behind the walls of the ruins, they waited for screams, but none came. For the next hour, there was only heat and silence. Even the sweating had stopped.

Fargo put a pebble in his mouth, trying to get some saliva to flow. It was getting hard to swallow. With three people, they could not hope to stand off an attack for long. When the time came, he would shoot Wellington first. Having never seen what Apaches did to captives, he would never understand what had to be done.

Someone suddenly cried out. It was not LaFarge. It was a man's voice.

Wellington and Hialeaha went to their portals. Fargo readied his rifle. A moment later, they heard the voice again, but it was not the screech of a war whoop. It was someone speaking.

"What did he say?" asked Wellington.

"He says that we are to die."

Fargo yelled out something in Spanish and waited for a reply.

Hialeaha glanced over her shoulder at Fargo. "What is it?"

"Something's not right," said Fargo. He called out again in Spanish.

The voice came back, speaking longer this time.

"More death talk?" asked Wellington.

"Some."

"Some?" questioned Hialeaha.

"He said we had desecrated a sacred place. I told him a witch had done it. I told him we killed the witch ourselves."

"Why did you say that?" asked Wellington.

"Because whoever's doing the talking is speaking old Castilian Spanish. Mexicans don't speak Castilian. Unless I miss my guess, the Apaches are gone. Those are Zuni out there. And I'd bet they're wearing green sashes."

Wellington cleared his eyes with a dirty knuckle. "Sakisti?"

"*Soy Tats-a-das-ago,*" yelled Fargo. "*Amigo de los Zunis.*"

The voice responded.

Fargo raised the Winchester over his head and slowly walked out of the ruins. He took a few steps and stopped. Without a sound, Zunis appeared from every direction.

Each warrior wore a green sash and turquoise around his neck. Most were armed with bows and arrows. Some held lances with iron points. A few wore metal breastplates and Spanish helmets.

From their midst, an old man stepped forward. He carried a lance, but his was tipped in polished silver. It was Pedro Pino.

Wellington and Hialeaha watched from behind a wall, unable to understand a word being spoken.

"There must be two hundred of them," whispered Wellington.

Hialeaha nodded. "It is up to Far-go now…to Tats-a-das-ago."

"What does that mean, anyway?"

"Quick Killer."

Wellington stared at Hialeaha for several seconds but said nothing.

Leaving Fargo standing, Pedro Pino turned and walked away. Within seconds, all but a handful of Zuni were gone.

Somberly, Fargo returned to the ruins but did not go inside. "We're safe now. They're satisfied with my story."

Wellington slumped with relief. "Thank God."

Hialeaha's eyes searched Fargo's. Words were not necessary. She could see what was in them.

"The Sakisti will help you get back to Zuni and escort you as far as Lamy," said Fargo. "Wellington, I'm holding you responsible for getting Hialeaha and Mahra back to Chicago. Guard them with your life. I'll find out if you don't."

"I will," said Wellington. Walking out of the ruins and toward the coach, he added, "You have my word on it."

Fargo avoided looking at Hialeaha. "The Apaches have LaFarge."

A long, knowing silence passed between Conway Fargo and Hialeaha the Cherokee.

"Then you must try to save her," said Hialeaha. "And Mahra will need me."

Together they went to the black gelding. Hialeaha handed Fargo his saddle blanket. He handed her his rifle.

"I have never felt this before," said Hialeaha.

Fargo slung his saddle over. "I have. A long time ago."

Hialeaha watched Fargo tighten his cinch. "Does such sadness pass?"

"Part of it does," answered Fargo. Still avoiding her eyes, he took the rifle and slid it into its scabbard.

With Hialeaha by his side, Fargo led the black down through the ruins onto the grassy plain.

"Will I see you again, Conway?"

Finally, Fargo gazed into Hialeaha's eyes. He gently ran his fingers down her cheek. "Only God knows the answer to that."

"Then go with God," said Hialeaha. She put her arms around him, and just before she kissed him good-bye, she whispered, "And always remember El Moro."

Epilogue

Pedro Pino took the sack of bones and laid them next to the shallow grave from which they had been taken. Leaning into the hole, he began digging with his gnarled fingers. He scooped up handfuls of sand until he reached a flat stone.

After brushing the stone clean, he motioned for help. Two Sakisti came forward. They worked their fingers under the corners of the heavy block of sandstone, and then lifted it up and set it aside.

Another Sakisti stepped forward, hardly more than a boy. He handed Pino a lighted torch.

Pino lowered the torch into the chamber and then looked down into it. The rows upon rows of gold plates and bowls, the armbands and belts, all made of gold, hung where they always had, and the piles of jewelry were undisturbed.

Pino had the two Sakisti men replace the stone. He spread sand over it, covering the entrance to the secret kiva. He ran his hands over the sacred earth, smoothing it flat.

Then, one at a time, the young Sakisti handed the bones to Pino. When they were in their proper place, the old man began sprinkling sand to cover them. They had lain there undisturbed for three hundred and forty winters. They were placed there the year before Coronado the invader attacked Hawikuh—the year before the poor, disgraced Padre Marcos led the Spaniards to Cibola, the city he claimed was made of gold.

27290224R00155

Made in the USA
Middletown, DE
15 December 2015